ALL THE
YOUNG
MEN

ALL THE YOUNG MEN

A Memoir of Love, AIDS, and Chosen Family in the American South

RUTH COKER BURKS
&
KEVIN CARR O'LEARY

Grove Press
New York

FIRST EDITION

Published simultaneously in Canada
Printed in Canada

This book was designed by Norman E. Tuttle at Alpha Design & Composition
This book was set in 13 pt. Spectrum MT
by Alpha Design & Composition of Pittsfield, NH.

First Grove Atlantic hardcover edition: December 2020

Library of Congress Cataloging-in-Publication data is available for this title.

ISBN 978-0-8021-5724-9
eISBN 978-0-8021-5726-3

Grove Press
an imprint of Grove Atlantic
154 West 14th Street
New York, NY 10011

Distributed by Publishers Group West

groveatlantic.com

20 21 22 23   10 9 8 7 6 5 4 3 2 1

For Paul & Billy

ALL THE YOUNG MEN

Part One

Chapter One

I watched the three nurses drawing straws.

The tallest one drew the short straw, which I thought was funny. She was a redhead, wearing a lipstick so purple you knew she didn't have a good friend to tell her it wasn't right for her.

I was at the hospital that weekend looking after one of my best girlfriends. Bonnie was stuck at the Med Center in Little Rock, recovering from cancer surgery. She was thirty-one and I was twenty-six —both too young for this stuff. She'd gotten tongue cancer and never smoked a day in her life. For years, Bonnie had worked at the newspaper, typesetting at night, but quit when she got sick.

They had her on a feeding tube in the hospital, and she couldn't talk, but she was good with a pen, and I was good at translating her scrawl to make sure she got what she needed. Bonnie spent a lot of time sleeping, so I spent a lot of time pacing the halls. I have never been able to sit still.

"Let's do four out of six," said Red.

"You said best two out of three," said the short one. She looked up at an older brunette who seemed to be in charge.

"Well, I am not going in there," said Red.

All three of them kept glancing down a long hall. At the end was a door covered in a blood-red tarp with a sign I couldn't quite read. As the nurses argued, I got curious. So I just casually started pacing down the hall, kind of walking on tiptoe so my heels wouldn't click on the floor. As I got closer to that red door, I saw there were about six Styrofoam food trays on the floor of the hall, left with no care, like they were feeding a dog. And right outside, a cart full of head-to-toe isolation suits and masks. I could read the sign now: BIOHAZARD.

There was the slightest sound coming from the room, and I leaned in closer to hear.

"Help."

It was so plaintive and small that I pulled the tarp aside to peek in. And there he was, this young man, stretched out on the bed and down to all of about eighty-five pounds. You couldn't tell him from the sheets. I stood right in the doorway. "What do you need, honey?" I asked.

"I want my mama," he said. I had a little three-year-old, Allison. She spent the weekends at her daddy's house. I knew from wanting your mama, and I knew his mother would want to help her sweet child.

"Okay," I said, stepping farther into the room. "I'm gonna call her. What's your name, honey?"

"Jimmy."

"Okay, Jimmy," I said. "I promise you I'll call her."

Well, I marched out to the nurses' station, this time letting my heels click on that damn floor so they would know I was coming. I had just become a blonde—thanks to bleach and my hairdresser cousin Raymond—and I found that I could get people's attention quicker than when I was a brunette.

"You didn't go in that room, did you?" said the older one.

"Well, yeah, I did," I said. "Listen, that young man, Jimmy, is asking for his mama."

"Are you crazy?" said the short one. "He's got that gay disease. They all die."

I'll admit, I got scared. This was in the early spring of 1986, and there was plenty of fear to go around about how you really caught

AIDS. When I visited my cousin Raymond in Hawaii, I had asked him about it because I was scared for him and his friends. We were all alone in his salon, so he could speak freely. "It's only hitting the leather guys in San Francisco," he told me. "God knows what they're doing to get it." I didn't know what the heck a leather guy was, but he wasn't dressed in leather, so at least it wouldn't happen to him.

AIDS was spreading, and people were swearing you could get it from gays sitting on toilet seats and using swimming pools, from doorknobs and licked stamps on envelopes in the mail. I lived in Hot Springs, the Sin City of Arkansas, a resort town an hour down the road from Little Rock. It had about a quarter of the population of Little Rock but untold numbers of visitors who came for a good time. Brothels, bathhouses, you name it. So if gays touching doorknobs was gonna kill you, we'd all be dead already.

"I'll call his mama if I need to," I said. "Would you please give me the number?"

"She ain't coming," said the old one in charge. "He's been here six weeks. Nobody is coming."

"Just give me her number," I said. "If she knew her son was this bad . . ."

"Suit yourself," she said, as the others smirked. She made a huge production of finding a next-of-kin form and scrawled the number down. Instead of handing it to me, she kinda tossed it, like now she was scared of me.

"Thank you," I said, all Southern charm and malice. I went to reach for their phone, and she pulled it away quick.

"Unh unh," she said. "There's a pay phone right over there."

I turned on my heel like I wouldn't want to use theirs anyway and went over to the pay phone. I picked up the phone, all bravado, but then I lost my nerve, thinking about telling the poor woman her son was dying. I turned back, and I could see those nurses eyeing me. I put the coin in and dialed.

"Hello," this sweet voice answered.

"Good afternoon, my name is Ruth Coker Burks, and I am trying to reach the mother of Jimmy—"

Click. She hung up. Now, I had a mean mom. And I'd had a meaner ex-husband. I'd stopped letting things slide. I put in another coin, cursing her as I dialed again.

"You hang up on me again, and I swear to Almighty God I will ask your Jimmy where he's from and put his obituary in your town paper with his cause of death." I knew I had her complete attention.

"My son is already dead," she said, not a touch of sweetness to her now. "*My* son died when he went gay."

"No, he is alive, just barely, and he is here begging for you."

"I don't know what sinner you've got in that hospital, but that thing is not my son."

"Well, listen to me," I said, turning to see those damn nurses hanging on every word I was saying. "If you change your mind, he is at the Med Center, fourth floor. And you better come soon."

"I will do no such thing," she said. "I won't claim that body either, so don't even think about calling me again. Burn it."

She hung up again. Now I had to figure out how to tell Jimmy his mama wasn't coming. I walked right by the nurses' station and refused to look at them for fear of giving them the satisfaction of being right. I click-clacked my heels past them and turned down the hall to his room, walking in before I changed my mind or they stopped me.

I went in, farther this time, walking almost to his bed but still keeping my distance. The room was dim, lit mostly by sunlight from outside. Jimmy looked even frailer up close, and so skinny. With such effort, he turned his head toward me.

"Oh, Mama, I knew you'd come," he said, in that small, reaching voice. I was so confused I just stood there, my feet glued to the floor. Then he started to cry. He was so dehydrated he could muster only one little tear, but his body was heaving in sobs, and it was so sad that I began to cry for him. Tears rolling right down my face as

I just stood there, dumb. But then he tried to reach his hand out to me. I couldn't *not* take his hand in mine.

"Mama," he said again.

"Yes," I said, squeezing his hand gently. "I'm here." I don't know if his vision was going or if he was just so close to dying his mind was seeing what he wanted most in life and death. This was probably the first time someone had touched him in six weeks without two pairs of gloves on. His face was grimy from sweat and drool. You could see the tear marks from the last time he was able to really cry.

"Let me clean you, honey," I said, in my softest voice. I filled a small basin with warm water, and the smallest amount of soap. I washed his face the way I did my Allison's when she was just a baby, smoothing a cloth slowly and softly over his skin.

"Mama, I'm sorry," he said. "I missed you so much."

"Hush," I said. "Do you remember what I used to call you when you were just a little thing?"

He paused a long time. "Your angel."

"That's right," I said, brushing back the hair they'd let get greasy and making it as nice as I could. "My angel. Don't you worry about nothing."

I pulled a chair over, and I sat with him, holding his hand for about an hour, until he fell asleep. I started to get nervous about abandoning Bonnie, so I gingerly got up and tiptoed out the door. The brighter light of the hallway shocked me into a realization of what I was doing. I'd gone down some kind of rabbit hole, but this was real life. I went right to a bathroom, turning the handle with my elbow and backing in like I'd seen surgeons do on doctor shows.

I grabbed a paper towel without touching anything and used it to turn the hot water on. There I was, scrubbing my hands and arms till they were red raw with about as much soap as they had, then rubbing soap on my face, paying special attention to my mouth and nostrils. I was so scared I'd breathed in something. I swished soapy water in my mouth to be sure, spitting it out, then looking up at my face in the mirror. I stared at that scared blond girl, dressed so nice so people would listen to her if Bonnie needed anything. I took a huge breath. Then another. Big heaving breaths to flush out the air in my body. "Okay," I said aloud. "Okay."

Bonnie made smiley eyes at me when I walked in, then furrowed her brow at my face.

"There's this young man who's real sick," I said. "Well, he's close to my age, but he doesn't have anyone coming, and I swear to God he thinks I'm his mama. Bonnie, I think he's gonna die really quick."

Bonnie took a pen to her pad. HE NEEDS YOU, she wrote. I'M FINE.

"You don't mind?" I think maybe I wanted her to need me so that I could stay in good conscience.

She shook her head, pointing again to her pad. HE NEEDS YOU.

So I went back to that hallway with the red door. Before I went back in, I stood there and had a little conversation with God. I knew that was Him working through Bonnie telling me I had to go back to Jimmy. "Lord, I'll take care of this young man if this is what You want," I said. "But don't let me get it, okay? I've got a daughter I have to raise." I looked up, waiting for a sign. That's the thing about God: He keeps you guessing.

When I went in, I took Jimmy's hand again. He seemed even weaker. I sat there with him all night. Thirteen hours in total. At one point, he got a really frightened look.

"What's gonna happen?"

"Oh angel, I'm not letting go of this hand here until Jesus takes the other one. I'm gonna stay right here until He says He is ready for you."

His face softened. People just want to be sure of things sometimes. I spent the next hours holding his hand, singing songs to him, as his breathing grew slower and slower. I had an ache in my belly from not eating, but I didn't want to leave him, for fear he would die alone. The nurses didn't visit one single time. No doctor, nothing.

It was just before midnight when Jimmy took his last breath. There was no big moment. He was just here on this earth and then he wasn't. The room seemed empty. I sat with him for a while after he died. And I cried.

I went out to the nurses' station and told them Jimmy was dead. It was a new shift of nurses, but they brought the same indifference to him. They seemed relieved, to be honest. Now they just needed to get rid of his body.

"What funeral home?" one asked. Like, let's move this along and get that thing out of here.

"Well, darned if I know," I said. "What do you usually do?"

"There is nothing usual about this," she said. "We need to think of our patients."

"That young man was your patient too," I said, but I was too tired to have a fight. "I'll call someone in the morning."

I checked in on Bonnie before I left. She was asleep, so I left a note on her pad. "The young man passed," I wrote. "See you tomorrow."

As I made the hour's drive home to Hot Springs, I thought about how cruel people can be. I imagined me in some hospital, lying there unloved and then unclaimed. When I got home, FooFoo greeted me at the door, slinking through my legs looking for dinner. My little house seemed empty with Allison at her daddy's, and before I went to bed I instinctively checked her room. The moonlight was flowing in, and I went in and sat on her bed. And I cried. I cried more than I did in Jimmy's room. I just couldn't imagine not caring what happened to my child. Allison got away from me once at the Arkansas fairgrounds, and the only one more scared than me was her. It was three minutes, and I couldn't breathe right until I found her and held her. It doesn't matter if your child's two or twenty-two. That's your baby. I couldn't imagine anyone deserting a child for any reason.

The next morning, I got out the Yellow Pages, and I proceeded to call just about every funeral home in the state of Arkansas. I started close to the hospital, but I had to expand my reach. Every call, as soon as they asked the cause of death, they refused to take him. This was the bubonic plague and leprosy all in one. Finally, I called a black mortuary over in Pine Bluff.

"We'll do it," the man said after a very long pause. "But we'll only cremate him. No viewing. And nothing in the paper."

I didn't have the money to spend on a cremation, so when I got to the hospital I told those nurses they needed to figure out a way for the hospital to pay for it, if they wanted him out so bad. This was the first set of nurses again, and when I walked up they all backed away. All of a sudden, they had a fund they used to pay for indigent cremation. There was just one catch: I needed to call his mother one more time to secure permission to cremate. So it was back to the pay phone.

"Jimmy passed, and I have one question," I said, not giving her a chance to hang up. I actually had a lot of questions, but right then I needed the answer to just one. "Are you okay with him being cremated?"

"Do whatever you want," she said.

"What about his ashes?" I said.

"They're yours now," she said. I heard the receiver click.

The funeral directors said they would only come after hours. I arranged to be there for Jimmy. They came late, wearing these horrible moon suits like they were from outer space. They shoved him in a bag and carried him off without one shred of dignity. I followed them as they hurried out the back door, keeping even this mercy a secret.

Bonnie stayed in the Med Center about a week longer, so when I visited, I saw that Jimmy's room was closed up for many days, biohazard tape all around the door so no air or germs could escape and catch someone by surprise. No one wanted to even go in there. In the meantime, Bonnie continued to get better and then went home. In Hot Springs, I had plenty to keep my mind off Jimmy. For one, the big drama was that Bonnie's fiancé, Les, who I think visited her once in the hospital, could not deal with the facts that she'd just had her tongue ripped out and she was bald from chemo and had radiation marks on her face. So he packed up and left her. And there was always sweet Allison to tend to and bills that needed worrying over. This was normal life.

Then Jimmy's ashes came in the mail. They'd just thrown them in a cardboard box. And I realized his mother was right. They were all mine now. And there was only one place I knew of to put them: Files Cemetery.

When I was ten, my grandmother died in an automobile accident and was buried, like all of our kin since the late 1880s, in Files Cemetery, a quarter-acre lot on top of a hill in Hot Springs. My mother had a big family fight with her brother, my uncle Fred, pretty soon after. At the wake, to be exact. Uncle Fred was standing at my grandmother's casket on the raised platform at Gross Funeral Home. He'd done something with family land. "Oh Mama, oh Mama, forgive me," he said, so loud we could all hear him. He was sobbing and rocking the casket. "The greed got in me, and I wanted that property. The devil got in me—"

Here came my mother, running down the aisle. "It's too late now, you sonuvabitch!" she screamed as she jumped on his back. She pounded on him, and they came rolling down the wheelchair ramp.

As vengeance against him for whatever he had done, my mother then, very casually, oh so quietly, used what little money we had, to purchase every single available plot in Files Cemetery. Two hundred and sixty-two spaces, to be exact. She put a *C* marker for Coker on each plot, so everyone would know they were hers. When she was done, she spoke to Uncle Fred one final time. "You will never rest with your kin," she told him. "You will be alone for eternity."

My uncle had to buy spaces at Memorial Gardens, among what he considered the common folk in town. He died when I was sixteen, and I drove my aunts to the cemetery because I was the only one who was still talking to all of them. Mama said she wasn't going, but *someone* hid behind the pillars at the entrance and shot off Roman candles over the hearse as it entered. High in the sky so they would fall over all of us. She wasn't missing that moment.

So, it would be kind to call my mother eccentric. I'm told she was nice once, before she was sent to the Booneville Tuberculosis Sanatorium when I was six months old. She was a nurse, and she didn't have tuberculosis, but she did have some rare lung disease. They didn't believe she didn't have TB and picked her up in handcuffs to take her up the dirt roads to Booneville. The sanatorium was built so people with TB would never have to leave. It was a village, with its own chapel, grocery, and fire department—and endless rules about contact with the outside world. They put her up on top of that mountain, sleeping on a screened-in porch, and whatever happened to her up made her lose her mind. They finally let her come home when I was four, just in time for my father to get sick with lung trouble of his own. He died in front of me on Thanksgiving Day when I was five.

In my teens, my mother and I would walk by the graves after church on Sunday. I would stop at my daddy's grave, still missing him so much. He was nearly sixty when I was born, and I nursed the memories I had of him to keep them fresh in my mind. The times he took me to his parents' homestead in Florida, where we would float in a tiny boat down the Peace River. He taught me not to be afraid of the alligators we passed or the snakes that hung from the trees. Or at home in Hot Springs, a singular moment I held onto, of me crawling to the TV, racing to the jingle of a Maxwell House coffee percolator commercial, and him putting his finger right in the top back of my diaper to hold me in place. His laugh as he picked me up to tickle me and love on me. That feeling of being lifted and held.

My mother was not the sentimental type, and each time we visited his grave, she would take a deep breath and make a sweeping motion with her arms. "Someday all this will be yours," she would say with this sarcastic laugh. Even as a kid, I would think, *Couldn't I just inherit a ring?* I was an only child. What was I going to do with a cemetery?

Now, I had Jimmy's ashes, and I felt like his soul couldn't really rest until he was safely returned to the earth. I knew I would have to do it at night. If word got out that I had buried an AIDS patient, much less taken care of one in a room for hours, there was not a judge in the state of Arkansas—or in America, for that matter—who would not have taken my daughter away from me and given full custody to her father. This was a state with a sodomy law that made consensual sex between two men punishable with up to a year in prison.

I couldn't afford anything nice to put Jimmy's remains in for burial, so I went to a friend, Kimbo Dryden, who worked at Dryden Pottery over in Whittington Park. He was a hippie, with long brown hair that made him look like the picture of Jesus that everybody's grandma has up in her house. But with a patch of snow-white eyelashes that I couldn't help but stare at. I asked Kimbo if he had anything he could spare. I didn't tell him what I needed it for. He had a chipped cookie jar he was willing to part with. I got home and poured Jimmy's ashes in it. Now I had to do it.

I waited for a full moon. Files Cemetery sits up on a hill covered with pines and oaks, plus one magnolia tree. It's right next to Files Road, so I had to be quick. The ground was covered all year in a carpet of brown pine needles that crunched with every step you took. The sound competed with the caws of mockingbirds, our state bird. The males will sing all night for love, sounding like a mess of porch swings in need of oil, creaking over and over again. I was strangely calm. I know there are people who are afraid of cemeteries, but I have always found them comforting. Especially Files. Maybe because I missed my daddy so much. He was a kind man. I knew that he would like what I did for Jimmy, so I decided to put the hole in the very center of Daddy's grave. This way I would remember where Jimmy was if Hot Springs found out and I had to get him.

I placed Jimmy by my daddy's marker to sort of introduce them. I ran my fingers along the raised letters reading "James Isham Coker" and "World War I & World War II." Born in 1900, he'd just made it into the Navy for the first one and then went back for the second one. When the legion of young veterans returned from World War II to kick out the Mob and run Hot Springs the right way, he was one of the older guys they treated as a respected elder. They were all good men.

"My daddy's going to look after you, Jimmy," I said. It's hard work digging in a cemetery, because they're always full of rocks. Cemetery land is never worth a damn. If you could grow something on it, it would never have been set aside for the dead.

I managed to pull out a neat circle of red Arkansas dirt. "I'm sorry we only had a short time together. But you're safe now, okay?"

I placed him in the grave, and I said a prayer for him. I rearranged the pine needles to hide what I'd done, and I looked around as a wind moved through the trees in the cemetery. Once he was safely buried, the magnitude of what I had done hit me. It felt like I was harboring a fugitive. A fear took hold of me that this secret would be my undoing. I thought: *What have you gotten yourself into?*

Chapter Two

It was spring, so the dogwoods were in bloom. White flowers filled the hills, which were dotted with lavender and pink dots of redbuds. That's when the white bass start running. They're mating, and everyone else in Hot Springs is too. If you find a creek where they're at, you can literally dip-net them. The fish, I mean, but that was also my friend Sandy's approach to men. In 1986, she was on a mission from God to get a husband. She was so fun, and she was the one who taught me how to be blond.

"I saw Richard last night," Sandy told me, adjusting her bikini straps for the sixteenth time to avoid tan lines and ensure a little attention. We were lying out on lounge chairs by the pool, sunning ourselves at work and not knowing how lucky we had it. We sold time-shares on the weekend at the Lake View Resort on Lake Hamilton. We did a two-hour tour of the condos at nine in the morning and then another at two. The middle of the day was ours to do with as we pleased at the resort, and we were encouraged by our bosses to sunbathe and get beautiful. Two blonds in bikinis, coming attractions for what you'd see here every day if you rented for a week.

"How's Richard doing?" I asked. He was a merchant marine bringing supplies from one ship to another in the Gulf, so he would be gone for weeks at a time. He'd arrive at Sandy's door, a man just out of prison.

"Good as always," Sandy said, sighing out the *always* and throwing her hands back.

"I like Richard," I said, which was true. It was hard to find a man worth a damn, and he was nice. Good-looking and funny, like Sandy.

"Ruthie, when are we gonna get *you* a man?"

"Aren't you the one who says I can't see any man you dated?" I asked. "You're not leaving me many to pick from."

"I can't help it if I'm popular."

"You can't help it, is right."

She would think I was stealing her man, and with the type of men Sandy dated, that would be petty theft. Not worth losing a friend like Sandy over. She was the only one I'd found as outdoorsy as me, and we could go on twenty-mile hikes in the hills and not run out of people to talk about.

"You gotta go where the men are," said Sandy.

"The only men interested in me have wedding rings," I said. If Sandy's was the I-saw-him-first rule, mine was no married men. "I didn't even like *my* husband, why on earth would I want someone else's?"

"How *is* that bastard?" she asked. We never said his name. It was a sort of superstition, and you're still not gonna hear it from me. It's like inviting the devil. "He's late on Allison's money again," I said. He was supposed to pay a hundred dollars a month, but the only thing reliable about him was that he wasn't going to come through. I married him when I was a month shy of twenty, because he was the first person that asked. He was thirty-five then. My mother had done a good job of convincing me I was born ugly and would die ugly, so I thought I wouldn't get another chance at saying yes to any man. My mother's plan for me was to marry the retread-tire man's son, because he would always have a job. On top of being just evil, Allison's daddy couldn't keep a job, so maybe I should have listened to her.

"Well, we need real men," she said. "Get Allison a better daddy than the one she got."

I shrugged. And there he was, right in my head. Jimmy. I pulled my hair back, trying to distract myself. I'd done this all week, ever since I buried him on Daddy's grave. I was so close to him in that hospital for all those hours. My hand still felt like his skin was on it. The look on the nurses' faces . . .

"Sandy, tell me again you'd take Allison if something happens to me."

"I do so swear," she said. "I'd raise Allison as my own . . . maid." She laughed, and I gave her a chuckle even though I didn't want to.

"I just don't want her daddy's family involved if . . . You know. Not that they would want her." One time, when Allison was a year old, we were out eating with her daddy's parents. They were taking a break from watching Pat Robertson on the TV. Their friend stopped by the table and oohed at Allison. "Oh, where'd she get that pretty red hair?" she asked. My mother-in-law didn't wait a beat: "That's what *we* wanna know."

Sandy sat up and lowered her sunglasses, but I wouldn't look back at her for fear she'd see I was really scared. "Nothing's gonna happen to you, Ruthie."

A husband and wife walked by us, so Sandy and I got quiet. He was doing that thing men do when they're trying to face front and not get in trouble with the wife, but they're straining their eyes to see you. The wife grabbed that hand of his real quick, so I made sure to say, "Hi there," just to her. People came here to look at the time-shares for the free lunch and use of the pool, and my job was to sell them something they didn't need. A week cost sixteen thousand dollars in the summer red week, but I was good at selling. Hot Springs actually had five seasons when you counted the racing season, and those were red weeks too. You could get a blue winter week for five thousand dollars, but I would always work to upgrade the renter and then get the sale from that too. Blue weeks were all Sandy really sold, but it was only because she thought she couldn't sell higher. "Sandy, *you* think that's a lot of money," I'd tell her every time she lowballed herself. "You need to quit thinking like that. *They* don't think it's a lot of money."

Larry swung by behind the couple and winked at us. "Ladies," he said. Larry Nelson was our boss, and he was a good one. One of the few I'd ever had who let me work and left me alone. I'd get a job, and they'd expect sex on top of my other work, so I'd have to quit. From the start with Larry, I had that "I'm not sleeping with you" air about me, so he didn't bother asking. I knew Larry's wife, and I also knew she thought I was sleeping with him, but I never was.

"Well, we should get moving," I said. There was an empty condo where we could shower and change back into our "let me sell you a time-share" clothes.

"Let's go make some more money," said Sandy. "Put on our lucky selling dresses."

Larry had us all up in this great big room we called the office. There were about sixty of us working selling time-shares, each at a little table, side by side. You could hear everybody's conversation; it was kind of like a circus. You took whomever came to your table, but if the people looked like they were going to be a waste of time, there were ways some sales people had to deflect them, like looking busy or suddenly having to run to the bathroom.

One time there was this little old man who came in wearing a stained T-shirt and overalls that were frayed at the bottom where he'd cut them. You could practically hear people saying, "I don't want him. All yours." Well, I didn't care what you looked like. He had come over from the Delta, and as he walked toward me I saw he had on these steel-toe boots that he had cut the toes out of.

He caught me looking. "Diabetes," he said.

"Well, it is a pleasure to meet you," I said. "I'm Ruth."

The guy didn't look like he had a penny to his name, but I gave him the same tour I gave everyone else. At the end, he reached into his overalls and pulled a snuff bag from behind the bib. And from that he pulled out sixteen thousand dollars in cash and put it on the table.

"I think I want one of these," he said. Everybody was just gob-smacked. So I had a reputation.

This couple I had that afternoon was more the usual type. They were in their thirties, he in a dark blue polo and she in a summer dress that looked new. They had a little money, I could tell, but these ones had their arms crossed tight, so I knew I had to warm them up. The tighter the buyers' arms were crossed, the tougher they were to crack. You knew they'd made a pact that morning that they weren't turning loose any money and they weren't listening to you. So you would sit with your arms crossed exactly the way they had theirs crossed. And you would just eventually, throughout the conversation, uncross your arms. A little bit at a time. And they would uncross their arms, a little bit at a time. Then, sometimes, they would pull them back up, and you had to start all over again. You had to keep breaking that pact, and it was always about the money.

I put my right hand over my left and leaned in. "Look," I said, lowering my voice as if I was leveling with them, even though I was about to tell one heck of a little white lie. "I bet you did the same thing my husband and I did when we first came here. 'Honey, we're not buying a thing today. We're not making a decision today, I don't care how great it is or how much we like it. We're not buying today.'"

They looked at each other and laughed, their bodies relaxing. It was always the same.

"I get it," I said. "Now that we've got that straight, let's do the tour."

As we walked over to the model condo, I talked up Hot Springs. I know a lot of people who love Hot Springs as much as I do but nobody who loves her more. My grandmother's grandfather, Grandpa Gardiner, came here from England in 1836 and opened the first general store and saloon. Well, one of the first. Everybody says theirs was the first. He owned the land from Central Avenue to Mount Riante, and he was always having somebody at his homestead digging a grave. "He lost another slave," the locals would say. "That boy from England, he doesn't know how to keep a slave. He buys 'em, and then they die on him."

They didn't know his slaves weren't dead. He was secretly putting them on the wagon train to the Indian Territory and freeing them. He hated slavery, didn't understand it at all. He would get the slaves when they came up the river, and he would buy them through his store, and then he'd help them escape.

"This used to be known as the Valley of the Vapors," I told the couple as we walked up a hill. "The warring Indian chiefs, way back about five hundred years or more, they would come into the valley where the hot springs were. It was the healing valley, so they couldn't bring their weapons in."

I paused for effect. "They would divert the water. I think there are forty-seven springs coming down from Hot Springs mountain, about a million gallons a day. It's hot, 147 degrees Fahrenheit, and they would divert the creek so that the hot water would come down and mix with the cool water. That way the chiefs just had their own little bath. They would soak out the problems and talk out what they needed and wanted. Instead of fighting about it. It was a sacred valley. It still is to me."

That was for her. I saw her put her arm in his as I continued. "You probably know Hot Springs was the original home of spring training for baseball. Babe Ruth loved it, but did you know Al Capone loved Hot Springs too?"

"No shi—" he said, and the wife pulled his arm but good. "Really?"

"Oh sure. He used to stay at the Arlington Hotel, and he even had his worst enemy living here at the same time: Bugsy Siegel. Hot Springs was neutral territory." Here came the trump card. "And Owney Madden, of course."

"Who?"

"Owney Madden? They called him 'The Killer.' The Mob sent him down to Hot Springs to cool off after he killed someone he shouldn't have. That was the thirties, and by then Hot Springs was the place to be in the South for organized crime. Wide open."

My grandfather was Owney Madden's doorman. I remember when Papa had his leg amputated and was recovering out at our house, and Owney used to visit him. This big black Cadillac would pull up, and a man would be standing by the car at all times. Owney always gave me graham crackers. I thought he brought them because he liked me, but when I got older I realized it was because I would just sit and be quiet because I had a mouth full of crackers.

We entered the condo, which was nice and big. Two-bedroom, two-bath—Larry really did do a good job. "Now, see how it feels to live here," I said. "It's not a museum."

She walked out on the balcony to look at the lake, closing the glass door behind her to keep in the air-conditioning. He sat on the couch and turned on the TV to find a ball game. This is how a lot of people want to live. Alone together.

"It's the life," he said to me, but more to himself. She turned back to look at him through the glass, and I busied myself straightening a pillow. I caught her nodding.

"Sold," he said.

I had the windows open the whole drive home in my little gray Toyota Celica. I'd never bought a new car, but I kept this one shiny enough that it passed. This was the first time I had four take-offs that were the same brand of tire, so I knew I had made it. I pulled into the driveway of my house, a buff-brick ranch, a thousand and change square feet.

I was doing all right on my own. Sandy was right though: I did want a husband. Just because you don't really need something doesn't mean you wouldn't like to have it.

I could hear the phone ringing as I got out of the car.

"Is this Ruth?" It was a stern voice.

"Yes?" I said.

"This is Sister Angela Mayer."

"Oh," I said, starting to straighten the kitchen counter as if this stranger could see me. "Hello, Sister."

"I'm an administrator at St. Joseph's Regional," she said. "I was given your name."

St. Joe's was the Catholic hospital in Hot Springs. "Yes?" I said, drawing it out.

"We have a patient that we need removed," she said. "We cannot care for him here."

"Do I know him?" I said.

"I don't know who you know," she said. "This hospital is not equipped to handle people with AIDS. It is not safe. And we don't want the reputation."

"Well, I don't see what I . . ."

"You'll come tonight?"

"Uh, let me . . ."

She hung up. I realized I hadn't asked his name.

I sat in the kitchen. The room was already darkening from the sun setting. I'd rushed in to answer the phone and hadn't turned on the light. Allison would be away until her daddy brought her back in time for me to take her to Sunday services.

I cradled my head in my hands for a minute. And then I picked up my keys.

"Well, shoot," I said to no one.

Chapter Three

Sister Angela Mayer met me by the giant cross in the lobby of St. Joe's. She wasn't in a habit, but she had the look of a nun to her, so I went up to her right away.

"Are you Ruth?"

"Yes," I said, extending my hand. She didn't even look at it. Pretended it wasn't happening. The Sisters of Mercy had founded this hospital a hundred years before. I wondered if she'd been around then.

"Come with me," she said, already moving to the elevator. She didn't say a word until the elevator doors closed and we were alone. "As I said on the phone, this hospital is not equipped to handle this case. We need to transport the patient elsewhere."

"Where?"

She looked at me, and her true voice glinted through her administrator voice. "I don't care what you do with him."

The doors opened. I wanted to press the L button. To get out. She must have known, because she moved her arm as if to touch my back to usher me out, but stopped just short of actually touching me.

The nurses were waiting but made no move to greet me, just stared at me.

"Can I see him?" I asked.

Sister Angela led me down a hall, and a nurse handed me a pile of protective clothing. It felt like I was getting ready to go into space. The sister stared at me, nodding, as I put on the booties, the gown, balloon-cloth pants, a hat, and a mask. Just like with Jimmy, the hallway had trays of food lined up on the floor.

Before I put on the mask, I turned to the sister. "What's his name?"

She looked at me. "It's on the chart," she said. "He was dumped at the ER doors."

She said it like it was an excuse. I don't think she even wanted to touch the chart, which said he was Ronald Watkins. I didn't know any Watkins people, and I knew a lot of people.

I walked in alone, and he was so far gone, I could tell death was a matter of hours. I could just tell, and if anyone had actually gone in his room they would know too. He was a skeleton. I walked out quickly to tell Sister Angela there wouldn't even be time to move him, but she was gone.

So I went back in.

"Ronald, I'm here for you." I sat down.

I held his hand, and it just felt wrong to do it with a glove. I took it off. I left the stupid space suit on, but I took off the mask and the silly cap. My hair wasn't going to get AIDS.

I sat and talked softly to him. I was talking to a body, he was that close to death, but it felt wrong to just sit in silence. Like Jimmy, Ronald simply stopped breathing, but this time I was less scared. I watched the artery in his neck pulse a few more times, slower and slower, until it too stopped. Seeing how long his soul would stay.

More calls started coming.

I guess the nurses and doctors all went to the same places to drink and unwind, because I later found out they got to talking.

"Oh my God, we had this insane woman come in, and she went right in the AIDS patient's room."

"Wait, you had someone come in to take care of him for you? What's her name? What's her phone number?"

They all wanted to get rid of them. I had two calls that first month, which I thought was crazy. Then three the second. Little Rock had the Med Center, a Baptist hospital, a Catholic hospital, and Doctors Hospital. Hot Springs had AMI Medical Center and St. Joe's. Those were the big hospitals. Then there are all these little towns around Hot Springs that had little clinic hospitals. If it was bad—and with AIDS, by the time the patient got help, it always was—those little clinics sent patients to a hospital in Hot Springs.

As the months wore on, they had more and more of these gay guys coming into the hospital emaciated, alone or left at the ER. They were all my age or younger, twenty-three or twenty-four. They'd been afraid to get help, or maybe just didn't know what was happening. It was a six-week thing from the first sign of symptoms. The diarrhea, a fever that wouldn't go away, night sweats, and what I saw most then, pneumonia. They wasted away, their bowels evacuating so much they were down to sixty or seventy pounds. By the time I was brought in, they were at death's door.

My work schedule selling time-shares was flexible, so I could work around that in emergencies. I imagined the commissions I was missing out on but put it out of my mind. Allison had turned four in May, and I had her in a KinderCare preschool day care five days a week. She spent weekends with her father, which helped. But when she wasn't with him or at school, she was right there alongside me at the hospitals. She often ate her meals there and already had her preferences. Allison thought the food at St. Joe's was the best, especially the pancakes. But the people at AMI were nicer.

Every single nurse and doctor thought they were the first person to tell me it was wrong to have a little kid there, but I didn't know what I was supposed to do. I asked a nurse, who wouldn't even go in the room, "If we go home, will you take better care of this man?" She nodded her head at me but walked away. Helping these men changed how I interacted with my daughter—I was constantly checking her for fever.

When I had to go to a hospital at night, I would wait until she was asleep and then put her on a pallet in the back seat and drive her to Bonnie's. Bonnie was the only person who knew what I was doing. I'd bring in Allison, still sleeping like a little sack of potatoes, and lay her on Bonnie's couch with her blankie until morning.

The hospitals were already mad they had to let them die there, so they needed the bodies out immediately. They'd heard I'd done it once, so they decided that was my job. I'd ask if there was insurance or next of kin, and they'd laugh. I learned that I had to have the person declared indigent by the county judge. Indigent burial or cremations are paid for by the county, as the funeral home has a responsibility to society to bury the person for only the actual cost. Hot Springs had long been a place where people had come to be healed by the waters, and so many indigent people had come here and died—whether of TB or whatever—that the county had set up a fund to pay for these burials long ago.

I started spending a lot of time at the courthouse, clicking my heels on the black-and-white tiles the size of nickels. I'd climb the stairs to the county judge's office, wearing something flowy in case I needed to distract someone. The goal was to get in and get out. Judges would all be excited when they saw me show up in a dress, and then their faces would fall when I explained what I needed. They weren't going to be making any time with me.

"They're indigent, and there's nothing we can do, and we've got to get them buried," I'd say. The judge is supposed to make sure there's been a diligent search for a family member with the means to pay or a church that would be willing to help with the costs. All I had to say was that this person had died of AIDS—there was no wasting time thinking that there might be someone to help.

I'd get the judges to sign off, then head back downstairs, slower now. An unfinished portrait of George Washington hung over a water fountain at the end of the hall, and we'd eye each other as I walked toward him and then turned right to leave.

Nobody once asked what I was going to do with the ashes.

Allison trailed behind me in Files Cemetery, still dressed for church. Her little white shoes crunched hard on the brown pine needles.

"We're just tending to the graves, sweetie," I said. Allison brought her little kids' sand shovel, and if we weren't dressed so nicely it might have looked like we were heading to the beach.

I was holding a tote that had two cookie jars in it. There had been two deaths that week. I'd been back to my friend Kimbo at Dryden Pottery a few times, but I never bought more than I needed. Superstition, I guess. I lied and told him I'd taken to giving the cookie jars as birthday gifts.

What's funny is that everyone's ashes are a different color. You might think the ash is powder, but it's tougher stuff. You see the fragments of bone, proof that this was a real person.

Today would be my grandmother's turn to take in two souls. "You'll like her," I said, taking the jars out of the bag and setting them on the ground next to her grave site. "She'll take good care of you."

I always brought a little plant with us in case somebody came along and wondered what we were up to. Even though nothing grew here, no matter how hard I tried to pretty it up with rosebushes.

"Ruth?" I said under my breath. "She's just planting flowers. Why in the world would you think she's burying AIDS patients? That would be crazy."

Allison knelt beside me, and I smoothed her reddish curls. "You are just the most beautiful angel," I said. "Now, help Mama dig a little."

I dug the two holes as deep as I could, piling the red dirt in a neat mound. Allison lost interest and started trying to do somersaults.

"Not in the cemetery, honey," I said, placing the jars of ashes gently into the ground. "And not in that dress. Keep that dress nice."

I smoothed the tote on the ground, and she knelt on it. I took her little hands and clasped them in front of her face so she knew that this was a prayer.

"Close your eyes and think about love," I said. "And we'll send it right here so the grass and flowers grow, okay?"

"Okay."

"God, I don't know these men but You do," I said. "Whatever their religion, we ask that You take them into Your care. Bless anyone who cared for them on this earth, and to anyone who has been kind to them who is now in Heaven, please greet them with love and mercy."

I opened my eyes and saw Allison's big green eyes looking at me. "Well, I think these plants are safe and sound and ready to grow," I said.

She looked down at the grave. "Good job, plants!" she said. "I love you." And she was off, skipping through the gravestones.

By the end of summer, I'd buried eight men from all the hospitals. It seemed like so many then. I had no idea.

They were always right at death's door, so there really wasn't a lot I could do. Except offer comfort. I had to make that clear as soon as I walked in, because I knew they could still hear me. Yes, I was another stranger coming in, but I wasn't going to be mean to them like everybody else had been. I just couldn't imagine being that sick and vulnerable and having people be nasty to you. I would sit with them, hold their hands, tell them they were okay now. Some would die quickly, but some would die over hours. I would tell stories to comfort them and me.

Sitting with them, I saw a river. I felt like I was taking these young men in my arms and carrying them across the river to the other side. And there were all the friends and family, people who wouldn't judge them, waiting to take them. I took them over that river and handed them safely to those who would love them.

And then I turned around and I was back on land, standing alone at the water's edge. I would get up, close their eyes and close their mouths, brush their hair, and straighten them up in the bed. Give them dignity.

A young man at St. Joe's changed everything. Howard.

He had pneumonia and what looked like bad thrush in his mouth when I got to him. I knew his doctor could see it, even if he was just standing in the doorway. The doctor was all done up in his space suit standing there, and he scolded me for not wearing a mask. He was a cancer doctor. They were sticking the patients with cancer doctors, because they still thought it was gay cancer. The doctors sure resented it, and they always let me know it, like it was my fault. Here, they'd just gotten into this moneymaking field, and now AIDS was gonna ruin their practice, and no straight people were gonna come anymore. I heard all that.

I went down to the cafeteria and got some buttermilk. Yuck, but I knew it would kill the thrush. I got this from my grandmother on my father's side. She and my grandfather helped settle the Florida Keys. They ran a fish camp down there, but she was the go-to person for medical stuff and could cure anything. She could diagnose things. I don't know if it was magic or voodoo or what she had. Maybe just plain common sense. But whatever it was, I've got it too—a lot of it.

My daddy would take me down there in the winters before he died. He taught me all that stuff, like how to make a poultice and put it on to draw out the infection. "Well, go pick this from that tree and pick that from this plant." There weren't doctors around them, and our family didn't have money to go to doctors anyway. So this is what you did.

I visited Howard three days straight, missing out on work while Allison was at her preschool. The buttermilk worked on him, and I tried to spoon-feed him yogurt, but he couldn't eat. He was in and out of it, but we could have snatches of conversation here and there. He had made it all the way to New York, right out of high school.

"If you have fifty cents and you're gay, you get on a bus out of Arkansas," he said. "Pick a coast and head for it." He got work assisting a bookkeeper. "It was off-the-books," he whispered, "which I always found funny."

"My rule is that I will take any job as long as it's legal and vertical," I said.

"Smart rule."

"I'm no dummy," I said. "I may be blond, but my roots are dark."

He started to laugh, and I felt so guilty because it started a coughing fit.

"Did you have someone in New York?"

"Ken," he said. "The most handsome man. That is what it would be like to be with him—you would walk around and see people react like, 'That is the most handsome man.' He got sick. I kept missing work, so my boss fired me. I think he knew. They hate us. Everybody hates us."

"I know, honey," I said. "I'm so sorry."

"He died at St. Vincent's. July 11. There were crosses on the wall, just like here."

We both looked at Jesus, as if he might join the conversation.

"Is it better there in New York?"

"Not really," he said. "Nobody knows what to do."

"Are people doing anything?" I asked. They had to be doing something about this in New York.

"No."

"Why did you come back here?" I asked.

"I started to get sick, and I thought my parents—" He stopped and swallowed. "I didn't have anyone. I had friends, but they started to disappear when Ken got sick. People are afraid to breathe the same air as me, so . . . We had a dog. A King Charles spaniel—our baby, Clementine. Clem. I snuck him in a bag the whole way down here. Mama said Clem could stay. She said, 'I pity this poor dog.' Dad stayed in his shed. Wouldn't come out." He took a long pause, then gave up on whatever he was going to say.

"Well, you were right to come here after all. There is nothing more beautiful than Hot Springs in the fall, right?"

"I loved the lakes in fall," he said dreamily. "They cool off, and the people are all gone."

"You can go out lake fishing and never see another person," I said.

"My daddy would take me and my brother out on the week-ends," he said. "I just wanted to see the leaves change again."

I started to cry too and looked around. There wasn't even a box of tissues in here. He started to fade again. "Well, if we are going to act like this, we need tissues," I said. "I will be right back, I swear."

He looked scared. "I promise," I said. I got up to go outside, and after I closed the door, I stepped on one of the trays of food they left by the door. I looked down at this pitiful baloney sandwich lying in spilled apple juice. Some dam in me broke.

I marched halfway to the nurses' station. Two nurses stood there staring, and here came another one.

"These trays on the floor?" I said, trying so hard to remain as ladylike as I possibly could, when I just wanted to scream. "He's not a *dog*. He's not gonna come out and eat off that tray. Stop it. I don't wanna see that again."

"He doesn't eat," said one.

"How can he? If you don't want to go in there, put a tray table outside that door and you put that there food on that table. Would you eat something off the floor? I wouldn't, and I am not gonna have you disrespect a human being like that. It's not right."

Sister Angela emerged, like some sort of devil. "You need to calm down," she said.

"*I am calm*," I said. Then I lowered my voice. "Look, here's the deal," I said, looking back at the nurses. "You might not like him. You may not want to go in there. But one of you, I know, will."

I turned to the sister. "One of you has God's love in your heart." Back to the nurses. "Why don't you trade off if you don't want to go in there, but don't be a jerk about it. One of you has the strength. *Find it.* Do what you do and help him."

"The patient . . ." Sister began to say.

"*Howard.* He went to New York. He had a whole life . . ." Sister Angela stared at me so I met her eye. "*I* could just go home," I said. "I could go home and not come back. This is the deal."

She curled her lip ever so slightly so I could see her disdain for me. She shot a look at the nurses and walked away.

"Now, may I please have a box of tissues?" I asked.

As they stared at me, I started to take off my space suit, removing the balloon-cloth pants and the huge top. A nurse handed me a box of tissues.

"Thank you," I said, throwing back my hair. I clicked my heels hard on the floor on the way back to his room, stopping to throw the space suit in the garbage.

I never wore one at any hospital again.

Howard became less lucid with each day until he died a few days later. It was like he was drowning in bed, he had so much fluid in his lungs. He never saw the leaves change again. His mother told me she didn't want him, so I asked to speak to Howard's father.

"He can't come to the phone," she said. I heard a dog bark, and she hissed, "*Lucky*, heel." I wondered if she had even changed his dog's name.

I buried him near Jimmy in Files. I told no one but Bonnie about the hospital visits. She was my sounding board, and we talked just about every night. Bonnie was adapting to her new life with a feeding tube and had managed to regain something like a voice. To be honest, she sounded a lot like Daffy Duck. And the thing is that Bonnie was so smart that she always used the big words. Maybe from all her years doing the typesetting at the newspaper. When I took her to her doctor, and he asked how she was, she might joke, "Resplendent." That would take about five minutes of decoding.

Her oncologist was Bruce Leipzig, a rabbi from New York. So, you know, he stuck out in Arkansas. He taught me how to care for Bonnie, help her with her medicines and her feeding tube. This wasn't new to me. I didn't have any medical training, but I had cared for my father when I was a little girl. His lungs would fill with fluid, and my mother would hear him gurgling in the night. She'd wake me up to suction him. She had married him for his military pension, and he had married her because she was a nurse, so it was a trade-off they both were aware of. She was sick, very sick, and sometimes she couldn't get out of bed, so I was her caretaker too. Daddy had a hole from a tracheotomy, and he would help me put the tube down his trachea and into his lungs. We would do one lung and then the other, usually filling half a jar with fluid. Which was about all I could carry at that age anyway. Then I would have to take the jar and empty it. I would gag, but you do what you have to do.

Bonnie was hardheaded too, and she wanted to live. When Dr. Leipzig told her she had only a three percent chance of living through the chemotherapy, she said, "I'm gonna die anyway, try it on me." He shrugged and smiled. "We'll try it then."

On one of the visits, I told him I'd heard about AIDS "on TV" and I wondered what he thought.

"You know, we doctors thought for a while that we had all the answers," he said. "Cut out the tumor, use this antibiotic."

"Done," I said.

"Right," he said. "I can tell Bonnie, 'Hey, let's try this.' I can tell another patient, 'This will prolong your life.' These people, what can you do? There's no answer. I can't imagine looking at a patient and saying, 'I have absolutely nothing to give you.' I mean, can you imagine?"

"No," I said, lying. Bonnie looked at me, knowing exactly what I was up to. "What do they think is causing it?"

"I guess they're saying it's a virus, and when you get it at first you have the worst flu of your life, and then it passes. But it starts to destroy their immune system. They're sitting ducks for anything that comes along. You have these young guys getting old man diseases."

"Like a monster movie," I said.

"I mean, as a doctor, it's fascinating," he said. "But it's people. I guess the only thing you can do is prevent it. There's talk about quarantining them, but how do you go about doing that?"

One day I was at St. Joe's looking for a doctor.

"Oh, I think he's looking up something in the library," said a nurse.

"The library?" I said. "You all have a library here?"

"Yeah, it's by the doctors' lounge," she said. "The medical library. They sometimes hide in there doing 'research.'"

I just smiled, but as soon as the coast was clear around evening time, I marched myself back there. The lights were off, and I turned them on to see shelf after shelf of not just books but also the *New England Journal of Medicine*, the *Journal of the American Medical Association*, the *Lancet* . . . I let out a breath, and then I started, taking the most recent copies of each and turning pages until I found any mention of AIDS. The articles confirmed what I knew: HIV was a virus spread through sexual contact, blood transfusions, sharing needles, or mother to child. It was not like the cold or the flu, and they had ruled out what they called insect vectors, which I realized meant mosquitoes. There were long articles about statistics and projections about AIDS, and letters about the ethics of mass testing and the importance of prevention in the absence of a vaccine or therapy. Even the words "epidemic" and "vaccine" gave me hope someone was trying to create a cure.

Then I discovered the larger library at the Med Center in Little Rock. Every week I had to take Bonnie to a social worker there who did touch therapy. She was an older woman named Tweed—"like the fabric," she'd say. She clearly cared about people, and we got to talking about what I was doing, and I told her I was on the lookout for any kind of information I could use. Tweed got me into the Med Center library, which was even better than the one at St. Joe's because this was a teaching hospital. It was larger and more formal, and there was always a librarian stationed at the front.

"I'm going in to do research, and she's helping me," Tweed told the librarian.

"Okay," was the answer. "How's your day going?"

"Oh, it's good, thank you," I said. And I was in. We went back several times, doing this routine where Tweed would leave to check on a patient and then simply not come back. After a few visits, I was able to go in without her, smiling at the librarian and maybe paying a compliment as an entrance fee.

Interns and students in their final years of med school, all male, used the library for studying and dozing off. I sat among them reading, and soon they were used to me too. The library had a microfiche reader, and I scanned through articles on-screen, taking notes. It brought back memories of using one in the school library when I was a kid. I didn't learn like other kids, and nobody—including me—figured out that I had a form of dyslexia. I just thought I had to work harder than everyone else. So I had spent hours in the school library alone, trying to catch up, reading the same sentence twice, three times if I had to, anything that would help. This was no different.

Bonnie had me help take her feeding tube in and out for when she left the house, but it hurt her so much that she just started leaving it in. She would unplug it and kind of tuck the tube behind her ear. People watched us as I took her around the grocery store. She was a sight. No hair, radiation burns all on her face and throat, quacking at me, with her feeding tube up in that jaunty tuck. "Here we come," I used to say to her whenever we walked in anywhere.

Bonnie didn't have two pennies to rub together and was living in a shotgun shack out in the woods. She was what my mother would call "froggy." Anyone poor and white, she said they lived out with the frogs in the woods. All Bonnie had for heat was a pot-belly stove to burn wood in. That first December after the surgery, the temperature went down to the twenties. I went over to check on her, and the house was freezing.

"Bonnie, you gotta put more wood on," I said. "You can't live like this."

"I'm fine," she said.

I went over to the stove and saw a box full of twigs. She had been gathering her own firewood herself, though she couldn't carry anything. Twigs was it, because they were light.

"Okay, that's enough of that," I said.

"It's okay," she said.

"No, it's not," I said. I had been doing so much to care for her, and she was living like this. "It is not okay. It is not right."

The truth is that Bonnie had lived that way even before she was sick. Making do. Her dad was a hit-and-run who probably didn't stick around long enough to even call it a full one-night stand, and that was back when having a single mom made them outliers. Her mother worked as a switchboard operator, so they never had any money. Bonnie was just used to running on fumes.

I called the housing assistance office for her, right there. Looked it up in the phone book and called before she could yell at me. They were giving me the runaround, so we just went down there. This was how I learned to solve all of Bonnie's problems. Just walk in with our little traveling show. If she needed a new form at the social security office or a hospital administrator wanted to charge for something, I'd wait until they got exasperated with me, and I'd say, "Well, here, Bonnie, you tell him." She'd pause, then start in with that Daffy Duck voice, and that would do it. Any place we went, they wanted us out so bad they would be like, "Well, here, take this chair with you. These flowers? Anything else you want. Just get out."

We found her a place on Music Mountain Road, another dilapidated shotgun shack so she'd feel at home. The rent was two hundred dollars a month, and housing assistance cleared that no problem. I couldn't get anyone to pay for her water though. But that's what got her out of the house and kept her social. She'd gotten to a point where she could drive again without me, so she'd go over to the cold-water fountain at Happy Hollow with her little bottles in her hoopty Toyota pickup. It's down the mountain from where there's a hickory tree with a nozzle in it, and that same water comes out of the fountain with the four faucets down below. People brought their milk jugs, their bleach bottles, whatever they had, and it was a social thing. You waited to see what people brought and started talking. Then she'd get a big jug of hot water from another fountain to bathe and wash her hair, which was slowly growing back salt-and-pepper. Bonnie could always spark conversations when she wanted to, even with that voice, so she developed a whole jungle-dazzle of friends there, a bunch of lost souls. She was like Hot Springs—she either drew you to her, or she sent you away.

As open as I was with Bonnie about helping people as they died, it was the opposite with my friend Sandy. I knew she hated gay people. "Why ruin a good dick?" she loved to say. "It's unnatural and against God." She wasn't a religious person, but you know how there are people who find religion when it's handy. And she really resented the ones that got the straight tourists looking for a bit of strange when they were in for a convention. "They have no reason to live except to take men way from me."

But at least Sandy kept everything very surface, and that was what I needed. She didn't want anything from me except an ear for her stories. We'd crash the hot tub at the Arlington Hotel, and on the milder days in December we kept up our winter tradition of canoeing down the Ouachita River. We'd rent the canoe from these hillbilly country people. Little kids and grown men staring at us in our bikini tops like we were aliens. We'd wear shorts or pants, because it did get cooler as the sun began to set.

"Did I tell you I had to kick this guy out last night?" Sandy said one day as we drifted on the water. "Dick like a cigarette."

"Sandy, one of these men is gonna beat the hell out of you someday."

"Oh, no, this was false advertising," she said. "Don't sell me Marlboro Man and then give me Virginia Slim."

"We should get jobs out at the Dairyette," I joked. That was where the country girls who weren't big on working would meet the guys with the company cars—work trucks from the water and sewer companies.

"Exactly, Ruthie," she said, playing along. "Get the sweet eye from one of the guys, and you give it back."

"Then he comes in later by himself. 'Where's the rest of the guys?' I'll say. 'I like that tooth you got.'"

"And you say you can't meet men," she said.

"Who needs them?" I asked. I turned my head as I heard a low roar in the distance. "Oh, here they come."

A jet was coming in low over the river. When we were out the flyboys from the military base in Jacksonville always flew as close to the ground as they could.

"Hello, boys," I yelled as the jet soared over us, so loud I could barely hear myself.

Chapter Four

I kept tidying up, walking quickly from room to room, like guests were going to stop by. But it was just Allison's daddy, and he wouldn't even get out of the car. Not that I wanted him to. When he brought her back from his place in Little Rock on Sunday mornings, I could swear that he drove slow just so I would get anxious about being at church on time. First United Methodist had two Sunday services: an 8:30 one that only the oldest and littlest of the little old ladies attended, then a 10:50 service that ended promptly at noon. We had to beat the Baptists out, or we'd never get lunch. Between the services, there was an hourlong Sunday school. I wanted Allison to be raised in the Bible, and I also wanted to be there for the Bible study for adults. It's where everybody talked, and if you weren't at the table you were on the agenda.

I went to First United because no matter what, God was always there. Every Sunday. I just felt His presence and love. I'd been raised Southern Baptist, but I wanted Allison raised in a softer religion. Her paternal grandparents were strict about church, and her daddy hadn't wanted anything to do with religion. He didn't care where I took her. What's good about the Methodists is they don't have enough religion to offend anyone. But from the first time I went into First United, it was sacred to me. Being in the building made me feel safe, and it felt like that's where God lived in Hot Springs. His vacation home.

A lot of people chose it because it was the social church—First United was where all the doctors and bankers went. Stone gray and built in a Gothic Revival style, it sat on Central Avenue and made Central Baptist across the street look like a poor relation. When I put my address in the church directory, I made sure to use a P.O. box, so nobody would judge where we lived. It was bad enough to be listed with the title of Ms. with no Mr.

When I finally divorced that man in October 1983, I moved him out to Little Rock. I went to his daddy and told him I needed his truck and why. I needed a truck that had a hitch on it for a U-Haul trailer. When my husband came home from whomever he was sleeping with, I had all his stuff packed up for him and told him he was moving to Little Rock. He didn't want to leave Hot Springs.

"Yes, you are," I said. I wasn't sharing my town.

By the time Allison was born I was already out the door mentally, but it took some time for my body to catch up. He was sleeping around, which you would think would make him demand less sex from me, but what did I know. Before I met him, he'd been married and had a son with a woman named Linda, and his parents still acted like she was their true daughter-in-law. Linda was invited to every holiday, and I soon learned that meant I wouldn't be. He didn't even have the nerve to tell me that first Thanksgiving. He let me get all dressed up, and I was confused when he took the turn to head toward Files Cemetery.

"I thought you'd like to be with your family," he said.

I got out of the car. He didn't.

"Linda's gonna be there," he said. "I'll come back and get you when it's done." He looked at me expectantly, and I realized he was waiting for me to close the door so he could leave. I did, and he drove off with the pies I'd made to impress his mother. Now they were Linda's to eat.

"Well, shoot," I said aloud. If I'd known I just had to impress the dead I wouldn't have spent so much time on my hair. So I sat with Daddy under the pines. He'd died on Thanksgiving, so I just kidded myself and decided it was God putting me where I should be.

Their son was about eight when Allison was born, and that boy hung, decorated, and lit the moon as far as his family was concerned. I liked him plenty too when I saw him, but I think Allison's grandparents had done such a terrible job raising her daddy that they thought that child was their second chance at proving they were good people. They showered him with love and gifts, and didn't even pretend to do that for me and Allison. Linda had all the power, and they worried that if they didn't pay her house off, or whatever the new thing she needed was, she'd take their grandson out to Jessieville, out north of town. Raise him out there as a country hick. She was no dummy, I'll give her that.

I was his third wife, though he told me I was just the second when he married me. Now he was onto his fourth, but that was her problem, not mine. His Aunt Gina was the one that set me straight on being door number three. We were all at his parents' house, some birthday party that wasn't important, so they could invite me. Ninety-eight years old, Aunt Gina always held court in the kitchen, with glasses so Coke-bottle thick you wondered how she even saw to put her red lipstick on. As I walked by the kitchen, I heard Aunt Gina refer to my husband before adding, "But that was the first wife."

"Are you talking about Linda?" I asked at the door.

She looked caught for a second, then narrowed her eyes behind those glasses. "No. I am not talking about Linda, you little tart, I'm talking about his first wife," she said, moving the heft of her body in my direction. "Linda was the second wife. You're the *third* wife."

I swiveled on one foot and yelled out to the living room. "You want to come in here and talk about this?" I chewed him out in front of everyone, all "You mean to tell me" and "What the hell?" As he sputtered an explanation, his mother looked like she was deciding if she was too embarrassed to enjoy *my* embarrassment. He said it was in college, and she was the dean's daughter. They thought she was pregnant so they made them get married, and it wasn't anything.

"It was something enough that she got the family silver," said Aunt Gina, looking at me with a silent *Not you*. She got the silver, and I was stuck with the husband.

When I got divorced, people assumed he hit me, because for a twenty-three-year-old woman to choose the social death of divorce in Arkansas, she must have been picking between that and getting beat to hell. But I wouldn't let a man hit me. No. No, no, no. Though I had to let him get right up to it once, just so he could see in my eye what would happen if he did.

That was Easter 1983, when we went to his parents' church for services. It was okay that Allison and I came to Easter services—that was for appearances and had the added bonus of saving her soul. He'd been picking at me all day. He got like that before seeing his parents. They'd been tough on him with the belt. His parents went to a brimstone church, the hard kind that would raffle a hunting rifle to raise money for the youth group summer trip or whatever. We were out of the car and walking alongside the church, him behind me. I had Allison in my arms when I said something about "getting this over with."

It was the match that lit him up, I guess. He got me cornered, and I almost dropped Allison as he pushed me against the wall. He reared back like he was going to hit me. Maybe because I thought he was going to accidentally hurt Allison, I just looked at him with some kind of fury. He could get one in, but a man has to sleep.

He had to do something with all that mad, so he took his fist and scraped his knuckles against the brick of the church. A bloodletting.

"Damnit," he said, to me or himself. "Damnit." I shook my head and walked in to sit next to my in-laws, who greeted me with their usual unspoken wish that Allison and I did not exist. He tried to hide the rash of his bleeding hand, wiping the blood on the dark of his socks until his mother, Imogene, finally leaned over and asked what happened. When he shrugged, she looked at me like I had let something happen to him.

He wasn't my problem anymore, except he barely paid child support. Still, he was a good father to Allison. He took her every weekend, and they had a relationship that was separate from ours. Though I had a strong suspicion he was only such a good dad to make me look like a bad mother, I wasn't going to take that away from Allison. Even though he made it clear he'd take her from me in half a heartbeat, just so I'd have nothing.

"She's burying homosexuals, Your Honor," I said aloud, looking out the window for his car. "Dragging my daughter into all this sick."

And now here he was, pulling into the driveway that used to be his. I fixed a smile when he drove up to the house, pleasant but flat, the way you do when seeing someone who thinks you owe them something. But I gave a real smile when I saw Allison jump out of the car.

"Mama!" she yelled.

He stayed in the car but called out the window to her. Some inside thing, real or invented for the moment. He always did this, and the charitable part of my heart thought he did this because it was hard for him to leave her. The harder part knew it was to break the spell of my reunion with her. Get her to look back and maybe make me really look at him. I didn't.

When he cut it close like this, I became a scold. It was the last Sunday before Christmas, so I had to get Allison into her pretty green dress before church. It had taken me weeks to hand-smock it myself. It was important to me that we always look presentable. I relaxed once we were in the car, holding her face for one last inspection. I reflexively put my hand to her forehead to check for fever. It had become a ritual. I went some place, set adrift for a second, until Allison pulled away.

On the drive over to First United, she got bored, or maybe sleepy because of how late her daddy let her stay up to prove he was the fun parent. I did my usual trick of pretending the cars in front of us were driven by monkeys.

"They're throwing banana peels. Duck!" I yelled. "Duck, Allison!" She squealed as I moved my hands on the wheel as if to swerve, bracing for some imaginary impact.

Sunday school was in the breezeway, and I helped lead the class while Allison was over in the nursery. I did it mainly because I wanted to be of use, and the women of the choir had made it pretty clear they didn't want a dyed-blond divorcée singing "Abide with Me" next to their husbands. Sunday school was always a nice little morning upper to go with the Bloody Marys people had had that morning. There were different themes to different classes, and this one was service—a lot of talk about feeding the sick and taking care of your neighbor.

I caught the Johnson brothers staring at me. They were my age and had been whip smart as teenagers. Now they were still as horny. When the class was over, they lingered at the door to watch me walk out.

I turned slightly, putting my hand to the back of my collar. "Is my zipper all the way up in the back?"

They both looked confused.

"Because you undressed me all during Sunday school," I said, "so I wanted to make sure you had me dressed back before I went out in public."

I stayed just long enough to see their faces go beet red, then went over to the nursery to pick up Allison. She was sitting apart from all the other kids, who were playing family and fighting over who was the mother.

We sat each Sunday in the eighth row, center pew, right on the aisle. Regulars at church picked a spot and kept it. It's why they got so bent out of shape at Easter and Christmas when the heathen hordes came in and took all their seats.

"Grace and peace to you in the name of our Lord and Savior, Jesus Christ," our pastor, Dr. John Hays, said as a greeting to us all.

He could give a good sermon, and I always marveled at how Allison actually listened and took what he preached to heart. He was older, his white hair still cut for when he took over the church in 1954, his look complete with dark heavy-framed glasses. His sermons challenged us to live as Jesus did, which was okay with the congregation, because that challenge ended as soon as he closed with "Amen."

When a lay leader got up to make some endless announcement, I kept my hand on Allison's shoulder to quietly hold her in place. As they droned on, my eyes went where they always did, to the stained-glass window high above the altar. It was Mary and the angel at the tomb, gorgeous, but you could barely see it because of the organ pipes in the way. It was just silly to block such beauty, but the organ was a hand-me-down from a theater they tore down.

I had big plans for after church, so I got right up when it was over. You could stand in line for an hour to shake Dr. Hays's hand as you exited the church, so I was both mortified and relieved when Allison hustled halfway through the crowd to get in line sooner. I made a small show of sweetly reprimanding her and looked back apologetically. The people behind us gave flatline smiles and looked away.

Dr. Hays kept glancing at me in line, and I looked down at my dress to make sure I didn't have anything on it. When I got to him, his voice was urgent.

"Ruth," said Dr. Hays. "I have been meaning to call you."

"Oh, really?" I said, my eyebrows shooting up. I instinctively picked up Allison and braced myself. I wondered if he had seen me at a hospital. Or the cemetery.

"I'd like to put you on the church's finance committee," he said.

"Me?" The finance committee was the most important group in the church, approving fund requests and handling all the pledges. It was all these important men in the town, and there had never been a woman on it.

"Dr. Hays, that would be such an honor," I said.

He put a gentle hand on Allison's head. "I think you'll bring a lot to the committee, Ruth."

"Thank you, Dr. Hays," I said. "I will do my best." I looked back quickly at the people behind me, and saw the flatlines of their smiles had curled just slightly into sneers. I smiled.

"Enjoy your Sunday," I told them.

I had to hurry to get on with the day.

While I was at a hospital in Little Rock that week, a doctor told me he had heard the darnedest thing. "There's a bunch of AIDS patients living together," he said. "Like three of 'em." A psychologist had given them a house. "In *Hillcrest*," he said. "Can you imagine an AIDS house in that neighborhood? Around all that money?"

I had to meet them. "Please, just give me a name," I said. "I won't say where I heard it."

I called the psychologist and was direct, putting on my doctor voice. "I have been, uh, seeing a lot of these patients," I said. "I would like the opportunity to meet with these men."

He got real funny, understandably. I'm a realtor at heart; I knew he'd never be able to sell that place. "I don't know what you're talking about," he said.

"I keep meeting people when it's too late," I said. "If someone—I don't know, eats some fruit or vegetable regularly or takes a different type of vitamin—and then doesn't get as sick, we can use that information."

"No," he said.

I thought how I would feel if someone called offering to help. I'd take it. I'd be so grateful. But maybe he had reason not to trust people.

"Listen, I just want to bring them Christmas," I said. "I can come by this weekend. I won't bug them or do anything else. I just want to meet them."

He paused, said the address quickly, and raced to hang up on me.

Now, in the church parking lot, I watched as everyone got in their cars to go for fancy lunches. They were all in their second-best red and green, saving their best outfits for the Christmas Day service. I got out two peanut-butter-and-jelly sandwiches I'd made that morning. I handed one to Allison.

"Allison, we're gonna get Bonnie and drive out to Little Rock to see some people who need Christmas, okay?" When I asked Bonnie if I could borrow her pickup to bring a Christmas tree to a bunch of AIDS patients who were living together, she immediately said she was coming too. She wasn't gonna miss the show.

Allison took a mouthful of sandwich and nodded, cross-legged in the passenger seat. She was four, the in-between of a toddler and a big kid. Depending on the light or her mood, she changed back and forth, from my baby to my girl, right before my eyes.

Dr. Hays had scared me. If people knew what I was doing, I could so easily lose her. Just the thought of it made me wrap up my sandwich and start the car. Sometimes if you're doing, you don't have to think.

Bonnie was waiting outside, probably to stop me from going in and checking on how she was living. I had a habit of surveying her medicines and food supply to make sure she was doing okay.

"So, I thought we'd try to get a tree first," I said, as I climbed into her pickup, getting it to a wheezing start. You always get what you think is going to be the hardest first. After that, the rest is easy. I didn't have money to spend, so I would have to talk people into donating. "Then I was thinking about Christmas cards, so they could write to their families."

"Are you going to say who it's for?" Bonnie asked.

"I think I have to," I said, pulling on to Highway 70. "I don't want to make up a story and be a liar." It would be a risk, but I would just keep track of who I told.

We pulled in to the Christmas tree lot and got out. The one guy there walked up, and I caught him doing a double take on Bonnie, then looking down at my legs, bashful, then up again.

"I'm hoping you can help us," I said. "And I think you're the guy." People want to help, I told myself. You just have to give them small ways to do it.

I took a breath. "You know, there's a house in Little Rock that has some AIDS patients, and they're not gonna live much longer," I said. "And I just think it would be nice if they could have a Christmas tree on their last Christmas."

It was a lot for him to take in. He paused. He could say yes or he could say no, and it would be done with.

"Sure," he said.

"Sure?" I said, catching myself before I gave him a chance to stop. "Well, that is great. I mean it, I am so grateful."

I thought he'd give us some shrub of a tree, but he picked out a nice one and loaded it into the pickup for us as Allison danced around. "I'll give you a stand, too," he said. I acted like he'd handed me a lottery ticket.

"Thank you," I said. "You have done such a wonderful thing, and I do appreciate it."

"It's nothing," he said.

"It's something," I said.

As we drove off, Bonnie finally spoke. "That went better than I anticipated."

"You're telling me," I said. "Okay, now, let's get the Christmas cards." I was a big shopper at Hallmark back then, so I figured that would be the place to go. Maybe I was a little cocky from how well it had gone at the tree lot. The woman who ran it was out on the floor, fixing up the displays of picked-over holiday cards.

"Good afternoon," I said.

She smiled wide at me. She had a tiny bit of lettuce stuck to the edge of her front tooth.

"I'm bringing Christmas to some people living with AIDS over in Little Rock," I said. She stopped smiling. "I wondered if you might be willing to donate a box of Christmas cards."

She kind of ducked and looked around to make sure no one else had heard that. Then she looked at me, just stumped.

I continued. "I thought they could send notes to their families or whoever—"

"Who would want to hear from them?" she asked.

"Well, I don't know."

"I don't agree with their lifestyle," she said loudly. Proudly.

"Well, they don't have long to live it," I said. "So, you don't have to worry."

She looked at me a long time, like I was somewhere between revolting and stupid. I smiled. I was a good customer. Finally, she yanked a box of cards off the shelf. "Well, here. I guess they're gonna die anyway," she said, handing me the box. "What's the harm?"

"What's the harm?" I repeated quietly. "These are lovely. I will be sure to tell them about your kindness."

"Don't bother," she said, puffing up her body to will us out of the store. Allison was already out the door, with Bonnie behind her.

I turned as I left. "And you have something in your teeth," I said. The air went out of her. "I just thought you should know."

We had one more stop, because I needed stamps for the cards. My best bet was a realty company that I knew was flush. A woman ran it with her son, Peter, after her husband died. He knew my dad, and I thought some of the goodwill would be passed on. Peter smiled at me, older than me and just a real sweetheart. I brought in the cards as a sort of proof of need. I told them about the house and that I had twelve cards and just needed twelve stamps.

"I cannot help with that," she said.

"I understand," I said. I wasn't going to argue with her about a dozen twenty-two-cent stamps. "Come on, Allison. Thank you for your time." *Just move on*, I told myself. I could buy them when the post office opened Monday. Maybe bring them another time. I wasn't sure how long I had, though.

I started the pickup, and the rumble-wheeze was just kicking in when Peter came running out. I opened the window, and he handed me a strip of a dozen stamps bearing a profile of the Statue of Liberty.

"Peter," I said. "Thank you."

"Okay," he said. There was a finality to it. I nodded, but I was happy to have the stamps. I turned on the radio and turned it up when I realized it was the Ronettes singing "Frosty the Snowman." We all sang, Allison knowing barely any of the words, and Bonnie quacking but singing nonetheless.

We pulled up right in front of the house. It was nice, a two-story Craftsman-type, with pale cream vinyl siding and a front porch bracketed by white-brick columns. I had built these men up in my mind so much that I had to remind myself I was a stranger to them.

"Allison," I said quickly, in the quiet of the truck. "I need you to be really, really nice today, okay?"

She knit her brow. "I *am* nice," she said.

"I know you are, baby," I said, unfastening her seat belt. I pulled the tree out of the truck bed myself and dragged it to the door and knocked. A man answered, tall and lanky, but looking like he was lanky even before he was sick. Which he clearly was.

"I'm a friend," I said, and named the psychologist. "He said you wouldn't mind if we brought you some Christmas."

He looked at me with the same confusion that the lady at Hallmark did, but then he softened. "That's so lovely," he said, his voice lighter than I expected. "Come in, come in."

The house was spare, like one of the staged apartments at the resort. A blond man sat on the couch with a blanket over him. "Don't get up for us," I said, not even sure if he could. A man with hair as short as Bonnie's came from upstairs, hurrying at the commotion. He had an artist's brush in his hand. They were all in their twenties.

"I'm Ruth Coker Burks," I said, shaking everyone's hand. "This is my friend Bonnie and my daughter Allison. I've been helping people with AIDS at the hospitals here in Little Rock and in Hot Springs. And I just wanted to come and meet you all."

It hung in the air for a moment. "I won't tell anyone why I was here," I said. "I mean that."

We got to setting up the tree, and the lanky one brought a radio from the kitchen to play Christmas music. They watched Allison twirl, and Bonnie laughed. She was so at ease with these men, explaining to them that she had cancer, talking more about her treatments and surgeries than I'd ever see her do with other people. They got each other.

The artist said we needed ornaments and had an idea. "Come," he said to me and Allison, "we can make some." Bonnie stayed downstairs with the other two men. Upstairs, the man had turned his bedroom, a sunlit room with just a mattress on the floor, into an artist's studio, with a beat-up, paint-stained table the only focus. Everywhere you looked, he had Scotch-taped paintings, dreamy suggestions of people and landscapes.

"Would you like to paint something?" he asked Allison. She nodded yes, her hands clasped behind her back. "These are watercolors. I love them," he said, dipping a one-inch flat brush in water and squeezing it out. "It's just paint and water and light. Here." He handed her the brush. "Any color you want, just dip it."

She chose purple, her favorite color. "Go ahead, he said, and she made a stripe across the white paper. "Gorgeous," he said, guiding her hand to dip the brush in the water. "Now, see what you can just do with water. Use the brush like a bird splashing." She dabbed at the purple, bleeding it out in stripes of a lighter pink.

"You're a natural," he said, and she beamed. "Now do that with a bunch of colors and see what you get."

She did three sheets, and we brought them downstairs. He taped them to the windows to dry, and they hung like stained glass. Then he cut them into shapes Allison called out. Circles and icicles, candy canes and stars. We undid paper clips to make little hangers, all of us smiling at such an unexpected gathering.

And then it happened. It was such a small moment, but there was so much in it. The lanky one went into the kitchen and came out with a glass of Coke for Allison. He asked her if she wanted some, and she instinctively looked to me for permission. Then they all did.

The question was plain: Could I let my daughter drink out of a glass that someone with AIDS had drunk from, even if it was washed? I had spent so much time telling nurses and doctors that the virus couldn't be spread by touching someone with AIDS or drinking from a glass. I could do it, and did so to prove a point. But my baby?

She had the glass in her hands, waiting for me to say yes or no. It was, as we say in Arkansas, when things get down to nut cuttin'.

I nodded yes, and she drank from the glass. I turned to the guys.

"I'm sorry that took me a moment," I said. "I'm used to it just being me." I didn't lie or dismiss it. I had fear, and I had to face it. But a barrier had fallen. We talked about fear and feeling isolated. People not wanting to breathe the same air as you.

One knew the psychologist, and I didn't ask how. He put them in the nicest house they'd ever lived in and came once a week to talk to them.

"Like a support group," I said. They had each had friends and lovers die, and now only had each other. I shared what I knew, symptoms I had seen, and what hospitals to avoid. They didn't ask what their deaths would look like. They already knew.

I remembered the Christmas cards and asked if they wanted to write to people. They started to write, and the room got quiet except for Allison's humming along to the Christmas music. The artist went upstairs and came down with something he'd painted. It was a self-portrait, though he looked older now. I watched him fold it into a small rectangle, then slip it into the envelope. "For my brother," he said.

They were afraid to put the house as the return address. "Use mine," I said. "I have a P.O. box, so it'll be nothing to them." I still had hope that they would get a response. "I'll bring them to you when they write back."

As they wrote, the room got darker and darker, and it was Allison who had to tell us to turn on the lights. We hadn't noticed. I felt at home, yet still at a distance from what these men were going through. When we left, Allison gave them all hugs, and we got back in the truck to drive home. The lanky one waved at the door and then quickly closed it.

He died after New Year's. The blond on the couch passed a week later, dementia setting in so fast he didn't know who I was when I happened upon him at the Med Center.

I closed the eyes of the artist in February. I never got any responses to their cards.

Allison asked when we were going back. I called the psychologist to see if he was still helping people with the house. No, he said, he couldn't go through that again.

Chapter Five

The calls would come either late night or early morning. I'd grown used to hospitals calling me, but these men were on their own. I don't know how they got my number, but they were told I was someone who might help.

The phone would often ring at first light, like they'd tossed and turned waiting for the sun and couldn't take it anymore. The calls came so regularly, I had to put a phone by the bed so I wouldn't wake Allison.

Most of them knew what was coming but didn't know what to do. They'd been living with a boyfriend who died or just taking care of a friend. Sometimes I would say hello, and all they could do was sob.

"I'm here," I'd say. And I'd listen to them cry for an hour, because they couldn't get it out or they didn't know how. "It's okay, just go ahead and cry. And if you can talk then you can talk. And if you can't, well, you know, you let me know when you want to hang up because I won't."

There was no medicine, so all I could offer was information. They were usually planning to return to Arkansas from someplace else, and I had to teach myself to stop immediately saying, "Don't." But most of them couldn't get a doctor to see them even where they were. They were literally thrown out of clinics because they were gay. Some didn't know the most basic information about what was happening to them. They were sleeping on somebody's couch, maybe somebody they were taking care of. And they went from sofa to sofa until they ran out of friends who were well enough to take care of them. I would meet them at the bus station in Malvern, a thirty-minute ride to Hot Springs. They carried their lives in a ratty suitcase or box. Often they were so sick they needed to go to the hospital right away, and I'd take them the forty-five minutes straight to Little Rock. I would take people to a Hot Springs hospital only if it was an emergency, and even then, I would tell myself that I could make up the fifteen-minute difference from Malvern if I floored it.

So many arrived thinking Mama would take them back. Sometimes I would go to their homes with them, mostly just to save me a trip of driving back out there when she wouldn't. The mothers were the hardest on them, the fathers off to the side. Most of these young men were raised Pentecostal, and Pentecostals just hated gay people. The churches were so powerful and set where the family stood in life. The women had probably seen an example made of someone else, about some smaller defiance. Men can sometimes do the deciding about who is exiled, but it's women who do the day-to-day work of shunning. They knew they'd lose everything if they showed mercy to their sons.

I went to a home one night with a young man from Mount Ida. Douglas was so terrified of telling his parents that he asked me to come inside with him. He was slight, and his nerves came in these little seizures of all-body shivers. At the door, I saw why. His mother was as short as him, but puffed out. Her whole presence was angry and red like a thumb that got hit by a hammer.

She eyed me up and down. Douglas told her he had something important to tell them and shook so violently I grabbed his arm and moved closer to him.

"Can we come in and sit down?" I asked.

"Of course," his mother said, turning to move fast, like she wanted to make the place look more presentable. She moved a newspaper off a couch, and as we sat she cleared glasses from side tables and brought them into the kitchen. A toilet flushed, and his dad came out from the hall. She told him their son had something to tell them.

Douglas said nothing, so I did. "You have a lovely home," I lied. "I see why he wanted to see you." I didn't see, but that wasn't for me to see anyway.

He told them. Blurted it out with a spasm that scared me. I put my hand on Douglas's shoulder to keep him on the earth. They looked like they'd been whiplashed.

"I thought—" she stopped. She looked at my hand on her son's shoulder. I had raised her hopes. I was supposed to be the problem. Pregnant. Or just some hussy in her twenties getting her dumb son in trouble. But at least that would have proved he wasn't gay.

"Why did you do this to us?" she hissed. She stood, and his whole body flinched next to mine. How many times had the gay been beaten out of him? He stood, his shoulders hunched down in self-protection.

"Your soul is rot," she said. She motioned to her husband, who was shaking his head, his lower lip pulled back to bare his teeth. A coward trying to look tough.

"I always knew it," she said. "But to come back and—"

"Okay," I said, walking to the door. "You've made yourself clear. Thank you. He wanted you to know." Douglas didn't say anything else; he was fading.

In the car, Douglas still said nothing. "I'm sorry," I said, which was about all I could say. He nodded. I told him he could stay the night at my house. It was Friday, and Allison was at her daddy's. In the morning we'd go to one of the tourist courts in Hot Springs. Tourist courts were like motor lodges, and there were lots of one-room apartments along Ouachita and Park because so many people came to town to take the baths.

I kept turning that phrase she said over in my mind: "Your soul is rot."

I put out extra sheets for him to make the couch more comfortable. I got up in the night to check on him. The sheets were still in the pile, folded, and he slept in the clothes he was wearing. Even sleeping, he seemed to be keeping his body as small as possible, not taking up any space.

More men called me before they came back, and when they arrived, I brought them to the tourist courts for a cheap place to live as long as they needed it. From working with Bonnie, I knew my way around the housing assistance program. They began to let people with AIDS get disability benefits from social security, so then I started getting them on that too. These were men who'd had jobs where they had lived, entire lives. They had invested in the system that spurned them. The only thing I had to do was get a signed note from a doctor. I mean, a *note*. It could have been on the back of a matchbox, and all it had to say was, "I'm his doctor, and I think he has AIDS."

There were two gay men in town who I thought would help me, but they didn't. They had jobs in social services, and the first few times, I tried to get in their lines, but I made them nervous. They were afraid people would find out they were gay. They were hiding in plain sight. It just went unmentioned because they were fun at galas and the Fine Arts Ball. I went to those parties too, with my best friend Sandy, and whatever guy and his friend she dragged in. Some guy would buy me a three-dollar drink and think he could cop a feel in return. So, with all the time I spent ignoring Sandy's guys, I had plenty of time to watch these two men as they socialized, perfectly acceptable because they played along. I didn't expect them to give some secret signal that I could use to get better treatment, but I was surprised at how much they wanted nothing to do with me or the guys I brought in. When I saw them, they started to look past me.

But we kept going. I would coach my guys for each line and each pencil pusher like it was a performance. A game we had to play in order to get things done. We were a team, and I treated them like stars. "Okay, we're going to the food-stamp office now," I would say. "The only answers you give them are *Yes, No, I don't know.* And if they get funny, I'll fill in for you." We'd walk out, reviewing the performance, and I would tell them how proud I was of them.

When I met them sick in the hospital, it was too late. But out there in the world, I seized on every bit of joy I could scrape out of the pan. These men had lived on the margins so long that coming into the light to ask for help scared them to death. I had to walk them through the steps, keeping things fun.

I realized this included death certificates. I had often been asked to fill out information for death certificates in hospitals, when I didn't know the most basic information about the men. I wanted them to have a death certificate so people would know that they had lived and they had died—they were here. Because they at least deserved that. They couldn't be "nobody's nothing" after what they had been through. At one point in early 1987 I had a few guys from all over, and I brought them together. I ordered pizza, and as we ate and laughed, I fired out questions like a game-show host. "What's your mother's maiden name?" "Where were you born, anyway?" I was always helping people with forms, so this wasn't that unusual, and I just said it was for the hospital, "just to have."

I wanted them to be counted, to have their lives matter, and I wanted them to have control over their destinies, no matter how limited they might seem to others. If I felt they were strong enough, I brought them to Files Cemetery and asked them to tell me where they'd like to be buried. I'd put so many on top of my family's graves, but those were the hospital patients I barely had a chance to know. And now there were people like Douglas, who were coming to an uneasy acceptance that it would happen *someday*, even though I knew we both realized it was soon.

John, Danny, Neil. I walked them around and told them who the people were and some history about them. "Or maybe you want

to be closer to the road so you know what's going on." The storytell-
ers liked that one, and the quiet ones often chose to be under the
oak. But after I gave them the lay of the land, I went quiet. "You go
out and wherever it feels right, you stand there, and that's where
you'll be."

I'd write it down in my journal and honor their wishes. Douglas
chose the oak.

Allison and I were at the church potluck, and the unspoken competition was in full swing. Everybody wanted to be the one that just
wowed 'em all with a sweet potato casserole. I felt exempt, because I
already knew I made the best fried chicken anyone had ever thrown
a lip over. It would bring a tear to your mama's eye, it was so good.
I put the flour and the salt and pepper and all of that in a paper bag,
and I rolled the chicken in it. And then I dipped the chicken in egg
and put it back in, to make that double crust. My mother was a terrible cook but made sure I knew how to cook, because she wanted me
to get married to that tire-retread guy. I had to be able to feed him.

Marie was hosting, so she had to put on *chi-chi fa-fa* airs, having
just had her kitchen remodeled. The women all had to take turns
oohing and aahing at it, but I got that out of the way quick. The
men sat around, all full bellies and small talk about Rotary business.

Near the end of the evening, I was in the living room with Allison when I heard a god-awful noise in the kitchen. I went in to find
Marie standing at the sink shoveling food down the drain.

"It just gets rid of everything for you," she said, trying to scream
pretty over the noise. It was a garbage disposal. People acted like
they'd never seen such a wonder.

"Well, that's not garbage," I said. The women turned to look
at me, half-smiles cocked so I'd have a chance to clarify my position in a more pleasing manner. I tried. "I mean, we can plate that
up . . . not waste it."

Marie paused and turned off the disposal. "Of course, Ruth," she said, her show interrupted. She looked at Allison. "If you all didn't get enough to eat—"

"No, we did," I said. "Everything was just lovely. And you have to give me the recipe for those Swedish meatballs, because Allison just loved them."

"I did not," Allison said, insulted. "I said they were—"

"Oh yes, you did. And, Mabel, this good coffee cake. I just mean we can share all this."

I'd done this before for Bonnie and some of the elders in the town after big parties. Like Miss Ann and old Miss McKissek. And Melba, of course, who always seemed so prim, just a sweet little old Lutheran lady, until you learned she'd learned all those manners running a St. Louis brothel in the 1950s.

Like after the Fine Arts Ball, I'd go in the kitchen and chat up whoever catered it, box things up, and take it around so people stuck at home could be part of the big night. I'd tell them where I'd been and who I saw. "Here's the food, and try this, it's really good." Melba and I would sit in her kitchen, and she'd read my fortune with regular playing cards, laying out my future on the tiny yellow checks of her plastic tablecloth.

I knew how much sharing that food meant to people, so why not do it here too? I started packing things up before she could say no. "Marie, you have all these paper plates," I said. "The good kind, of course, nice and sturdy. I would expect nothing less! Doris, will you pass me that foil?" I got them all enlisted in helping me, whether they wanted to or not.

Then I saw my fried chicken. Practically untouched. "I guess nobody liked the chicken," I said. I'd only had a little so that there would be plenty for everyone. I knew it was good.

"There was just so much food," Marie said quickly.

"Well, I'll find a home for it," I said, just as quick, putting the foil top right back over the big pan. Allison and I started a relay team to my car, and the men began helping because anything that was going to get them home quicker was fine with them. Soon my back seat was full, and we drove off.

"Hold on," I said to Allison. I stopped by the post office and reached over to the glove compartment. I'd started keeping thank-you notes in there with stamps and a blue pen after getting those donations at Christmas. I'd even sent one to that awful woman at Hallmark.

"A Southern lady knows the power of a thank-you note," I said to Allison. "Whoever Marie gets in the mail first gets invited back." If you did it right, you also had a detail that would make them think of you every time they saw it. "From the minute I stepped on your beautiful lawn, I was just stunned by the home you keep," I said aloud, writing against the steering wheel. Marie needed to be better than all her neighbors, so that would be good.

I went to lick the stamp and Allison stopped me. "No, me," she said.

"Okay," I said. "But put it *on* the envelope. It's not a sticker for you, okay?"

"Ta dah," she said, proud of her work.

"Good job," I said. "Now run it to the mailbox so we can go bring this food to people."

We spent an hour driving around, stopping in on my guys who were living at the tourist courts and also at the homes of old Miss Ann and Melba. Lonely people tend to be night owls, so I knew they'd be up. We were like reverse trick-or-treaters, ringing the bell to give them something good. "You don't even have to heat up the chicken," I told everyone. "Those meatballs need all the help they can get, but that cake will forgive any sin."

I'd watched all these men just waste away, and I thought that if I could keep weight on them, they'd have a head start and maybe stay ahead of it. I was tired of waiting for them to die. I was actually trying to help them live instead.

I started cooking for them, and on a day off I would make enough meals for the next week. It wasn't easy on my budget, but I could cook anything, and I was inventive. My next-door neighbor had a huge backyard garden, as much as his front yard with the house on it. In the summertime, he was always looking for takers for his extra vegetables. I would cook them on their own or use them to stretch meatloaf as far as your eye could see. In winter, he had plenty of collard greens and turnips to spare. I wasn't fond of turnips myself, but a lot of the guys I looked after were from the country, so that was a taste of home. I also didn't mind stopping if I saw a tree that was heavy with peaches and grabbing a bunch to make a peach cobbler for everybody. I can't even guess how many blackberries I picked, or apples, which were everywhere from August until the edge of winter.

Or I'd go up the country to Collier Springs, because the old-timers swore by the nutrition in the watercress that grew wild in shallow streams. You needed to find it growing within a few feet of a fresh spring, so you'd know it wasn't contaminated, and you had to watch out for snakes. They loved to make a home curled up in the watercress, so the trick was to bring a rake and lift the plants out of the water first. Give the snake a chance to move out and find a new home before you stuck your hand right in.

My cousin out on Amity Road had cattle, and he'd call me when he sold a cow. "Come out, girl," he'd say. "I got something for you." After breaking it down for his customer, he'd have all kinds of hamburger left over, and the cuts of meat nobody else wanted. I could also do that at McClard's—the most famous barbecue restaurant in Hot Springs—asking politely if they had any ham bones or scrap meat to make a big pot of greens or, even better, beans. White beans cooked with a big old ham bone from McClard's just needed a bay leaf thrown in to be magic for my guys. Sometimes they gave me enough scrap meat that I could make people pork sandwiches, delivering them the same barbecue that people paid the big bucks to eat. "Here it is," I'd say. "You don't even have to wait in line for a table. It's delivered right to you with a pot of beans."

In the fall and winter of deer season, people were excited to show off their kill, and I'd be there with a hand out. "Could I just have a little bit of what you're not going to use?" I would take the neck bones of anything, because there was always a lot of meat there. But the gold was the marrow that I could draw out to make the bone broth for the ones that were too sick to eat. I'd take a hammer to break up the bones, add one capful of vinegar to really draw out the good stuff, then put it on simmer and let it go all day and night. They could just have that in a mug, and when they weren't strong enough to hold up a mug, I'd hold it for them. And when even that became too hard, I'd feed them by spoon.

But there were still groceries and things I needed to buy for them. Bonnie and I were at Kroger getting groceries, and she asked me what army I was feeding.

"I'm bringing food 'round to my guys," I said. "It's really making a difference. I can just tell."

"Well, let me help," she said.

"Bonnie, you are many things, but you are not a cook."

"I mean my food stamps," she said. A woman looked over when she heard that and primly nodded, like Bonnie deserved food stamps on account of how she looked.

"Really?" I said.

"Eating's an aberration for me anyway," she said; we blended her food for the feeding tube. Bonnie started giving me half her food stamps, and we'd get groceries together.

But they still kept dying. I learned that if hospital patients needed something, I could advocate best during the graveyard shift and weekends. The night shift didn't care if you hung around or what you did, just don't get them in trouble: "Burn the place down but have it back together by shift change in the morning."

Unless it was an emergency, I'd drive my guys to Little Rock. AMI was our backup in Hot Springs. "If AMI burns to the ground, go to Little Rock if I'm not here," I'd tell them. "Do *not* go to St. Joe's." I had more fights at St. Joe's than at any other hospital. These doctors, men who I respected from town, would shove a finger in my chest and tell me that I was going to die. That was bad enough, but they told me I was bringing in people who put everyone's life at risk. Dr. Porter, a cancer doctor who was furious to be stuck with AIDS patients on his oncology floor, thought I was disgusting because I went in the room while he stood at the door. He became enraged with me once because I took a chart into a patient's isolation room. He was screaming at me so much he was spitting.

"Doctor, there are sick people here," I said, trying to calm him down.

"Don't tell me there's sick people here!" he yelled. I think he truly believed the chart was infected. I know Dr. Porter is why the nurses thought it was okay to leave the trays outside patients' doors again. It was so upsetting, because now I knew these dying men. I'd fed them, from chicken sandwiches to broth in a mug. And now they were trapped in these places that did the very least for them. I thought I could shame Dr. Porter into doing more.

"Have you heard about the pizza and pancake diet for AIDS patients?" I asked him.

"What are you talking about?"

"Pizza and pancakes—you just slide 'em under the door," I said. "It's more than your staff is doing."

"Well, I don't want 'em in the hospital."

"They don't want to be here."

"Well, if I get an infection from one of them—"

"Wear a condom when you go in."

He stalked off. I had these small moments of release, because otherwise the anger was too painful. There were people in the hospital I could do that with, but mostly I tried to act as professional as possible. I called it my doctor costume. "If I have to get the doctor involved . . ." I'd say to nurses.

"Oh, no, you don't need to get the doctor involved." Anything but a doctor on their ass. Even an imaginary doctor. And I felt like *I* was becoming that doctor. I read everything I could, and I was so proud that I was getting the glossary: the cytomegalovirus retinitis that would make some of them blind if they lived long enough; the pneumocystis pneumonia that would fill their lungs and always get them. I kept notes on everything in my planner, noting that the only people I ever saw with Kaposi's sarcoma lesions had been on the coasts. Those were the purple and red blotches that the national news showed people having, in the rare times they talked about AIDS.

I wrote all this down, thinking knowing the names would help them, or at least I would have information when the cavalry or the federal government showed up to take over. It was a way to tame the chaos. To at least feel the power that comes with naming something. But saying "this is pneumocystis" did not help when a guy was shaking so hard because it was impossible to keep him warm, no matter how many blankets you grabbed from other rooms. The only thing you could do sometimes was wrap yourself inside with him just to give him some heat.

Saying "this is cytomegalovirus retinitis" didn't help the men whose vision had started to go, first in a light fog they could deny and then in a closing curtain that left them blind. To block out the beeps and the chatter of the nurses, I closed the door and read to them. At first, it was the Danielle Steel and Nora Roberts books that gave me comfort and distraction. On my own, I would read three at a time and flip between them like TV channels. But they seemed too superficial, and it seemed cruel to read a cliffhanger to people next to a cliff. I understood why people read the Bible to people who are dying. There's a sureness to it, a sense that this journey had been done before. But I never wanted to bring the Bible in, because these guys had been hit in the head with it enough.

I started carrying an old tour book for the Florida Keys in my bag with me at all times. I'd had it since I was a kid, and after my daddy died, I read it to escape back to memories of him taking me there. As I read it to my guys, we'd leave whatever hospital we were in, and go somewhere beautiful, away from trouble and worry. They'd all come home to Arkansas, a place that had birthed them but wouldn't claim them. So we left.

The first stop was always Key Largo. I would read the description and tell them about the times when I was a kid visiting with my dad. Then I'd take them on down to Islamorada, where we swam with dolphins and dived down into the water, which changed from a clear turquoise to cooler blue as we swam through angelfish, darting around us in streaks of electric yellow, purple, and blue, seeming to be lit from within. We'd put our hands on the coral reefs that had grown over shipwrecks, riots of green and purple covering the skeletons of abandoned cargo ships and freighters. We'd dry ourselves on the beaches, which are made from coquina, disintegrated shells that turn to stone after eons and eons.

At the end of the guidebook, we'd made it to Key West. I would skip sections to get there sometimes, if we needed to, pressing the gas on the Seven Mile Bridge on the Overseas Highway to make better time. For us, Key West was a gay mecca we lined with as many gorgeous men as there were lavender and pink flowers. By the time we got there, we had an understanding that there was no judgment. We'd smile or just sigh, and they might point out a guy in short shorts riding by on a bike or a swimmer who looked just like the first guy they ever kissed.

We went someplace else, where they were safe and warm. Where there was nothing to be hidden and nothing wrong with admiring the way the sun shone down on the beauty of men. As if it existed for that very reason—to be admired and loved.

Chapter Six

It was a Friday morning in April 1987, and one minute I very much cared that Allison asked for two Eggos and then didn't even eat half of one—and then I didn't.

I caught the first words from a morning news show on in the living room. Princess Diana had visited a newly opened AIDS ward in London the day before. I stood in front of the television, then kneeled to get closer. "The Princess of Wales showed not the slightest apprehension about her visit to Middlesex Hospital and its new AIDS ward," said the British correspondent, the same one they always had on to talk about how Diana and Prince Charles were in a royal soap opera. "All the speculation had centered on whether she would wear gloves when shaking hands with the staff and nine patients of the new ward."

"She didn't wear gloves," I whispered, watching her walk, so tall and beautiful in a knee-length blue dress with long sleeves. She shook hands with all nine patients in the ward. *A whole ward devoted to AIDS*, I thought. She stayed more than an hour but was not filmed with any of the patients. "They were worried about public exposure," said the correspondent. They were worried, not her. Someone they interviewed from the hospital said the princess sat on the beds of patients when they couldn't stand.

They flashed to a picture of her, seated and smiling, facing some-one we could see only from behind. "Only this patient agreed to a still photograph with the princess, and then only with his back to the camera." The slender neck, the dark, thinning hair. He looked like one of my guys. I wondered how long he had. Diana's smile was broad, just on the edge of looking forced, so I could tell she knew he didn't have long. She could feel his frailty in her hand.

Then the news moved on, but I stood there. Maybe things were changing. Allison yelled from the kitchen. "I'm not hungry."

"It's fine," I said, walking, taking sure strides like Diana's. "Let's get ready."

I picked out a blue dress for work and double-checked Allison's backpack. Her daddy would be getting her at school, and I always sent her best clothes along. I crammed them into her little school bag so she didn't look like a little ragamuffin every Friday.

Work was busy, but lately everyone had been showing around more sightseers than buyers. I got only one couple, in their fifties and sweating, even though it was just seventy-eight degrees. During the tour I could tell they each wanted to say yes, but neither wanted to be responsible if it was a mistake. I needed this sale, and I thought I had them on the way back to the sales office to sign the papers. But when I motioned for them to sit, she started to and he didn't.

"I need time to pray about it," he said. I saw her face fall, and she leaned on the chair like she never had any intention of sitting. This girl Roxanne who I couldn't stand was next to me. I didn't have to look to know she was smirking.

"I would think so," I said, matter-of-fact, like it was a necessary formality. "Are you Christian?"

"Of course," he said.

"Well, so am I," I said. "Would you pray with me now?"

"Right here?" she asked.

I took their hands and I knelt, right there in the sales office in front of all the other time-share staffers. The couple had no choice but to join me.

"Well, Lord, here it is. You brought these fine people here, and we ask that you guide Harry as he makes this important decision. In Jesus's name we pray."

"Amen," they said, moving slightly, as if to get up. I remained silent and rooted to the ground, so they did too.

After a long beat, I whispered, "Did you hear that?"

"What's that?" he asked.

"That's God's voice."

"Really?"

"Yeah," I said. "That's God telling you, 'You better take a break and take a vacation.' Because the only other way He tells you is when you have a heart attack."

They laughed and bought. Hallelujah, they bought. How could they argue with the Word of God? Roxanne shot me daggers until Sandy came over.

"Roxanne," she said, all smiles. "That dress you're wearing, it's so—comfortable. And Ruthie, *your* dress."

"Thank you," I said. Roxanne huffed off to judge someone else.

"Let's take it out," she said. "Don't waste such a nice look on work."

"I can maybe meet you out later," I said. "I need to run some errands. Where will you be?"

"The Arlington, but hopefully not for long," she said. She looked down at my contract. "But if you do catch me out there, drinks are on you."

"Praise the Lord," I said.

My errands were actually just one, and it was stopping by a house out on Highway 70 West.

*   *   *

Bonnerdale was about twenty miles west of Hot Springs, and when I drove up to the address I had, I was surprised to find it was a fairly nice house. It was probably one of the nicer ones spared back in 1935 when they tore down neighborhoods to build the highway.

A tall, sinewy man was leaning on a weathered pickup out front with the hood up, his jean shorts cut as close as Daisy Duke's. He was wearing black work boots, and a cigarette dangled from his lip. He took a long drag on it as he turned to watch me get out.

"Tim?"

"Who's asking?" He had light hair and dark eyes. His sandy blond hair was sheared off, and he had a tiny little mustache. He was wearing a cologne that was so loud, I could smell it as I was coming up the driveway.

"I'm Ruth," I said, going to shake his hand. "We spoke on the phone."

"Oh," he said, relaxing and taking another drag off his cigarette. "Yeah, I'm Tim Gentry. You're prettier than I thought you'd be."

"I could say the same for you," I said, pointing to his shorts. He let out a laugh, did the smallest dip, almost a curtsy. A hillbilly dandy.

"Nice truck," I said.

"Not mine," he said. "We were just working on it. The drive belt is loose. Well, *he* is fixing it." He turned to the house. "Jimmy," he yelled to the house. "We got company."

He was at the screen door almost immediately, shorter but tougher looking than Tim. A Budweiser in his hand like it could be a weapon. He had a mop of thick, curly dark hair, with just a little salt in it. He had grease on his shirt.

"Jimmy, this is the lady," Tim said.

He softened, only a little. "You wanna come in?"

"That would be nice," I said, moving to shake his hand. "I'm Ruth Coker Burks."

"Jim Kelly," he said, still formal, like I was from the government.

They were living with Tim's parents, who were watching a game show in the living room. Tim's dad was almost in his eighties, and he made no effort to hide that he was staring a hole through my dress, and it didn't matter much, because his wife was sitting on the couch suddenly trying hard to not look drunk. I shook their hands, Princess Ruth greeting everyone. When you went into somebody else's world, you had to enjoy how their life was, not bring your world into theirs.

"I don't want to interrupt," I said. "I know you're working on the truck."

"Right," said Jim. He gestured to Tim, cocking his head, meaning we should follow him outside. I wasn't sure if that was the end of the visit, but Tim grabbed a plaid vinyl lawn chair and brought it over to face the hood. He opened the door of the truck and sat in the driver's seat, leaning back like he was in a lounge chair.

"Do they know?" I asked.

"Oh, sure," Tim said.

"I'm glad you could tell them," I said. I went into intake mode, getting all the vitals. Tim and Jim were doing odd jobs to get by, fixing cars for people who couldn't afford a real mechanic, working at convenience stores. The kind of jobs you could come and go through.

They'd been together a few years, meeting in Gainesville and then moving up here to live with Tim's parents. Tim had started a heavy-duty love affair with heroin down in Florida, but had quit when he moved back home. Tim told me he got a real bad flu, which I assumed was pneumonia, but I let him talk. He went to AMI for it and tested positive. Then Jim tested positive too.

"Timmy said you help people," Jim said, starting to relax as he tipped back his beer and then went to work on the truck.

"I do."

"What can you do?"

"Well, for one, I can get you social security," I said. "Get you some income." They nodded, so I got out my little planner to get their information. "I am also trying to figure out why some people get this," I said. "How, I mean."

"You know, I don't know how I got it," Tim said, seeming genuinely mystified. "Because I always slept with nice-looking men who wore suits."

"A suit will do it, right?" I said.

"Always," Jim agreed. There was a sudden drawl to his voice.

"The South just jumped out in your voice," I said. "Where are you from, Jim?"

"Perryville," he said, like he hated to admit it. Perryville was about fifty miles north of Hot Springs in the middle of nowhere. It's five square miles of not many people living as far from each other as possible.

"How'd you get to Florida?" I asked. It's hard enough to get to Perryville, and it's even harder to get out.

"Navy."

"That'll do it."

"Babe," Jim said, then threw Tim the keys. By now I was invested. The truck hummed, not great, but not bad either.

"No more squeak," Jim said. He closed the hood and did a slight bow as I clapped. Tim moved to sit on the hood, crossing his long legs. We stayed out talking until the sun set purple and pink across the sky. These were like the good old bad boys I grew up with, not hurting anybody but always up to something. When I left, I promised to be back with forms to get them services.

I drove over to the Arlington Hotel feeling like I'd made new friends and excited to see my old friend Sandy. I never got over how grand the Arlington was; everything about it was big. The lobby was more like a palace court, and it looked the same as when it opened, on New Year's Eve in 1924. Sure, it was haunted, but so was a lot of Hot Springs.

I found Sandy at the lobby bar and stood back a minute to watch her in the wild. She sat with her back arched in an impossibly unnatural pose, scanning the bar. Sandy's floral dress blended with the huge mural of flowers over the bar. It was like a nature documentary with the female of the species being the aggressor.

"Is this seat taken?" I said in a low voice, sidling up to her.

"I'm waiting on somebody," Sandy said. "He's taller than you and very rich." She laughed. "Wait, I forgot you're buying. You'll do." She turned to find the bartender, who was already waiting. She feigned surprise at her luck. "Oh! We're all here, how perfect. She's buying me a vodka soda."

"And a club soda with lime."

"What time do you have to be back at the convent?"

"I'm easing into the night," I said.

"Well, Sister, maybe we can find you someone to sneak in."

Our bartender brought us our drinks and asked if I wanted to open a tab.

"Yes, she does," said Sandy. "And don't be a stranger."

We clinked glasses. "To friendship," I said. "Thank you for putting Roxanne in her place for me today."

"Oh, I'd do that even if I didn't love you, Ruthie. She's a bitch."

We caught up on office gossip. Sandy wasn't selling enough, but now I felt like it wasn't her fault for not putting more effort in. There were just fewer people buying. "There's no chickens left on the side of the road," I said.

"What are you talking about chickens?"

"You can tell how good or bad the economy is by how many dead chickens you see on the side of the road. They jump off the trucks, and you see 'em if things are good. If it's bad, there aren't any because people have stopped to take 'em home and eat 'em."

"I haven't been seeing chickens," she said.

"See?"

"Well, when I die, that's when the credit card will be paid off," Sandy said. She took a long draw on her drink and scanned the room. "I'm going to need someone to drive me home."

"I can."

"Um, no."

The next round, I ordered a vodka soda too. "I can't let you drink alone," I said. We clinked glasses, and as we drank, I loosened up a little. I thought how much I wanted to tell her about the work I was doing. I still felt I couldn't. So, when Sandy started in again on me needing to find a man, I felt the need to at least say that truth.

"You think I don't want someone? Not just for Allison but for me? All I want sometimes is to be a wife and be in the Junior League."

"You've got the haircut for it."

"Doesn't work, though."

We sighed. I still had hope.

When I finished my drink, Sandy knew I was heading out. She didn't try to stop me, because I think she was ready to focus on finding Mr. Tonight. We went to the ladies' room, and since it was empty but for us, I took my chance.

"Sandy, I want you to start protecting yourself," I said as she primped in the mirror, reapplying lipstick. "I am not going to harp on this, but AIDS is real, and you need to be careful because you could get this disease."

Sandy rolled her eyes, but I continued. "You need to use a condom every time. It's not just gay men, no matter what they're saying." She looked mortified.

"Shush," she said. "Dear *Buzzkill Magazine*, have I got a story for you—"

"I'm serious," I said, opening my purse. "I am giving you these." I had a stash of condoms I'd bought for my guys to have.

"Oh Lord."

I wasn't going to harp on it, because nobody wants a friend to do that. But I had to.

"Why do you have condoms?" she asked.

"Let's say *hope*," I said, with a laugh. "You never know what's gonna happen."

We walked out, and she pretended not to notice a table of men looking at her, not realizing they were the prey.

Chapter Seven

W hen Marc had called two days before, he kept saying that he'd be wearing a Yankees hat, intent that I not miss him at the bus station. He told me three different times that he was getting in at 7:40 a.m. I think he was afraid of being marooned back in Arkansas. "I'll see you," I said.

Of course I would spot him. Though they were strangers, I could always pick out the guys who came for me. Even Allison could. They were always surprised to see her waiting with me, but she went wherever I went, especially in summer.

Marc came off the bus nearly last, circular glasses on top of a sharp nose and a chin that was just as angular. He was tall, bundled up in a sweatshirt and brown leather jacket. So many layers for August.

I waved, and he came over. These moments could be awkward, because you had to read if they were nervous talkers or if they just wanted some silence. And I also had to look them over real quick and quiet to see if the next stop had to be the hospital.

But before I could figure him out, Marc said he needed the bathroom badly. I pointed quick; it was clearly an emergency. He fumbled with his duffel bag, so I took it. He came back and apologized.

"Nothing to be sorry about," I said. We started the drive to one of the tourist courts. He was hoping that his family would take him in, but not naive. They were Pentecostals down in Arkadelphia, so he wasn't going to go straight there.

He waited until he closed the car door to talk. "The pills are a nightmare on my stomach," he said.

"Really," I said, more as a comment than a question. He had told me he was on AZT, and I had so many questions for him but was afraid to overwhelm him. Marc was the first person I met on AZT. The FDA had rushed it to approval in March, after a study showed at least fewer people died while on it. But supplies were small, and doctors had to go through a lot of hoops just to get it prescribed. They would have to call the pharmaceutical company, Burroughs Wellcome, and make a case for why their patient needed it. Deserved it. I could barely get a doctor to go in a room. You had to have a real Boy Scout of a patient, because the dosage was every four hours, night and day, to the minute. The article I read about it said it was ten thousand dollars a year. It seemed doubly cruel to tease people with the idea of having a year *and* to make it the most expensive drug ever made at the time. Here I had my guys on Medicaid, sometimes relying on the fountains in Hot Springs for water. Not a pot to piss in, or a window to throw it out of, yet they were supposed to have a beeper to remind them when to take a pill. But I wanted the medicine for them.

The irony was that Marc told me he had gone through all his savings just to qualify for Medicaid. Now he was stuck. I'd warned him on the phone weeks ago when he first called with his plan to come down. "You can't get AZT here," I told him. "Tell your doctor there and see how much he'll let you stockpile. Try to get three months of prescriptions and *then* come home."

When we got to his room in the tourist court, he seemed relieved that it was really there. I mean, I guess when you leave your whole life behind, you don't really know where you're going to land. I would get him housing assistance, I assured him again.

"Can I see them?" I asked.

He knew exactly what I was talking about. He had a black nylon fanny pack, which he kept up front under his sweatshirt, and when he unzipped it to reach in I saw what cash he had. And a wide bottle.

He handed it to me. I let out such a sigh, and the weight of the moment made me sit down so fast that Allison came over to see what this precious thing was. I showed her, turning it in the light like some magic elixir that could save the village.

"Here she is," I said aloud. I read every word on the bottle. Azidothymidine, and the name of a pharmacy on Bleecker Street in New York City, Village Apothecary.

"May I?"

He nodded. I opened the bottle and looked at these tiny white capsules with blue bands.

"I love them and I hate them," he said.

"You feel they're working for you?"

"I can't tell what's me and what's them. It feels good to do something. I get headaches, brain fog. I'm sick all the time with diarrhea. God knows what it's doing to me."

"But you're doing something," I said. My guys needed that, but it seemed impossible.

"Yeah." Marc took off his glasses, wiped them on his sweatshirt, and grimaced. "It doesn't save everyone, I know that," he said. "I have friends on it that I know I'll never see again, even if I'm just down here a few months."

He thought he would go back. I'd had a lot of guys who told themselves that a cure was on the way. That we'd all line up for a vaccine, with the sick people pushed to the front. But there was a little more to this hope. He thought he could go back to his old life.

"I'm sorry they're so far gone," I said carefully, trying to keep that hope fully intact. "Uh, when they die, does the doctor or someone come and take the medicine back?"

He laughed. "No," he said. "Oh, you're serious."

"It just seems like it would be . . . valuable."

"Nothing's valuable when someone dies of AIDS," he said. "Walk around SoHo and the Village, you're gonna see incredible art left by trash cans. Families or just landlords show up and throw everything out that doesn't look valuable. So, pills? For AIDS? No."

It took the wind out of me. Even if these pills were just hope, it was hope.

"Well, I have to get going," I said. I'd promised Tim and Jim that I would take them to Wal-Mart that morning. "We'll let you settle in." I gave him the drill again, repeating that I would help him get in the system here and bring meals by when I could to supplement what he could get with food stamps. I hugged him goodbye, and Allison did too, quickly squeezing his legs.

We drove over to Tim and Jim, and I found myself feeling that we were stopping in on friends, not patients. I would take them up to Collier Springs or Mount Ida with me to hunt watercress for the meals I made my guys. These country boys made it fun, squealing when we found a Cottonmouth hiding in the stream. Jim would act like he wasn't scared, but you never saw someone jump so fast in your life. There was so much laughter when they were around, and they asked Allison questions, truly interested in a five-year-old's take on which one of them was right about something. There was always something to discuss, because they would make a drama of everything. "Jimmy says he hates cream cheese, Allison," Tim might say. "Now, you tell me, where do you stand on cream cheese?" She would laugh, then laugh harder when one pretended to be devastated to hear her verdict.

They were waiting for us. I didn't even have to get out and ring the bell. Jim was out first, and then Tim. *Oh dear*, I thought. *The Daisy Dukes.*

"Tim, honey, we're going out in public, and I know we're just going to Wal-Mart, but you cannot wear those shorts."

He smiled, posing quick. "You don't like?"

"Yes, I love them, and yes, I love you, and yes, you look fabulous, but I can't take this at Wal-Mart."

He laughed and went inside, coming back in sweat shorts that at least left something to the imagination. "I'm sorry," I said, as he joined Jim in the back seat. "They're gonna run me out of town if I'm not careful."

"Pitchforks!" said Tim. "Get her."

"You laugh, but if people knew what I was doing—" I stopped myself and made it a joke, eyeing them in the rearview mirror. "Hanging out with degenerates who don't know what fork to use. Allison cover your ears a sec."

She did. "You know why Junior Leaguers hate orgies?"

"Why?" they both said, playing along.

"Too many thank-you notes," I said. "And they never know where to put their elbows."

They laughed, and Allison said, "I heard you."

"We're just talking about oranges," I said. "Orange you glad I didn't say banana?"

We laughed, but we knew we were right, that people would disapprove. Even walking with them through Wal-Mart, I was conscious that people were staring at us. The people I recognized smiled wanly and kept going, and the people I didn't looked at us like we were a puzzle they couldn't figure out.

Tim and Jim mostly got groceries covered by their food stamps—ready-made stuff like Chef Boyardee. I couldn't imagine anyone in that house cooking. I needed to get Allison a backpack, so the guys humored us by going to the back-to-school section with me. She was starting kindergarten at St. John the Baptist Catholic School in a few weeks. It was the best education around, and I didn't mind that she'd go to Mass every morning.

Jim and Allison pretended to chase each other, scurrying between the circular racks while I tried to find things that wouldn't break the bank but still looked like we had money. Tim was acting funny, a little impatient.

"If you want to go smoke," I said, "you can just meet us at the registers."

He was watching Allison and Jim. "I have a daughter," he said. I nodded to let him keep going. "I was married in Florida. She's six."

"Is she as pretty as her daddy?"

"Prettier," he said. "Long blond hair."

I pictured his sandy blond hair falling long on the sharp shoulders of a girl. "Do you get to see her?"

"Uh, not really," he said. He swallowed, then reached for the Marlboros in his pocket. "I'm just gonna . . ." He didn't finish the sentence. He turned to head out the front.

When he was back, he was his usual fluffed-up self. I decided I wouldn't bring it up if he didn't. And he didn't.

I lined Marc up with a doctor in Little Rock, and when I drove him to his first visit, I had Marc go in with the pills and explain how he took them. I think the doctor cared more about being shamed that a New York City doctor had access to a drug than that it would actually help people. But whatever the reason, I was able to get him to prescribe AZT to another one of my patients, Owen, a mild-mannered guy in his twenties who was almost homebound. He was sick enough to deserve it but not so sick he would be considered a lost cause.

I took the prescription to a pharmacy in Little Rock, the one the doctor said he had the best relationship with. I thought I hit the jackpot, because the pharmacist was my age and seemed so normal. He was flirty, and I just dropped it off and practically ran, acting like I worked for the doctor and a patient needed whatever this was and didn't the day turn out nice after being so gloomy this morning and I must be going.

A few days went by, and I hadn't heard anything, so I went to see if it was in. I walked in, and the pharmacist was there with an older one. He turned to say something to the older guy. I put on my smile and kept walking toward them.

He stood there waiting for me to talk. "Good morning," I said.

"I wasn't supposed to fill that," he told me. Gone was the cute smile. He glanced back at the older guy, who was stocking pillboxes like he was mad at them.

"Well, you did, so I guess it's still back there," I said, all smiles. "I can't . . ."

"Yes, you can. You ordered it. The doctor prescribed it. I can call him. Right now. He won't be happy, but I can call him."

He shook his head, willing me away.

I leaned in and said softly, "You can just give it to me and take my money."

He looked past me. "Hi, ma'am, are you next?"

I turned. It was an older woman, who seemed confused about why she was suddenly next.

"I can't find the eye drops," she said slowly, eyeing me suspiciously, like I was here to run a bad check.

The young pharmacist leapt at the chance to get away from me. "Oh, of course, I'll show you where they should be."

The older pharmacist stared at me, contempt in his eyes. "I know what this drug is for," he said.

"Well, it's a good thing you're a pharmacist then, because you can help people with all that know-how."

He walked toward me. "I don't believe in all this stuff."

"I don't believe in AIDS either, but it's here."

He winced at the word and my volume.

"I don't believe in that gay stuff."

"You know, it's a human body," I said, trying to soften the moment. "It's the same thing."

"No," he said coldly. "It's not." But he put the bottle in a little paper bag and threw it on the counter. I grabbed it to put in my purse before he changed his mind and reached for a pen to sign for it.

"You keep that pen," he said when I was done. "And don't come back."

I put the pen in my purse. "Thank you," I said.

Eventually I'd have a coffee can full of pens from pharmacists who kindly asked that I never come back. I had one pharmacist grab a big gold can of Lysol and spray it at me as I walked out. I refused to run away, and let it fall on me. It was winter, and I drove away with the windows down to try to air out the smell of Lysol. I pulled over where no one could see me, and I cried. Then I got back on the road to try another pharmacy.

By 1988, I was looking after more people than I could say grace over. It was still the network of calls from the hospitals and gay men giving out my number. Jim called to tell me Tim was at the hospital with another lung infection. They had him in isolation. "There's this nurse running things . . ."

"I know the one," I said. "The charge nurse." She despised gay men and went out of her way to make sure they knew it. I could only imagine what she made of a free spirit like Tim.

"He's real depressed," Jim said, trailing off.

"I'll go cheer him up," I said. On the way over, I started to get mad, imagining ways the charge nurse was humiliating Tim. A lot of the nurses had let go of wearing the full space suit, I guess seeing that I kept going in and here I still was. But she never did. I'm sure she was the reason he was in isolation, too. I'd seen her be unnecessarily rough with people, usually when I'd sat so long with someone I'd become wallpaper to her. But I knew from patients that she was one of those "You did this to yourself" whisperers.

I passed a real hoopty Road Runner gas station, one of the dirtier ones in town, and I had an idea. Those men's bathrooms often had vending machines for condoms, usually novelty ones. I knocked on the door before opening it, and sure enough, right there by the door was a coin-operated dispenser with French ticklers. They're the jokey condoms with the spiky bulbs at the end, supposedly for "her" pleasure. Fifty cents later, I had a pink one. I put it right in my pocket.

When I got to the hospital, I waited until I was right outside his door to unfurl the French tickler and safety pin it to my blouse like a brooch. When I walked in, I got a puzzled smile out of Tim, and I knew the charge nurse was about to come in and scold me for not wearing the paper gown and slippers. Sure enough, she came tearing in, yelling at me.

"Does a condom prevent infection?" I asked, still facing Tim. We smiled at each other.

"That's what they say," she said.

I turned to show her my brooch. "Well, I'm wearing one."

She stared at me, confused, then embarrassed. Tim laughed, which infuriated her. She looked past me to talk to him. "You are a danger to everyone on this floor," she said.

"No, he is not," I said. "My wearing a condom does just as much good as wearing all that god-awful stuff."

She turned on her heels and stormed out.

"Well, that was fabulous," said Tim.

"Wasn't it though?" I said, pulling a chair over from the corner. "Now, you and I know I am a lady, Tim. So all of that was for you."

"I appreciate it," he said. He looked sad. "I want to be home."

"I know," I said. "This is a bump in the road. You've got more road left and more bumps too. We'll get you out of here."

I meant it and wouldn't have said it if I didn't mean it. We chatted for an hour, when a smaller nurse came to the door, decked out in the space suit. She pushed a tray on wheels with a needle and vial. Her eyes widened when she saw me.

"You must be new," I said kindly. She was terrified.

"The doctor wants a blood sample," she said. "For the CBCs."

"That's to count your white blood cells," I told Tim. "That's good. Nice to know." I turned to her. "So, you gotta stick him?"

"Yes," she said, her voice shaking. She was probably the only one willing to go in because she was too new to say no.

She prepped him, making a big show of finding a vein, even though you could see Tim's from space. It was the first time I really looked at the skin on his arm, and I could see the light scars of track marks.

Her hands shook, and she stabbed at him once, then withdrew in panic. Tim winced and she looked like she might pass out. She tried again, and she just couldn't do it. Tim had had enough.

"Just give me the damn needle," he said. She was confused but willing to do anything to get out of this. In small fluid motions, Tim rewrapped the tourniquet with his teeth and right hand, shoved the blood needle in his left arm, and pulled the draw. I put the cotton on as he withdrew.

"Honey," he said to me, "I'm going to have to teach you how to do this. These girls aren't ever gonna get it."

The nurse sat in the chair, slumped to a point that I thought she had fainted, but she hadn't. "You did great," I told her. "Sometimes you just have to know when to get out of the way."

I sat with Tim after she left. I had an idea.

"Will you really teach me how to draw blood?"

"Oh sure, Ruthie," he said. "I have to."

"I am just thinking," I said, the notion still formulating in my head. "A lot of the guys who come to me didn't get tested until they were sick."

"Like me," he said.

"Like you. But if you tested earlier, maybe before you were sick, you could maybe have gotten in front of it."

"Yeah, but who was I gonna ask for an AIDS test that wasn't gonna kill me or put me on a list?"

"Exactly," I said. "But if *I* did the testing . . ."

"That'd be a different story."

"And we need a different story than the one we've got."

We made the plan right there: I would start testing people who wanted to know. There was no such thing as an HIV testing kit—it was just a glass blood needle, a tourniquet, and a vial. Then they'd bring the vial to the Arkansas Department of Health in Little Rock. I could do that.

I was in and out of enough ERs and doctors' offices that I could get supplies. The nurses turned a blind eye. Any time they made me and my guys wait, I'd just rifle through the drawers and put all kinds of stuff in my purse. Needles, cotton balls, bandages . . . Go in with a five-pound bag and come out with it weighing fifty.

When Tim was home and well enough, we started our lessons right in the living room. Jim had the radio on, singing lightly along with Reba McEntire, wondering what in the world she was going to do about some man.

I had seen blood drawn many times, but I was so scared to hurt him. Tim had no time for it. "Honey, give me that handkerchief," he said, and tied himself off. "Look, this is how you do it."

He did it in what he thought was slow motion for me, but he could do it twenty times in a minute, he was so used to shooting up. "Okay," he said. "Your turn." I aimed at his vein.

"No, you go in like you're landing an airplane," he said, "not like a helicopter. Catch the vein, that's it."

I did it, filling a glass vial, and finally exhaled. "I'm not a phlebotomist," I said, "but I play one on TV."

Tim's mother volunteered to be my next guinea pig with a new needle, and again Tim coached me through it. "It's gonna be gin," he said under his breath, but she laughed. I wanted a "control" so I knew it worked when we got the results back. Hers was likely negative, and his would be positive. Then I'd know it worked.

I had a Styrofoam cooler—a little minnow bucket I used for fishing—and put the labeled samples in there with some ice.

"Wish me luck," I said. Off I drove to the Arkansas state health department, which I had seen but never been in. It's an imposing fortress with a long row of about a dozen steps out front, so you know the people there come down from on high.

I generally don't do front doors, because they're easier for people to close on you. So I drove around to see if there was another way in. Down an incline in the back, they had a loading dock, with more vans and pickups parked around it than the fancy cars in front.

"Here we go," I said. I got out, adjusted the shoulder pads of my white blazer, and marched up to the back of the building. Next to an overflowing dumpster was a ramp that led to a door. I walked up and went through it like I owned the place.

There were two guys, each of whom seemed more than a little surprised to see me.

"Good afternoon, I'm Ruth Coker Burks, and I think I am all turned around. How do I get to the drop-off for blood samples?" I hid my minnow bucket behind me.

"Uh, you want to go this way," one of the guys said, pointing down a passageway, "then left. The public health lab."

"Thank you," I said. "And what is your name?"

"Earl."

"Earl, thank you so much."

I went toward the intake desk. A woman in her fifties looked up from reading a magazine. We exchanged smiles. "I love your nails," I said. If you have a hard time finding a compliment to give someone, go for the nails.

"Oh, thank you," she said. She looked down at them, like they were prized possessions.

"I have two blood samples that need to be tested for HIV."

"Ewww," she said. There went that smile.

"You don't have to fall in love with it, just get it where it needs to go."

"Okay," she said, stepping back from her disgust. Maybe she wondered if I was someone important. She seemed surprised at the bucket.

"There's two," I said.

"Do you have the test request forms?"

"Shoot," I said.

"Here," she said, handing me two.

They wanted names. "It's anonymous testing, right?"

"Right."

"Good, because I am not sure I got their real names," I said, writing down "Ronald Reagan" and "Nancy Reagan."

She eyed the forms suspiciously but gave me a number to call. "End of day tomorrow," she said.

"Perfect, thank you." I walked to the back, and thanked Earl again. "Are you gonna get out on the water this weekend, Earl?" I asked, now waving the minnow bucket.

"You bet."

"Well, good luck to you."

I got the call that Ronald Reagan had tested positive for HIV, and Nancy Reagan had tested negative. It worked. Now we could get in front of this thing.

I started to think about the rules of the game changing. But then the game got turned upside down.

Chapter Eight

I knew there was trouble when I saw the crowd outside the resort, but I couldn't have guessed how much.

We were locked out; there were chains on the gate. Sandy was already there, cursing up a storm. "It's been seized," she said.

"The feds?" I asked.

"Well, somebody with locks. It's done."

The way I came to understand it, the resort was financed by a savings and loan that fell. Right on our heads. What I did know for sure was that the resort owed me about thirty-five thousand dollars in commissions that I was counting on for the rest of the year. And that vanished.

"What are we gonna do?" asked Sandy. Allison was at school, and I had this feeling like I needed to fix this before I picked her up. I saw our life falling away, and I needed a plan.

"Sandy, there's about six more weeks to the racing season, and that's probably the only place hiring right now," I said. "We need to get over to Oaklawn." Oaklawn Park was the racetrack, still the big draw to Hot Springs back then, but the horse races were only in town from January until April.

Sandy made a face. The people in town were raised to call people who worked at Oaklawn "racetrackers," which was as good as saying "trash." These locals and church people, they didn't mind going and betting, but they didn't talk to any of racetrackers. I remember when kids used to come to school because they'd moved here with their families for racing season; they'd get stuff thrown at them all the time.

"Well, I'm going," I said. I drove right there, realizing over and over how much trouble Allison and I were in. Her daddy certainly wasn't going to suddenly start paying child support. And my guys. Gas to get to Little Rock, food . . .

I stopped behind a little yellow Chevette signaling to make a left into the racetrack. They had to pass two lanes of oncoming traffic on Central to get there.

"Just edge into it," I said aloud. A tourist bus was behind me, and the driver leaned on the horn. "How's that gonna help?" I asked.

The car wasn't budging, and traffic wasn't relenting. The bus honked again. I got out of the car, closing the door lightly. I signaled to the bus driver with one finger that said "Hold on," and then I walked up to the car. It was a little black lady, and she was terrified.

"Let me ask you this," I said. "If I stop all this traffic, will you go?"

She nodded. "Yeah, but ya can't do that."

"We're gonna do this," I said. There was no median, so I was right in the middle of the road. I held up my hand to the first lane. A car whizzed by. The car behind him slowed, and I took a step into the lane, basically forcing him to come to a full stop. I did that lane by lane, standing in the center of Central Avenue. I directed her to turn. The bus started beeping in short bursts, and I waved to him to make the turn. I knew he had a schedule.

I looked at the faces in the two cars, and put my hand to my heart in a sincere thank-you. I ran to my car, assuming they'd start up again, but they waited, even with cars behind them honking up a storm. Sometimes you have to hang a lot on small mercies.

I got a job selling tickets at the track, but that wasn't going to last. I was pretty, so I got a lot of people coming to my window. After a week they put me in the private club, where the good tips were.

"Maybe you'll find a husband," the manager said when he told me they were moving me. I smiled but thought, *What do I need a gambler for a husband for?*

But that would be only through April. And I had all my guys to feed. Even with half of Bonnie's food stamps, I couldn't afford to keep this going.

I began to go to some of the elders of the town for help for my guys. I had impressed a lot of them while working with the church finance committee, coming up with fundraising ideas and always knowing who in the church might want to make a larger pledge that year to clear their conscience over some affair or business deal. I never ratted on anyone, I was just observant and kept a mental list.

Many of the elders just knew me as my father's daughter. I was a toddler when my daddy would let me tag along to sit as the menfolk talked on the porch at the house of Raymond Clinton, a powerful figure in Arkansas politics. He helped lead the GI movement that got veterans to run for all the offices in Hot Springs and Garland County. Raymond owned the Buick dealership, and if you wanted anything done in Hot Springs, you had to go through him and get his blessing. In the evenings, all these veterans would meet at Raymond's house out on Lake Hamilton. It was kind of a hideout. My daddy was twenty years older than the other men on average, and as they figured what it meant to be a veteran, they looked up to him, as someone who had been in both World War I and World War II.

The women would be in the house, but I didn't have a woman to be in the house with me. My mother was in the TB sanatorium. So I would get to stay out on the porch with my daddy and the men. Daddy was already so weak he couldn't really walk anymore. Raymond's nephew Billy would help him in and out of his car and get him to the porch. Billy was Governor Bill Clinton now, but then he was just a high schooler. Even then, we all knew he was going places.

All the talk was about politics, and Billy would use visiting with me as an excuse to stay out on the porch. Billy would throw me up in the air and catch me as I laughed, eavesdropping on lessons on how to gain and maintain power. When my daddy died when I was five, I sat on Raymond Clinton's lap at the funeral.

As long as I didn't push it, I could go now to these men for donations: Mr. Johnson, a sniper in World War II who came back the quietest man, so meek you'd never know what he'd seen. Mr. Wallace, a Marine in twilight, treating Rotary like his service. Another two men who were presidents of the big banks. These gentlemen still ran the town, but quietly, and I think that they respected that I worked quietly too.

I had to rely on their discretion and know who I told. But they knew all the secrets in town, so this was only one more. I just had to be careful not to wear them out and not make it their issue. I would make an appointment to meet in their offices and just privately say, "You know, I've got these guys, and they don't have food." Or they don't have rent while I'm getting through the paperwork of housing assistance. Or whatever. They would make a phone call. And it would be done. "Put fifty dollars on Ruth Burks's tab."

I had to be up front about this being about AIDS, because I wanted it on their radar. AIDS was something we had to deal with here in Hot Springs. I also knew that if I made up a story then I would have never gotten any more money. I would have been a liar in town, and I didn't want *that* reputation. Let people say I've got AIDS, but don't call me a liar.

I also wanted to make sure Governor Clinton knew what was going on in his hometown. I wrote him these long letters, detailing patterns I saw. Bonnie would proofread them, going over them with me two or three times, suggesting changes to this or that. By the time I was done, they would be fifteen pages long. Stories of the men I'd seen waste away. I knew he knew gay people. Bill was always someone who knew there was a world outside of Arkansas. But I knew he didn't know the gay men I saw—the poor, the rejected, the ones with nobody to care for them. I always signed it Ruth and Allison

Burks because I didn't want anyone thinking a single woman was writing the governor. He already had a reputation, and all of us in Hot Springs grew up very protective of him. When I went to the health department, I might stop by to take a big, thick envelope to the little state police headquarters just past the front door of the capitol.

"We'll get it to his office," they said. Who knows what they thought of this blond woman all dressed up?

Sometimes he would call my house and thank me for the information. He asked questions about their lives, how they were getting by.

"You're doing good work," he said. We were both in a bind, each feeling only able to do just so much for fear of being run out of town.

There were only so many times I could go to the elders of the town for grocery tabs. I knew keeping weight on my guys was helping, but even with Bonnie's half of the food stamps and all my foraging, I was coming up short.

And then the answer was right there at the Piggly Wiggly.

It was early morning, and we needed bread on the way to school, so I swung by the Piggly Wiggly on Park, and we popped in real quick. On my way out, I saw the dumpster was so full they'd left the top open. It wasn't a huge bin, just about chest-high, and right on top was a clear bag full of plastic-wrapped loaves. The bread I'd just spent money on.

As Allison got in the car, I walked over to get a better look at the bag. Through the plastic, I could see that all the bread had a sell-by date of just a few days from then. I thought of all the sandwiches I could make my guys and the dressings or the ways I could stretch meatloaf.

I grabbed it. The whole bag. And once you're taking food from a dumpster, you're in. So, what was I going to do but look to see what else they had? Vegetables and fruits with the slightest bruises, some perfectly fine. Dinged cans and the like, probably put out earlier that morning as they went through inventory. It was like the potlucks and galas—all that food gone to waste when it would be gold to the people who weren't invited to the parties.

The Piggly Wiggly was right on the corner, so the lot was wide open to traffic. I knew cars were driving by, but I had the focus of someone who'd dropped her keys in there. "I saw that crazy Ruth Coker Burks this morning," I said aloud to no one. "*Dumpster diving.* 'Well, maybe she's working there?' Nah, she's out with the trash at the track."

I grabbed as many bags as I could, taking two trips to the trunk of my car.

"Yuck," Allison said through the window as I was between trips.

"It's not yuck," I said. "This is perfectly good food. We can help a lot of people with it, and it's a sin to waste it."

I got her to school and worked out a plan. I'd give the fruit and vegetables a bath in hot water from the downtown fountain with a tiny bit of Clorox, make sure I rinsed everything real good, and I'd break off stuff we didn't want so I could make a big pot of vegetable soup.

Then it occurred to me that if the Piggly Wiggly had good food, what about the big Kroger out on Airport Road?

"Well, let's pay a call," I said to myself, turning the car around to drive to the lot behind the store, where the trucks came and went for deliveries. At least this one was behind the store, but it was much larger. I really would have to dive in.

It was worth it though, even in heels, because sure enough, there was a banquet. A lot of it was in date, as if whoever had done the clearing said, "Oh, what the hell, I'll have to throw it away in a couple of days anyway."

It became my secret routine. I would go gathering at the dumpsters in the morning, because it would spoil by afternoon. Usually on the way to school, I'd check the one on Park because it was by the house. Drop off Allison, then hit the Kroger dumpster. I usually didn't have to be at the racetrack until noon, so I stopped by the hospitals to check on people. "I just stopped by for a bucket of coals," I'd say. That's from the old days, when you needed to start your fireplace. Somebody would stop by to get enough coals from your fire to start their own fire. But they had to get home quick so the coals didn't burn out. It's a way to say, "I just stopped by for a quick minute." I'd maybe adjust an IV someone had for antibiotics or just be present so the staff knew someone was checking up on the men.

The Piggly Wiggly must have seen what I was up to, because they stopped putting the really good stuff in the dumpster. They left it nice, outside the dumpster. Like presents under the garbage tree. No one who worked there ever said a word to me.

There was a milk truck, a big refrigerated eighteen-wheeler, that was sometimes parked behind Kroger. The driver used to take away all the stuff that was about to expire and deliver the new goods. I think he saw me enough times to know I couldn't be doing this just for me. One day he was staring at me as I picked up the day's haul.

"Hi, there," I said. He was bald, and it was like he'd smirked as a kid and his face froze that way.

"You help people, don't you?" he said. I told him I do my best but moved a little quicker in case this was going to be a thing.

"I'm gonna leave the door open on my truck by accident, so all that stuff I'm supposed to take away that's still good is gonna be right there."

I nodded.

"But you don't know that, do you?" he said.

"Nope," I said. "I don't know a thing."

It was such a blessing. Cheese, milk, yogurt, ice cream . . . The gold-standard butter and Bulgarian buttermilk I put into everything to get my guys more calories so I could keep the weight on them.

Whenever I saw that truck, I knew it would be a good week for my guys. I could be like this little grocery-delivery person. Bonnie of course loved all this, because it was like getting something over on the system. As I went around bringing food and meals to people, I especially loved bringing her anything that seemed exotic. The stuff you can't get with food stamps.

She brought up food stamps once as an option for me, and I changed the subject, saying I didn't qualify when we both knew I did. I didn't go on welfare, not just because of my Southern pride. It didn't bother me to get everybody else resources they needed. But I was being realistic about my hopes. I knew nobody around Hot Springs wanted to marry someone who'd been on welfare. I'd rather be eating out of a dumpster that nobody knew I was eating out of than ante up food stamps and trade my future in.

Pride doesn't pay rent, though, and my daughter couldn't live in a dumpster. It got to a point that Allison and I needed to move, and I could only budget about two hundred a month in rent. I found a place on Sixth Street, an ugly tan pile of bricks, but it had two bedrooms, so at least Allison could still have her own room. I was relieved there was a phone line in my room.

Our first night there, I put Allison to bed, for once glad that she still slept with the light on. I knew if I turned it off the roaches would come. I'd probably need to keep the lights on for a month before they got the hint to leave. I stayed up long after she was asleep, maybe from nerves about the new place. Then I heard this low guttural voice, barely intelligible. "*Heeeeeey sleeeeeee.*"

It was coming from Allison's room.

I panicked, grabbing a broom as I ran to her room. I burst in to find her still asleep.

The voice again. "*Waaaaaaaaa.*"

Whoever it was, he was in her closet. I freaked out, and I remember thinking, *This is so weird. I don't freak out.* But I was. I picked her up and backed out of the room to the living room to call the police.

I took her out on the porch to wait for the police but could still hear him inside, this terrifying voice. I must have sounded scared on the phone, because a cop showed up so fast.

"*Uhhhhhhhhhhhhhhh.*"

The cop heard it too, and he drew his gun. "Probably a goddamn junkie," he said, walking in as scared as I was. As he made his way to Allison's room, I put her down on the couch, afraid to leave the cop alone with this guy. I stayed at the doorway while the cop twice put his hand to the closet door to open it, each time pulling back in fear. Then he just did it.

"All right!" he screamed. "Okay!"

"*Uuuuuppppppppp.*"

He put his head down, and sighed. "Ma'am, you have a Smurf."

"What?"

He reached in and grabbed Allison's Smurf alarm clock. It was two Smurfs sawing a log, its alarm sound a usually chipper voice saying, "Hey, sleepyhead, it's time to wake up." The battery had run down so it just sounded demonic.

"Well," I said, "that's my entrance to the neighborhood. I'm really sorry."

"I was scared half to death," he said.

"Death by Smurf would be a helluva way to go," I said. He left, but I noticed he kept popping by for about a month after, just to check in. Usually at night, hoping to get in. "We're good, Officer." I'd say. "No Smurfs here."

The real problem was the rats. I had to put a board under the washing machine to cover the hole so the rats wouldn't come in. *We'll make do*, I told myself.

My problems were continually put in perspective. My guys kept bringing me people to test. I'd go to an apartment to bring food, and another man would be there. The closeted ones would be in their work gear, nervously rubbing their hands together. There were people I recognized, though I pretended not to know anything about them. And there were some I could just tell had it. They had an old age look at a young age.

Across the board, everybody would be so nervous. But they trusted that I knew how to do it. Well, I didn't know how to do it, but I did it somehow. I was afraid to stick people repeatedly, so I would hold my breath as I did it. I thought of Tim—"In like an airplane, not a helicopter"—and in the middle of doing this fluid motion I would realize, *I can't breathe*. And then I'd start to breathe.

Telling people was the worst, but I knew I could deliver the news better than some mean person or someone who would use a needle and dive right in to the vein to hurt them. It was a fact, something to adjust your life to so you could manage it. In the end, though, it was telling somebody they were dying, because that's what it was. I could offer this bit of hope about AZT and getting into treatment, though I was starting to think that all it did was turn your fingernails black. But it was still hope. My guys would take their AZT until the day they died because they knew tomorrow they would come out with a cure. If they just made it there.

I fanned the cupcakes with a folded newspaper, trying to get them to cool enough so I could ice them. Allison turned six on May 28, a Saturday. I kept her for the morning, and then her daddy would take her to Little Rock. The temperature was already creeping toward the eighties, and we had no air-conditioning, so I was fighting a losing battle with the fan.

The plan was for a morning picnic with school friends in the park, nothing at our house. Allison gave out little invites at school, but I hadn't heard anything back from the other mothers. There were eighteen cupcakes, white cake, and the icing was vanilla. I was anxious about the picnic, so while I waited for the cupcakes to cool, I turned the icing a pale pink with a few drops of blood orange. I just wanted it to be nice for Allison.

The cupcakes would have to be just cool enough for the icing, because I wanted to have time to do her hair. Her strawberry-blond curls had naturally straightened, falling down to her shoulders. A gorgeous color on my beautiful girl.

She was watching cartoons, and as I iced the cupcakes I realized how rare it was for her to be here on a weekend. She had a whole routine of favorite TV shows that I'd only heard her mention.

She wasn't excited about her birthday, which I just didn't get. How can you be six and not want a party? I had to snap her out of the trance of cartoons just to get her to look at the cupcakes, and she finally smiled when she saw them.

I had her sit so I could comb out her hair. "Are kids excited for your party?" I asked.

"No."

I ignored that. We drove over to the picnic spot just before the time I had asked people to come, and I laid out a red gingham cloth in the center, then a few blankets around it. I kept the cupcakes loosely covered with foil to keep away the bugs.

The stage was set, so we sat. And we waited. I smoothed the red gingham over and over, trying to keep away what I slowly realized was happening.

"It's early yet," I said, fifteen minutes in. Then I stopped saying that.

No one came.

She didn't cry. She knew nobody was going to come long before I understood. Allison had never been invited to a single birthday party. I just assumed the other children didn't have them. She'd been invited to one, but they'd accidentally put the wrong time on the invitation. We showed up, and it had been over for hours. Allison told me it was on purpose, but I told her it was a mistake.

Now, I tried to talk to her about it.

"Mama, stop," she said. A finality to it. Something pushed away.

I took her to McDonald's, and said I wasn't hungry. "I want you to get whatever you want," I said. I watched her eat, remembering the kids who taunted me because of my mother. She'd had a horrible reputation in town because she was so mentally ill. The kids who teased me, I realized now, were hearing that from somewhere—that my mother was "crazy."

I took Allison home, and her daddy showed up to get her. I hugged her so hard. "I love you, I love you, I love you," I said. I didn't know what else to say. I felt defeated.

The cupcakes sat on my counter, still covered in foil, their presence taunting me like those kids in the schoolyard. Those kids were right about my mother, and no matter what they heard, they didn't know the half of it. And now what had I done to Allison?

I never let myself go back to that time, my childhood, because I was afraid I would get stuck there. But here it was, unbidden.

We are living on Lake Hamilton. I am six, Allison's age, and the house still feels new. Mama burned down our original house when I was five. A white clapboard home that was too regular for her. She had come home from the TB sanatorium broken and wanted a new house before Daddy died. He would get it on credit life. Credit life is when they'll pay off the balance if you die, which she knew he would.

She waited until my daddy was out one night to start the fire. I was on the sleeping porch, and I think I was supposed to go up with it. I was asleep when somebody jerked my ankles and pulled me to safety. I don't know who. Not her.

The house she built was blood-red brick. A two-bedroom with a beautiful view of the lake. And when Daddy died, it was in this house that she lost her mind.

It starts like this: she works at Children's Hospital and comes home late with stories about how the kids climb into her lap while they eat dinner. She loves the kids at Children's Hospital. She hates me.

I have a dog. She drives it out to Mount Ida and lets it loose because I don't deserve it. I come home from school to find she has piled all my clothes into a heap by the water. She throws gasoline on them and tells me I don't deserve nice clothes. She lights a match and hands it to me to set the pile of my clothes on fire. I do.

She drags me to Salvation Army and buys me clothes two sizes too big so she doesn't have to do it again. Before second grade, she takes a scissors to my hair, and I scream as she gives me a short, uneven boy's cut that will take years to grow out. She tells me how ugly I am.

There is always something wrong. A bad grade on a report card, or I laugh too loud. The sun could have set wrong. You never know. You never know.

From time to time, she drops me off at Hillcrest Children's Home, an Assemblies of God orphanage in Hot Springs. The kids there have no parents, and they resent that I am so bad that my mother doesn't want me. They bully me, and I am usually there for two days at least, sometimes a week. Longer in summer. Each time she takes me there, I pack my belongings in a little red suitcase, filling it with the toys I have collected for myself—acorns, pine cones, and interesting leaves—because my mother will not let me have Barbies or other dolls. I keep it under my bed at the orphanage. I am constantly scolded for checking to make sure it is there. But I am convinced that my mother will come and take the suitcase when I am not there, proof that I have nothing and that she has left me there forever.

The people who run the orphanage finally tell her she needs to stop bringing me. "*They* don't even want you," she tells me.

She beats me constantly, and one day she whips me with the electric cord of a coffee percolator. She breaks the skin on my legs, and I run away, barefoot, through the woods to the house of an old woman. She is sweeping her front porch. I turn and lift my dress just a little so she can see the blood running down my legs.

The old woman sweeps me away with the broom. "I don't wanna see it, I don't wanna get involved," she says, brushing my feet with the hard bristles of broomcorn. I wash the blood away in the waters of Lake Hamilton.

In a manic stage, my mother buys me a bicycle. At seven, I get on it in the mornings, and I am not allowed back in the house until dark. I spend entire days exploring. The Oosters have a smokehouse, and I stop and get a sausage end or a baloney end and then go on my way.

I ride through the woods behind our house, a vast forest of pine by the lake. My sanctuary. Any given day, I find one of those pine beddings where there is no grass, and I make my fort and stay back there. I hide for so long that I forget I'm hiding. I fall in love with Hot Springs, and I want everyone to feel safe in its arms.

Now, in the living room, I let myself cry. My mother did everything she could to ruin my life. I'd spent my adult life letting her back in and then exiling her again, never asking her why she was so cruel to me. We were on another break. I needed to keep Allison safe from her.

And now Allison was as lonely as I was.

I stood up, smoothed my skirt, and went to the kitchen to get the cupcakes. I drove them around to my guys. They all knew Allison, and I told them she wanted them to have them. I never wanted to burden them with our problems.

Chapter Nine

The last Friday in June, a jazz orchestra gave a concert in the Arlington's Crystal Ballroom. This was a little bit of a last hurrah for me. Monday I would be starting a job working at the Weyerhaeuser sawmill, pulling wet grain plywood off the assembly line on the graveyard shift. It was the only job I could get, and it was part-time, just half the week. Allison's daddy would have to take her for longer, and Bonnie would pick up the slack. I'd applied at so many places, and the ones who brought me in for interviews made it clear sex was a requirement of clerical work. I did two days at a sales office and quit when I realized the boss thought touching my ass was a friendly greeting.

"Now that you don't work for me," he said, "can we go out to the car and you give me a blow job?"

I got up from the seat in front of his desk. "I'm the one out of a job now," I said, turning to go out the door. "Don't you think I should be the one needing something?"

So, the sawmill job was the best I could do. But I could still dress up for something like this night at the Arlington. A curling iron and a tube of lipstick can hide a million stresses.

People were dancing, and I wished Sandy had been able to come. I looked at the elderly couples dancing, and I didn't begrudge them their happiness, but I wanted it for me too. I leaned against the wall as a vocalist took center stage to sing, "A Pretty Girl is Like a Melody."

He was in a tuxedo, singing about a woman who haunts him, and I closed my eyes, transported back seventy-five years, with all the ghosts of showgirls and gangsters still in the building coming down to dance.

"I know what you're doing."

He was on my right, appearing beside me. It was a doctor I barely knew, part of a clinic in town. His specialty and mine did not mix.

"And what's that?" I said, staring at the singer.

"I know you're testing people."

"Testing?" I said, like it was a word I'd never heard.

"AIDS."

Well, that was that. I wanted to ask how he knew, but I didn't. Maybe he was confirming a rumor. I braced for what was sure to be next, the "I will ruin you" or the "How dare you?"

Instead, he said, "I don't mind testing for you."

I turned to look up at him. Now it was his turn to look away and focus on the singer. "Really?" I said. The Doctor was tall and had an air of superiority about him. It wasn't until the early eighties that they let outside doctors come in to Hot Springs. It used to be you couldn't be a doctor in Hot Springs unless you father or father-in-law was.

His voice was halting, rehearsed but still unsure. "Bring them to the clinic. At night. The back door. Give me warning, and I'll leave it open. If it's locked, leave."

"Whatever you want, yes."

"Where do you bring the sample?"

"Health department," I said. "Little Rock."

"Refrigerated?"

"On ice," I said. "Minnow box."

He suppressed a smug chuckle. "You keep bringing the blood to the lab. Nothing to do with me or the clinic."

I nodded.

"Don't tell anybody."

I turned to look him in the eye. "Never. I can't thank you enou—"

He moved on. The singer ended with a flourish, holding the last note. I let out a breath as he finally took one. The Doctor was married with a mess of kids, and I knew one of the rules was that I not ask who told him about me.

The first time I took someone, it was a scared friend of one of my guys. I can't remember his name, but I was nervous myself. I picked him up, and we drove to the back of the building. It backed up against some woods, so no one would see. We went through a plain white door, and the Doctor was waiting. He did what he would always do when I brought people: he shook hands but did not introduce himself. He'd get right to it, but at the moment of the needle, he was especially gentle. "You can look away if you need to," he said softly to them. "You're okay."

I took the sample home and put it in the refrigerator to take to Little Rock the next day. Allison never knew what she was going to find in the fridge.

The first two times with the Doctor, the test was it, and that was plenty. The third time, the Doctor asked if I needed anything. I took that as a signal that I was doing okay by his rules. I told him about a patient who wasn't responding to antibiotics. "What are they doing for it?" he asked.

I named a drug, and he suggested a switch to another, writing it down for me. In the hospital I repeated what he said with an air of authority. "What about . . . ?" The doctor at the hospital said it wouldn't work, but I went back later and saw he had prescribed it. I didn't point it out, just wrote it down in my little planner.

I finally had an ally, someone who could help me. And it inspired me to ask someone else for help.

Right before the night's finance committee meeting at First United Methodist, I stopped in at the office of Dr. Hays, the lead preacher for the church. He commanded a large room with dark wood and thick rugs. There was a conversation area with leather couches, but he only ever talked to me from his desk, a huge clock behind him to remind me his time was valuable. Crosses here and there to remind everyone who had paid for our sins.

We said some pleasantries, and he looked at me, expectant. The clock ticked behind him.

He is a good man, I told myself. *He likes you. Just be direct.*

"Dr. Hays, I have been helping some men with AIDS, and I have met a few who have been newly diagnosed."

He looked at me. I kept talking.

"Could I have one of the Sunday-school rooms, just one hour a week, for a group support, uh, support group meeting? In the breezeway?"

He straightened himself up in his chair. "Surely you're not talking about bringing *those* people into *this* church?"

That did it for me—the "those." We had spent every finance committee meeting talking about paying for the new house we had to buy Dr. Hays. We put down new grass for him, and then the sprinklers wouldn't work to his specifications, and the pattern on the cloth on the chair next to the back door wasn't the right shade of whatever color. Our answer was always the same: "Well, yes, Dr. Hays. We'll take it back and pay to have it reupholstered to make you happy, Dr. Hays."

"Oh, no, Dr. Hays. I'm talking about bringing them across your new lawn we paid for. And into the house we paid for. And sitting their butts down on the thousands of dollars' worth of furniture the church bought for you."

"You are—"

"That's what I'm talking about doing with *those* people."

"Go."

"It's in the breezeway," I said, walking out as he stood. "Those germs aren't gonna crawl out and find their next victim."

I went outside to cool off before the meeting. I got in my car so nobody would hear me let out a yell. I felt foolish for thinking he would help and that I just needed to summon the courage to ask for it. "Of course, Ruth," I said aloud. "What do you need? Can we set up a ministry for this? I can't believe you've been doing this on your own. How can we help?"

That felt better. That's what he should have said. That's what Jesus wanted us to do. I got out to go back in. I could smooth this over. He wasn't going to help. At least I knew where I stood.

I went in, and the men of the finance committee were at the table. My plan was to just keep my mouth shut.

Dr. Hays looked up. "Uh, uh. You're not on the finance committee anymore?" He said it like a question. Like I should know this was the decision or like he was unsure he could actually do it.

"I'm not?"

"You're not."

"Why?"

"Uh, this isn't the place to talk about it."

I looked at the men, these leaders of the community, who had grown to respect me, not simply as my father's daughter but as someone who had both new ideas about how the church could raise revenue and good ones that widened our scope of pledges. Now they seemed confused.

"No," I said, "this is exactly the place to talk about it. Right here, since y'all are gonna talk about it after I leave anyway."

"Well, we were going through the records, and we don't see where you tithe," he said. "We have to have people that commit to tithing, so we know how much money we have to commit to the church."

I didn't have the kind of money that I could promise ten dollars each week or five. "I give ten percent of what I have," I said. "And sometimes when I have a five, I want to ask for change out of the offering plate. But you don't remember the time there was five hundred dollars wrapped with a rubber band?" I asked. "That was me. Jim Edwards won so big at Oaklawn that he gave me that, and I gave it right to the church. I didn't know I had to sign off with anyone."

The men shifted uncomfortably. Some of them had helped me. Picked up a phone and made a problem go away with fifty dollars. They couldn't know how they extended the lives of my guys, but they did know that I cared.

"I just asked Dr. Hays for a room, one hour a week, to help some people with AIDS who need supp—"

Fred Kurtz from the chamber of commerce piped up. "Are you out of your mind? We have to think of the safety of the church and this town. I won't let you put up a vacancy sign for perverts!"

"We have church business," Dr. Hays said firmly, looking away from me.

"This *is* church business," I yelled. Then, catching myself, continued softer: "The business of the church should be helping people. That is exactly what we should be talking about." Dr. Hays still wouldn't look at me. "Gentlemen, I thank you for this opportunity to serve the church. I have learned a lot."

I walked out and drove home to put on my uniform for the sawmill.

The next day I checked in on Tim and Jim at home with Tim's parents. It just seemed like everyone in that house was trying not to be the last one to die. Tim's dad was just old—though he sure liked to joke by lifting my skirt with his cane—and his mother loved the bottle more than it could ever love her back.

"Do you ever think about getting a place in Hot Springs?" I asked. "I could get you housing assistance. I know you qualify." They were living on Tim's social security check, which was three hundred dollars a month. For some reason, Jim never wanted to apply for it, and I didn't push it. He didn't want to be in the system, and I wondered if he'd maybe gotten into some trouble years back.

"Our own place?" Jim said.

"Just you two," I said. I'd never gotten a place for two men together, but why not?

Well, housing assistance was why not. I was up front with them, saying I had two men with AIDS, and they needed a place and they were together. A studio would be fine. A few weeks went by, and when I called they gave me such a runaround on the phone, saying I had to resubmit forms and prove eligibility. How dare they do this? I knew Tim qualified.

"We'll just come down," I said.

"Well, that's not necessary," the man said, an edge of panic in his voice. "It won't change the fact that—"

"Okay, see you soon," I said.

The file was in Tim's name, so I called him and asked if he didn't mind going down to the housing office with me. He said, "It's a date."

He was waiting at the house and walked to the car. I looked at his outfit: plain black shorts and a tight polyester button-down.

"Tim," I said. "You know those Daisy Dukes you love?"

He nodded.

"Go put 'em on," I said.

The housing building is set low, and to enter it, you have to walk down a really wide, long set of stairs outside. It's all windows on the side, but the building is set so deep you can't even see the parking lot. Why they built it that way I don't know, but I guess the thought never occurred to anybody that disabled people were the ones that need housing assistance.

But that day it was a stage, and I could see everyone inside staring at us—Tim's long legs in those short shorts, and me in my highest heels—making our grand entrance down the stairs. If he was with me, they knew he had AIDS. And Tim left no doubt that he was wonderfully, unapologetically gay.

We were taken care of in five minutes. Approved. Anything we wanted, just get out.

As we walked back up the stairs, Tim turned to wave at the people behind all that glass, still staring at us. They didn't wave back.

"They kind of look like they're in a zoo, don't they?" I said.

"And they think *we're* the animals."

"Right?" I said, in an earnest, confiding voice, as if the same thought had occurred to me but I was too polite to say it. Tim started to laugh, a big shaking cackle he aimed upward, which made me laugh too. We stood there, laughing until we cried, our arms around each other for fear that if one of us looked back again at those jaw-dropped, wide-eyed faces, it would send us rolling down the stairs. We took another step only when we'd finally wiped our tears, whispering "Okay, okay" to each other.

Chapter Ten

I stood outside Allison's school, on top of the hill, and cursed her daddy. "You know what?" I said out loud to myself, "that jerk is not gonna be here. He never shows up for anything."

We were high enough that I could see the highway from Little Rock in the distance. He was still working out there but had moved back to Hot Springs, much to my displeasure. As the sun started to set in the September sky, I could see the prettiest little thunderstorm in the distance, like gray and white cotton gathered into a neat pile.

Allison's Catholic school was having an evening open house for first grade. They had it on a Monday night in September, so the dads could show up, look at what their kids had done in their first week in school, and not show up again until the father-daughter breakfast in June. I sent a note to him with Allison, and I even had to talk to him to tell him the date. From the door, but still.

I wasn't going to put on a show like we weren't divorced, but I remembered never having my daddy at anything because he was dead. Kids, even six-year-olds like Allison and her classmates, notice everything, even if they don't get the whole story. I'd invited Imogene, my ex-mother-in-law, to come as a sort of insurance policy. I wanted somebody up there with me to show her teacher and the other parents that Allison had real family. I had to promise to pick Imogene up and drop her off, making the obligation as small as possible. She was already inside, probably saying something about Catholics and idols, so I gave up and went in.

"Where's Daddy?" asked Allison. I scanned the room and saw all the dads were here, awkwardly talking to one another. The women used loud voices to praise their kids' drawings, then looked around to see who was impressed.

"I think he's held up," I said, glancing at Imogene, who sat awkwardly in a little chair sized for a first grader. Her eyebrows were arched, but her eyes were beady, judging everything. Not even for sport or fun, just out of habit.

Allison's teacher talked a little about the curriculum, and I was impressed. I was glad she was here, even if Imogene thought nuns were zealots. I hadn't even told her that Allison and her classmates went to Mass every morning. Allison even had a little prayer book, and when she and I buried someone in the cemetery, she would sometimes read from it. I definitely wasn't telling Imogene *that*.

The open house went longer than I expected, but Allison's daddy never showed, no matter how many times she looked at the door. We got in the car to drive Imogene home, and we were all quiet. When we got to her house, I had no illusion we'd be invited in. I wanted to ask Imogene if she could ask Allison's daddy why he couldn't do even the one thing I asked him to do.

"I wonder why Maggie's here?" she said. Maggie was Allison's daddy's new wife. The fourth one. She had a nice car, of course, and there it was parked outside Imogene's house. *Yeah, I wonder why that bitch is here?* I thought, but just shrugged. Imogene went in the house, and I drove off. While I was in the area, I stopped at one of my guys' apartments, just to make sure he was doing okay. They'd given us a packet of Allison's drawings at school, and he made a big deal about admiring them.

The Doctor had given me a bunch of pill organizers he got from some pharmaceutical rep pushing blood pressure medicine or something. As Allison explained her drawings, I divided up doses for the week. Whether it was a side effect of the AZT or an early sign of some kind of dementia, it was sometimes hard for my guys to keep track of their pills and whether they had taken them. This was such a simple way to be useful, and I found the divvying up to be like a meditation.

When I got home, the message button was flashing on my answering machine. I was tired and hoped one of my guys hadn't left a distress call. I pressed play and walked away.

It was Imogene.

Allison's daddy was dead in a car crash. I turned to shut off the message to spare Allison, but Imogene spoke so fast I couldn't. Allison stood there, a look of shock on her face, like she was replaying what she'd heard to make sense of it. She looked at me, waiting for me to explain how she had misunderstood. Waiting to hear from me that I would fix it and her father was fine. I couldn't.

He'd been driving out where the interstate turns to Highway 70, right where I'd seen that little thunderstorm. While I had watched from high on the hill, cursing him, Allison's daddy was lying dead in the rain, his car smashed against a bridge abutment at the bottom of a steep curve. Two women were working at a dairy bar right there at the bottom of the hill, and they saw it all.

They said he was speeding and passed a car against the line. When he tried to get back in, he swerved on the road, slick from rain after a dry spell. His car went spinning, turning again and again, gathering momentum until it crashed. One woman stayed to call the police, another ran to the car. She said he had slid to the passenger side, dead, but not a mark on him. In the seat as if he were waiting for the driver to come back.

Despite all the death I'd seen I couldn't come up with words to comfort Allison. The morning after we got the news, I called Dr. Hays, the head of our church, to tell him what happened. Allison really liked Dr. Hays, and I thought he could offer some solace. He'd been cold to me since I asked for the room for the support group but still polite. I made a point of waiting in line to shake his hand on Sundays because I knew it made him uncomfortable.

He said he was sorry to hear that. I asked if he would please come to the house to talk to Allison. He paused too long. "Yes, I can."

Dr. Hays drove up just before noon. I was waiting and opened the door to greet him. I could tell he was never in this neighborhood, even though the church secretary lived right by me. He walked gingerly, like the very ground might soil his shoes.

"Thank you for coming, Dr. Hays," I said. "Please come in."

"I think it's best if I stay on the porch," he said. "Is Allison—"

"You won't come in?"

"I cannot," he said quickly, glancing around. He looked anywhere but at my face.

"Why not?" I willed him to look at me. He did.

"You are a single woman, and it would not look right for me to come in to your house."

"The Persistent Widow," I said. Luke has Jesus talking about her in his Gospel. The widow who won't give up until she gets justice from a corrupt judge. She goes to him for help against her "adversaries," and it's never clear if she is talking about other people or something else that plagues her. I knew what I had wanted help with. I was still deeply hurt that Dr. Hays wouldn't even give my guys a place to talk to each other.

"You're not a quite a widow," he said.

"No, not quite," I said, smiling with no teeth so I wouldn't roll my eyes. "But I am persistent." I turned and called to Allison.

They talked on the porch while I waited inside. I couldn't stand to listen to him. I stood at the sink, holding the edges to steady myself. I had no idea how I was going to do this. I hated Allison's daddy, but he'd been a good parent. A better parent than me sometimes. I had no idea how I was going to do this alone and still take care of people.

When Dr. Hays left, we drove to Maggie's house, just so Allison could be with family. On the way over, Allison said she wanted one of her daddy's shirts. A long-sleeved button-down she pictured him in. "That's very nice," I said, swallowing a little hiccup of emotion. When my daddy died, I would wrap the sleeves of his shirt around me too.

We got to Allison's daddy's house, and I reminded myself to be nice. I don't think even Maggie liked him, and she was still married to him. I rang the bell and fixed a look on my face of compassion. Maggie was not as good an actress. Her face fell when she opened the door.

"Ruth?" she said. "What are *you* doing here?"

"Allison wanted to be with her family."

Maggie didn't look down at her. "This isn't a good time."

Past her shoulder, I could see his ex-wife Linda was inside with their son.

"I can, uh, I don't need to stay—" I took a step back, placing Allison at the forefront. Maggie didn't budge.

I mouthed, "Really?" and Maggie shook her head. I leaned in to speak softly but directly. "She would like one of his shirts."

Maggie looked aghast, like we were there to ransack the place. For a shirt. "Oh," she nearly spit, "it's just like you to have to come in and try to take something you want so soon."

I looked down, intent on keeping Allison from being further hurt. "Well, we just wanted to pay a call on you, Maggie," I said, only for Allison to hear.

Allison wanted me to take her to the florist. I had asked Terry Wallace, an announcer at the racetrack who had money, if I could borrow a hundred dollars for Allison to have a dress for the funeral and to buy flowers. First I had asked Imogene to help out, and she'd said no. So I was forced to ask someone who was basically a stranger to me. But he was a nice man, and I knew he wouldn't tell me no.

Allison was insistent that she choose the flowers for his funeral herself, and we stopped at home to pick up an angel candlestick she'd recently painted at school. She had a vision, and I had a need for her to have a win. When I parked, she turned to me as I unbuckled my seat belt.

"You can stay in the car, Mama."

"I'd like to help."

"No."

"Yes, I will help by staying in the car. Yes. That is what I will do."

She was in there so long that I thought maybe they were waiting for me to come in and pay. So I snuck in softly. One of the people who ran the shop, Suzann, had come from behind the counter. They were crying.

Suzann saw me, and I nodded, putting my finger to my lips. "I want it to be special," I heard Allison say. My six-year-old had prayed over so many people as we buried them together that I lost count. She understood the importance of a funeral, the ritual, the sacred meaning of being put to rest. I had a hunch where Allison's daddy's soul was going to end up, but I had to keep my mouth shut about that and just be there for her while she sent him off.

At the service, they wouldn't let us sit with the immediate family. His own six-year-old daughter. Her flower arrangement with the angel candle was indeed lovely, and I asked the funeral director if he could bring a little stepladder over or something so Allison could see her father in the casket.

"Well, can't somebody just pick her up?" he asked.

"No, she needs a moment alone with her father."

"Well, I will have to ask the family."

"She's his daughter," I said. "Isn't that family enough?"

Maggie said yes, but I got the sense we had crashed the funeral. Allison's daddy would be buried in Memorial Gardens, where my mother had exiled her brother for eternity so long ago. That seemed fitting. Allison wasn't allowed in the family limo over to Memorial Gardens. I understood me not being welcome, but not his daughter. Allison had a rose that she had quietly plucked from the casket spray, one she had studied all the way from the funeral home to the grave site. She had put all of her energy and love into it, and now she wanted to put it inside the casket quickly before everyone else got to the grave. The funeral director was put out and brushed us aside, again saying he would have to ask the family. I took him by the lapel and dragged him to the limo Maggie and Linda had just arrived in, sitting side by side. I ripped open the car door.

"Maggie, tell him that it's okay to open the casket so his six-year-old daughter can see her daddy one last time."

"Well, I guess."

Allison never got that shirt. They gave her a paperweight. Just a little globe with some plastic that meant nothing to him or them. But she put it in her room where she could see it. Allison's daddy told me he had a fifty-thousand-dollar life insurance policy payable to his daughter. You know where that story went.

He left us destitute. Because Allison's daddy had been married four times, I had to fight to get social security for Allison. It dragged on and on, and we were already out the money he was behind on child support. Bonnie helped watch Allison while I worked, but I was so stressed I went down to a size four. Bonnie didn't say much about it. If Bonnie didn't have a solution, she wasn't going to offer advice.

I was home one morning when there was a small but insistent knock on the door. It was Imogene, standing on my front porch, scowling. She was wearing a camel-hair coat that was expensive at one time, but that time had come and gone. She had her arms holding each shoulder, acting as if she was either so cold or so offended to even have to be at my home.

"Your friend told me you need help," she said.

"Who?"

"The sick one."

I laughed to myself. "Well, you'll have to be more specific."

"Bonnie," she said, as if she hated admitting she knew anything about me. She handed me a wad of cash. "Here. That's the best I can do. And don't ask again."

I waited until she was gone to look at the amount. Two hundred dollars. Money to go away, I guess. Well, I paid the rent and then took a tiny piece of that money, two dollars, to buy a flat of eggs at a hatchery. And I put it in the passenger side and drove over to Memorial Gardens.

Before I could think about what I was doing, I brought the eggs right over to his grave. "You sonuvabitch," I said, throwing a fastball egg right at the stone, aiming for his dumb name. "You sorry sonuvabitch. You left us all alone. Your child and her mother. Your useless parents won't see us."

I grabbed another and another, tears running down my face as I lobbed them right down. "Two hundred dollars." The yellow muck piled up on his grave. "One month's rent. *One*."

It was just a few hours before dark, and this would be a buffet for the coons and other varmints that would come out to feast on his grave.

Then the cops pulled up. I wouldn't even look at them. Just kept throwing egg fastballs. As an officer slowly approached, I said, "What do *you* want?"

"You're upsetting a lot of folks over here."

"Well, I'm sorry about that, but I've got some business I've got to attend to."

"It's not nice to throw eggs at graves."

"It's not nice for ex-husbands to leave their child penniless." I grabbed another, punctuating it with a "Destitute!" I grabbed two more. "It's not *nice*"—*slam*—"to have your child living on"—*slam*—"nothing."

"I'm taking those eggs," he said.

"That's just gonna waste your time," I said, finally turning to look at him. "Because I'm just gonna get more. And you'll just have to come back here."

He swallowed.

"Because," I continued, "there is something I have to let my ex-husband know."

He paused. "I get it," he said. "Just keep it down." As he walked away, he called out. "You're just lucky it's gonna rain."

"I guess I am," I said, picking up two more eggs. "So damn lucky."

Tim and Jim were giddy in the elevator. We were closed in tight because the elevator was a small one, beige with wood paneling. Tim danced like that was what would power it to the eleventh floor.

"I tried to get you the penthouse," I said, "but it's the one below." Jim was doing his "we'll see" act, but I could tell he was excited too. It was a big thing for these country boys to move uptown. Housing assistance set them up with a large studio in the Mountain View Heights building, right by the national park. It was a high-rise by the standards of Hot Springs, where even being in an elevator was a big deal.

When we got off the elevator, I walked them through the building as if I was their realtor, listing off the amenities. "I love this open walkway," I said, pointing out to Hot Springs Mountain and the park. The leaves were just started to fade to red and orange. "That's about the best view there is. The other side has a view too, but this is the one to have to see what's going on." Jim grabbed Tim's hand and squeezed it, real quick, but I saw it. If this was back at the resort, I knew I'd have a sale.

An older black woman walked by us. "New blood," I told her, making a point to stop her to introduce them. If they were gonna be here, they were gonna be here, so the neighbors needed to meet them. This was government housing, mostly seniors. She shook their hands, and we continued on to the apartment.

I held out the key. "Who's doing the honors?"

Tim put his hands to his face in excitement, and just as Jim went to take the key, Tim squealed and grabbed it to put it in the lock. They ran in, and Tim started exclaiming. "Oh, honey," he said to me. "Oh, honey. It's just so beautiful."

"Here's your kitchen," I said, waving to the left, "and the bathroom there." There was a large partition wall, making a front room with space for a big couch and a place for a bed on the other side. "There's that view again," I said, pointing to the picture window.

I led them to the back where the bed would go. "Here are all your closets, and on this side, you have a view of North Mountain."

Jim nodded at Tim. "You happy?" he asked.

"I am," he said.

"You're uptown now," I said.

They moved in quick, not having much. I drove them around in Bonnie's pickup, finding them things here and there. I'd gotten used to slowing down at dumpsters. We got a nice glass-top coffee table for the front room, just gorgeous, and a love seat we found on the side of Highway 70, like someone hadn't tied it down and just left it when they hit a bump and it flew off.

One of their favorite parts about the new place was the proximity to the trail up the mountain. By then I understood that they were not monogamous, and though that wouldn't have worked for me, it worked for them. They understood the risk and used protection, and the rest was none of my business, except for keeping them supplied with the condoms I started collecting from the health department. It wasn't a shock to me that men had sex in the park; the surprise was the joy with which Tim and Jim spoke about it. The foreplay of walking by someone and looking back. Leaning on one tree, looking at someone doing the same. The subtleties of signaling that you are friendly, joining in like a dance. I wanted to know about how things happened, so I could better understand how to talk to people about navigating risk and pleasure.

"Do you all go at night?" I asked.

"Twilight," Jim said.

"Guys getting off work, heading home," Tim said. "And also in the morning. That's when the executives who have the wives and children can say they're going in early for a meeting. It's tougher to swing that at dinnertime."

"A quick stop," I said.

"A quick stop," said Jim.

Advent, the four weeks before Christmas, is about waiting for something big to happen. A bunch of weary souls hanging on for a reason to feel the thrill of hope in winter. So it was funny that I finally got social security that first week. I had spent the summer digging in boxes in records rooms and warehouses, trying to piece together the employment history of Allison's daddy. He'd had and lost so many jobs that I couldn't keep up, and Maggie and Imogene wouldn't help me at all. They said I was just greedy, trying to make money off their husband and son. But there was a man, Marc Bergup, who worked the window of the press box at Oaklawn Park. His nine-to-five job was at the social security office, and he offered to help me when he found out what we were going through. He got me a partial check that first month, and without it, I don't know what I would have done.

It would be enough that I didn't have to work a full-time job. I could quit the sawmill, and Allison and I would be okay.

They lit candles at First United on the four Sundays of Advent, each candle symbolizing a different longing: faith, hope, joy, and peace. Allison wanted to be an acolyte and have a turn lighting the candle. Kids did it with their parents, and we'd never been asked. She was having a hard time dealing with her daddy's death, so I asked Dr. Hays right away.

"No, it's just for families."

"Well, what are we?"

"You're not a family," he said. "You don't have a husband."

I'd had it with him. "You know what? We are a family. And if we're not a family because my daughter doesn't have a father, it's because he just died. Remember? You were at the house—well, on the porch—when he died? So we would like to light a candle this season."

I wanted joy, but I settled for hope. I still had it, at least.

For Christmas, I asked Allison's daddy's parents if she could please go to their house, just to give her a sense of normalcy. "I will drop her off," I assured them.

Imogene said she could come for exactly two hours on Christmas Eve, not Christmas Day. "Fine," I said. Imogene was crying when I arrived with Allison, so I let myself in to make sure things were on the up and up in there. Pat Robertson was on, like always in their house, swearing God was speaking through him like some ventriloquist's dummy. He said God's hatred of homosexuality caused hurricanes, tornadoes, and fires—so of course it caused AIDS.

"What's wrong?" I asked Imogene. I had never known her to show any emotion, much less to cry in front of *me*. She preferred to not see me, a living embodiment of her son's sin of divorce.

She gave a dramatic pause, then looked up in absolute grief. "I was just thinking of him," she said, naming her accursed son. "I was just thinking that he's in hell."

I thought, *Well, you're right.* He was a mean, terrible person, and she knew he was. But I just looked down because Allison deserved to think well of her father. I drove home and used the time alone to work on cooking, starting with peeling a ten-pound bag of potatoes. There'd be a dumpster Christmas feast for all my guys, because the people at Kroger and Piggly Wiggly seemed to leave out more for me before the holidays. I had a giant free turkey from Piggly Wiggly, green beans, and sweet potato casserole to make from scratch. All the things I would want. For dessert, I'd saved a magazine recipe for Cuisinart's competition for best cheesecake, even though I only had a hand mixer. I made it thanks to my milk-truck friend. I wanted the men to have the best.

The next day I drove everything around with Allison, everyone assuming we were just stopping in on our way to our real family holiday. They didn't invite us to stay and share the day with them, not knowing that all I wanted was to be asked. It felt wrong to invite myself and my daughter to stay. But the truth was we didn't have anywhere else to be. Nobody wanted us at their table either.

The Arlington always did a big thing for New Year's Eve, so of course Sandy wanted to be at the dance. Bonnie had no use for what she called amateur night and said she was happy to watch Allison so I could go.

I wore my hair down but big, with a curl to it, and put on a black silk evening dress with a bow on the back. I walked in and saw Sandy, who nodded in approval when she saw me. I did a little half spin for her benefit.

"You look like a bottle of champagne," she said.

"Whatever you're drinking, keep at it," I said. "You're not so bad yourself."

"This old thing?" she said, looking down at her red dress. "Well, actually, it's brand-new."

"So new it still has the tags, right?"

"Like a Mercedes," she said. We laughed and I watched her eyes scan the scene. She swiped two flutes of champagne off a tray, smiling at the steward. I had missed this. The shorthand of our friendship. I had no time to go canoeing with her anymore.

She motioned to two seats at a small table out in the open. "Starting point?" she said.

"Perfect." We sat down. I had missed just being with her.

"This year has to be better than 1988," I said.

"Lord knows it can't get worse," she said. I wasn't so sure.

"How's Allison doing?"

"It's hard," I said. "She misses him something terrible. She's mad he's gone, and so am I. But we have different reasons."

"You gettin' the money straightened?"

"I just finally got the social security," I said. "Allison needs it. I think they may have been holding it up on purpose because I am always bringing my guys around for help."

"Your guys?"

"I've been doing a lot of . . . I have been helping people. People with AIDS."

There was no pause. It was a look of disgust. "Ruthie, I may not be smart, but I am not dumb either. I have heard things, and every time I see you, you mention some funny thing some guy said. Some queer, I can tell, and then you clam up like you're in some secret club."

"Well, we're taking members."

"No," she said. "I don't know what kind of blinders you have on that you think no one knows what you're doing."

"Well, they need help," I said. "And they're good people."

"*You're* good people," she said. "You need to stay away from those people. They are ruining everything. I can't open a bill from Dillard's without worrying some faggot licked it."

"Sandy, please don't talk like that."

She leaned in to whisper. "And then I have you telling *me* I have to use condoms because these people are everywhere."

"Well, are you?"

"Yeah," she said, "The first time, yeah." She tipped her champagne glass to empty it.

"What if it works out and you—"

"If it works out it's enough that I made him wear it once."

"Sandy, that makes no sense," I said. "You have to use one every time. Every act."

"Oh, listen to you. You see? 'Every act,' like animals. Ruthie, you have had less sex than anybody I have ever known. And now you're some sort of expert because of these perverts. Ruthie, you need to quit going around those people. End of story." She got up to get more champagne from a tray as the waiter passed. She only took one this time, taking a big gulp. She looked back at me, and for a moment I wasn't certain whether my best friend was going to sit with me again. But she did.

We didn't talk about it again that night. At midnight, Sandy and I clinked our glasses with strangers, all of them drunk on the possibility a new year brings. As we sang "Auld Lang Syne," I looked over at my friend, my old acquaintance, and worried I was losing her.

Those first minutes of 1989, I was haunted by something she had said. *What kind of blinders did I have on that I thought nobody knew what I was doing?* God must have put them on me. I couldn't have done all this if He hadn't.

Allison's daddy was dead. Nobody was going to take her from me if people found out what I was doing. Certainly not her grand-parents. And now I had social security. If someone fired me, they fired me.

I realized I had nothing to lose.

Except time. People were dying. I'd been too quiet. If I told the papers about this, the news maybe, then everyone would know what I knew. They'd say, "We gotta get to Hot Springs."

If I sound the alarm, I thought, *the cavalry will come.*

Part Two

Chapter Eleven

In the South, a lady had her name in the paper only three times: her birth, her marriage, and her death. You were otherwise never mentioned in the newspaper, and if you were, it wasn't good. If you were on TV news, it better be so people can pray for your safe return from whoever it was that kidnapped you.

KARK-TV filmed me outside because it was warmish for February. I am not someone who calls ahead, so I just went down to the station in Little Rock, and they agreed to do a story. I gave them some basic facts, not about me and what I was doing but just about the presence of HIV in Arkansas and how important it was that people had basic information.

There was some discussion as to when the segment would go on, the morning or the evening. I let them figure that out. I was just relieved it was done. I didn't know what would come of it, but I knew how alone I felt out there and how I would react if I saw someone on TV talking about AIDS.

They showed it on the morning broadcast, and calls to my house started about ten minutes after it aired. They were different than the midnight calls from men afraid of dying. These people were tentative, feeling me out to see if I was a Holy Roller or a heathen, depending on who was calling. If they were calling for a friend, I knew "the friend" was the very person I was talking to. If it was for "a friend of a friend," I probably had a boyfriend or friend on the line.

I'd sometimes purposely slip up and say "you" to show that would be fine too. People sometimes needed to be told.

I waited for someone in charge to call me. Someone from the governor's office or the CDC or the FDA—any of those abbreviations —just to say, "We had no idea. We'll be there tomorrow. We'll take care of this." I waited and waited.

I dressed extra nice for church that Sunday and got there a little bit before Sunday school. I was completely convinced that I would be approached by people who wanted to help, and I wanted them to be able to be discreet about it if they needed to be. But the people who were there milled about, each finding polite ways to avoid eye contact. I busied myself making the coffee for all of us to have.

The place started filling up with more and more people, most pouring themselves coffee.

"Ruth made the coffee," someone said as the Bible study began. I didn't see who. But I looked around and realized everybody had set their cup down. Every last one of them. The Bible study continued, and while there was all this talk about what Jesus would want you to do, I thought about all the times something like that had happened and I just hadn't understood. The potlucks I left with my food untouched, the birthdays Allison spent alone. All the times I picked her up from the church nursery, playing alone.

I always knew I was different because I was a single woman. You couldn't stay single in church, because then there must be something wrong with you or you're too busy sleeping with married men to settle on one. Sandy told me I was foolish to think nobody knew. They did know. How long had we been shunned while I was just too naive to realize it? How long had our church home wanted us to leave?

"Allison, sweetie," I said later. "Do you get teased at school?"

She didn't answer.

"What do kids say?"

She paused a long time, and when she spoke, there was a hard-ness to her voice. "People say not to play with me," she said. "They say I'll give them AIDS."

"Kids *say* that?"

"No, grown-ups tell kids that."

"Who?"

"Everybody," she said. "It's been my always. Everybody knows."

"I am so sorry—"

"It's not your fault," she said, almost dismissively. Like it was something she had come to terms with long ago on her own. "It's what we do."

It's what we do, I thought.

For some reason, it wasn't until I was in the local paper that I started to see the real backlash. Maybe because if AIDS was in the *Sentinel-Record*, it was in Hot Springs. The editor wasn't fond of me, I don't think, but she did a story. The paper's photographer took a photo of me, and as the flashbulb went off, I knew that was different than just talking on TV. This was something you can tear out, hold up, and show to your husband. "Look at this degenerate."

I opened the paper, and there I was, above the fold. I would be in homes all over Hot Springs. I dropped Allison off at school, like always, then bought a second paper, so I could send the article to Governor Clinton, not knowing he got the newspaper right off the press. Maybe it would give him cover to do something big.

I got home, and the phone was ringing. You think crank call-ers just do the night shift, but when they hate you enough they'll make time in the business day. This one came at nine thirty or so.

"This is Ruth." I had started saying that when I answered, because people were scared enough to call for help, and I wanted them to get to it, knowing, yeah, it's me.

"The sooner those faggots die, the better off they are." They'd practiced that one, I could tell. Said it over and over in their minds for who knows how long, waiting for a reason to say it, and here I was in the paper.

"That's not true," I said, like I was in customer service. I wasn't giving them the excitement of hanging up just so they could call back.

"They are ruining our kids and recruiting." The voice was clumsy now, off-script. "Our kids are gonna be that way? *No*."

"No one can make anyone gay, any more than they can make them straight."

That was like a math problem, and it kept him busy just long enough for me to cut this off. "Look, you called *me*. So, if you need some education, I can help you, but otherwise I am busy."

They hung up, and then I did have one big body shiver. Like I'd successfully caught a moth and let it loose outside, shaking off the feeling of an insect fluttering in my hands. I stared at the phone, waiting for it to ring again. It didn't. "That's right," I said to the phone.

I needed a manicure, because people treat you better when you have a little armor on you. I stopped by the nail salon on the way to doing rounds at the hospitals. They sat me next to this nice-looking brown-haired girl I'd never seen before, with a chunky baby boy next to her in a pram. She looked at me like she was dying to talk. She was just getting started, and her nails already looked fine, but I remembered the loneliness of my first year with Allison. Finding excuses to leave the house.

"That's some child you've got there."

"Thank you," she said, like he was the last thing she wanted to talk about. "I love your dress." Her accent had the flat *a*'s of Mississippi. She was a recent transplant for sure. No tourist brings a baby to Hot Springs.

"Oh, thank you," I said. "It's actually two separates, but that's our secret."

She laughed. "I took a shower today for the first time this week," she said. "That's my secret." We talked about parenthood, and I was right she was from Mississippi, from an old-money family from Ocean Springs. I thought, *Oh good, a friend.* One of the nail techs followed her out. I assumed she'd forgotten her card or hadn't signed the check right.

Whatever was said, she looked through the window at me. She looked disgusted and raced off to her car. The next time I saw her was at Kroger, struggling with the cart and the pram right at the produce section where you enter.

"You gotta push one and pull the other behind you," I said.

She turned, and her smile contorted to a scowl. She didn't say anything, just went to the register to check out. I stood behind her in line.

"Can you tell me what you heard?" I asked.

"Enough," she said. "They said, 'Don't you let her 'round that baby.'"

"I—" I stopped myself. I nodded and decided I'd shop tomorrow. I put my cart back neatly, went to my car, and burst into tears. I didn't want to be a pariah. I had dreams. I had even hung some corkboard on a wall in my kitchen and pinned pictures torn from magazines. They were scenes of how I wanted my life to be—vacations, a family with their back to the camera at the beach, a pretty but modest home. I'd picture myself in those scenes. I wanted a man who would love me and take up for me—to say, "You can't talk about my wife that way. You can't say that." I just wanted a normal life. I didn't want everyone in the whole town to think I was trash and hate me.

I tried to get used to feeling so hated, to develop a callus where things got to me, but things still did. Not long after that new mother was turned against me, I went to my P.O. box, where I received ashes sent to me from funeral homes. When I opened my box, I saw there was a bright blue Hallmark envelope inside. There was something about getting a card in the mail that was exciting to me, a holdover from when my aunt in Florida would send me a birthday card every year. I opened it right there. There was a bass on the front, leaping out of the water, just begging to be caught. "To the Best Uncle on His Birthday."

I opened it. Someone had written in an angry scrawl: "You are the scum of the earth."

That was just the first card I got. The cards were always something that had nothing to do with me. Everybody seemed to have the same idea: A christening card. For Grandpa on Father's Day. Happy First Birthday! People had cards lying around and would send them to me. I guess Hallmark didn't make a Screw You card.

I told myself these were strangers, people who'd seen me on TV or in the paper. But I knew better. I'd listed my P.O. box in the church directory. These were people I knew, who smiled at me on Sunday, took Communion behind me.

I went on TV again and then again, as I was now the local station's AIDS expert. They would have me come over and settle things when people were in an uproar. Some politician wanted to "send all those AIDS people to Guantanamo" or "quarantine 'em on an island." I'd be that one voice saying, "That's not right." Jesse Helms, the senator from North Carolina, had said, "We have got to call a spade a spade, and a perverted human being a perverted human being." My response was, "Well, at least now he's acknowledging we're talking about human beings. Now, about that other part . . ." I gave them sound bites, I showed up on time with my hair done. I wasn't going on to be a TV star. I mean, when I was younger I'd dreamed of being the weather girl. But I wasn't planning on being the AIDS girl. I just wanted to get the word out.

I talked about funeral homes, trying to get people to care about the stigma. I thought that if people understood that even in death these men faced hate, maybe they'd care about them in life. I made an offhand comment: "I've sometimes had to bury them myself."

Maybe that's what started it. I don't know. But I began to get ashes in the mail, anonymous and with no return address. Sometimes there was a note with a name, often not. Usually when I received ashes, there was a tag, a little coin with the funeral home's name and the assigned serial number for the deceased stamped on it. It was usually a stainless-steel coin, blackened and charred from going through the heat of the cremation process. The tag might be attached to the bag of ashes with a twist tie, or just thrown in with them. I'd have to dig down into the middle of the ashes to find it.

But these would have no tags. Maybe to keep it secret, or because the person who sent it had taken the coin to keep as a memory. So who knows whose life I held in my hands? It was disturbing to me, burying complete strangers. I assumed they were from people who'd been entrusted with them, a lover or friend. Or someone had arranged it for himself, in literally a last-gasp effort to ensure his soul would be at rest: "When I die, send me to her."

Some likely came from funeral directors who didn't want the cremains traced back to them. A lot of them were in the closet. Nobody expected any woman to marry a funeral director, so it was a job where they could hide in plain sight. It's possible that the senders were people who were willing to do just enough for someone who'd died indigent. The county would pay for the burial, but they did not want it traced back to them. I'll never know.

I would put the remains in a jar, and with Allison trailing behind me, I would carry the ashes slowly through the cemetery, kind of like I was divining for water. "You tell me," I'd whisper, until I was seized with a feeling of being rooted to the ground. It wasn't a jolt, just an easing into a final resting place after wandering for who knows how long.

It was hard to explain to Allison, who was so curious about the lives of people. The first time, I thought it was just too complicated to explain to her that I had no idea who this person was. It almost felt undignified to admit in front of the ashes that they were unknown to me. I addressed them merely as "you."

"Rest now," I said, using the same soothing voice as I did with the dying.

"But what was his name?" Allison asked.

"Just someone special." I said it quickly. Allison was going to be seven in a few months. She no longer took what I said as gospel.

"But what was he called?"

"I don't know," I said, too quickly, my voice harsher now that I wasn't talking to the dead. She crossed her arms in anger, very much alive in front of me.

"I'm sorry," I said. She thought I was withholding something from her. She had made the connection between the men we visited and the jars we buried. She cared too. And that care carried a weight, even if I thought I could protect her from it. I went to hold her hand on the way back to the car. At first, she resisted, and I was so relieved when she took it. "I'm sorry," I said again, though I told myself she had already moved on.

People at church looked at her differently. I still thought I could fit into the Christian community, but we were tolerated outcasts. And sometimes I worried we would arrive one Sunday in our nice dresses only to be turned away. I clung to the normalcy of those Sundays, and I still felt God's comfort there. I couldn't imagine being turned away, but it had happened to my guys, so why not to us?

If there was any doubt about how people felt, it was made clear when someone sent a leftover Valentine. "Why are you talking to those people?" read the message. "They are going to hell anyway, and now you bring that hell into our church." Then in all caps: "EVERY PLACE YOU WALK, IT FALLS OFF YOU LIKE DUST."

I read those words over and over again, because they were right. They sensed what I felt. I did feel like I had the dust and the bones and the ashes on me. I didn't feel dirty or "contaminated." It was a very, very fine dust that just fell off me, but to me, it floated down in a trail of gossamer and gold. I didn't understand how people couldn't see the shine.

Chapter Twelve

I t was pouring down rain, so I knew what was coming.

"Mama, can I sleep in your room tonight?" Rain had made Allison nervous since her daddy died in that thunderstorm, so I always had to give her a little extra attention and love when the skies really opened up.

"How about we make a deal?" I said. "You pick out some books, and we can read in my bed until you get sleepy."

She padded off. "Brush your teeth," I called after her. It was a Friday in mid-April, just a month and change left of her being six. There were flashes when I was aware that these moments don't stick around.

Allison crawled into bed with three Amelia Bedelias. I admit I hated those books. That stupid maid who didn't have anything to teach my daughter. I was debating how bad a parent I would be if we read my Danielle Steel together instead, when the window lit up with lightning.

"Allison, honey, there's about to be—"

Too late. The thunder shook the house's windows and with them my little girl. Even our cat, FooFoo, jumped. I had to fix this.

"We are blessed to be safe and right here," I said softly, slipping into my bedtime voice as I squeezed her closer to me. She didn't say a word, staring at the cover of her book.

"When I was little, I used to go see my Aunt Ruth in the Keys, and she loved the rain," I said. This was before Daddy died. "In Florida, it rains down there for about an hour every afternoon. Big thunderstorms. It just depends on where the east coast sea breeze and the west coast sea breeze meet—that's where the storm is gonna be."

"Every day?" she said.

"Oh yes," I said. "My aunt Ruth, we would be outside, and she would say, 'Okay, it's getting ready to rain.' And that's when I would take my nap."

"You could sleep with the thunder?" she asked.

"Oh sure, because I was safe inside with people who loved me. And I knew that when I woke up, we'd go out and pick limes for limeade. That's where I learned to make it."

Aunt Ruth, who I was named for, would take me out barefoot through the wet grass, and she'd reach up to pick the limes. At each pluck, water from the tree would rain down on us and we'd laugh. She and my uncle never had children. I guess they were never able to, but she was so wonderful.

I took a long sniff of Allison's hair, still smelling like the yellow Johnson's shampoo from her bath. She was getting that dreamy, warm limpness of a child relaxing into sleep. This was the parenting I liked, not the running around and the constant questions.

"Her kitchen was yellow," I said, and I was right back there. "And she had a pitcher with red flowers painted around it. I'd sit there watching her cut the limes, and smell 'em, and oh, I love limes to this day. Every time I see them I think of her."

Allison's breathing slowed as her eyes closed. *I don't need you, Amelia Bedelia*, I thought.

And then the phone rang.

Allison's eyes popped open, and she grimaced. "Damnit," I said aloud, speeding through my mental Rolodex of patients.

"This is Ruth," I said.

"Ruth Burks?" He sounded surprised I'd answered.

"Yes," I said, looking right at Allison, who was getting a faraway look in her eyes.

"Well, hi, Ruth. Jack Butcher told me I should give you a call. My name's Mitch. Mitch Stanley."

I could barely hear him, because it sounded like he was out in the pouring rain. Jack Butcher? Jack was one of the wealthiest businessmen in town.

"Okay," I said. "Uh, what can I do for you?"

The man laughed. "I'm here at the Hilton in North Little Rock having drinks with Jack."

"Well, you sound like you're outside in the rain to me."

"Well, you sound pretty smart, because I am. I'm at a pay phone, and I would like to be inside, but Jack said this was something I needed to do."

What in the world was Jack Butcher doing have drinks with someone with AIDS?

"So, what *is* it you need?"

"Well, I was wondering if I could take you out to dinner?"

I sat up and nearly dropped the phone right on Allison's head.

"When were you thinking?"

"How about tomorrow? Jack told me to tell you I'm all right."

"Did he tell you I have a daughter?"

"She didn't come up," he said and laughed. "Look, I hate to rush you, but I would like to get in out of this rain. So, can I take you out?"

"I'd have to bring my daughter."

"I'll pick you both up at eight."

When I hung up, I must have looked crazy, because Allison asked what was wrong. "Nothing's wrong, honey," I said. "We're going out on a date."

"What's a date?"

"I think I've forgotten," I said. "We're gonna have to see."

*   *   *

As I got Allison dressed, I kind of wondered whether the doorbell was really going to ring at eight o'clock. Maybe I hoped it wouldn't. I combed her hair in the bathroom, wondering what on earth I'd been thinking, saying I had to bring her along.

"I need you to be on your best behavior, okay?" I told her in the mirror.

"I *know*," she said, not at all well behaved. I sighed as she ran into the living room to watch TV. At least this guy would know what he was in for.

"And if we're not having fun, we'll just leave," I called after her.

I looked at the mirror and rehearsed my smile. I pictured opening the door, easy breezy.

"Hi, my name is Ruth," I said, turning my face this way and that to check my makeup. "You must be . . . a homicidal maniac. Anyways—"

The doorbell rang, and I jumped. I smoothed my dress one last time and started to walk to the living room, only to find that Allison already had the door wide open. Standing in the doorway was the most good-looking man. A built-up Elvis in a dark blue business suit, an impossibly white dress shirt, and no tie. He was in his thirties, with wavy salt-and-pepper hair and a mustache.

"Mama," she yelled back to me, though I was right behind her.

"Yes, Allison," I said, softly. "Hi, I'm Ruth."

"Mitch," he said, reaching for my hand as he quickly looked me up and down. Our eyes met on his way back up to my face. He grinned, caught, but it was somehow charming on him. He'd probably gotten away with a lot just for the way he looked. The same way he had a mustache but somehow didn't look like a car salesman.

"Are we ready?" he said.

"Yes," said Allison.

"Let me just get my purse," I said. I went into the kitchen and exhaled, safe from view. I glanced at the bulletin board but reminded myself that most men weren't worth a damn and I shouldn't get my hopes up.

He drove with the same languor with which he walked. Purposeful, but not in a hurry about it. "I thought we'd go to the Villa," he said.

It was a new place on Central, but I'd never been. It was nice, with an area under glass that looked out on a garden. He nodded at the hostess, and she gestured to the restaurant, giving him his choice of tables in the main dining area, which was like a stone grotto. She cocked her head at me and Allison, but smiled, and I wondered if he was in and out of here with a lot of women. When he didn't even look at the menu, I figured this was his date place.

There was live music, a woman with long curly hair playing the violin. Allison stared at her, but I thought that was fine, because what else are you up on that little stage for if not to be seen and appreciated? The waitress came by, and I made a big show of listening to the specials, and they did sound good, but I knew I was going to get the cheapest entrée, which was the penne alla Norma.

"How about you and I share that?" I said to Allison. I didn't want to owe this guy anything.

He chuckled. "I'm good for two dinners," he joked, and then turned to Allison. "What's your name again?"

"Allison."

"Allison, do you like spaghetti and meatballs?"

"Yes."

"Great," he said, looking at the waitress. "It's decided." He ordered a steak and a beer I'd never heard of, and looked at me. "There's a really nice Pinot Noir . . ."

"Can I have a Coca-Cola?" Allison asked me.

"Yes, you can," he answered for me.

"Water's fine for me," I said to the waitress. I took a sip as she walked away. I'd never had someone answer Allison for me in my presence.

"Jack tells me you're a model," Mitch said.

A dribble of water fell down my chin as I jumped. "A model?" I said through my napkin.

"You're not?"

"No, why would he say that?"

"You could be," he said. "He says you model furs."

"Oh God," I said. "That was a benefit for the Fine Arts Ball. I was just helping out." I'd done that as a favor for someone last year, kind of hoping she'd throw in a fur as a thank-you.

He smirked. "I bet you made them a lot of money."

"I wasn't gonna let it sell cheap." He put his head back and laughed, and I admired the crispness of his white shirt against the tan of his neck.

"That's why I was surprised you were home on a Friday night," he said. "I figured you were some kind of party girl."

"Tea parties, maybe," I said. Allison made a face. "And not even those. So how do you know Jack?"

"I work for him," he said. "With him." Jack sold to Wal-Mart, and Mitch was one of his parts guys, like a broker. He flew around internationally, ordering the parts and negotiating the price. "I've actually got a lot of jobs," he said. "I don't like to be tied down."

Message received, I thought. The beer and Coca-Cola came, and they each gave their drink an admiring look. Allison took a huge gulp through her straw, which was a bit of a relief, because if she spilled it there would be less everywhere. Mitch took a sip of his beer, held it for a moment, and nodded. "With wine, you drink from the front of your mouth," he said. "And beer you drink from the back, close to your throat. There's a fullness to it—"

Allison had gone through her whole Coca-Cola, and her straw was making a loud sucking noise.

"*Allison*," I said.

"It's okay," he said. He raised a finger, and the waitress came right over. "Can we get another Coca-Cola?"

This man was buying my daughter two Cokes? What miracle had I walked into? The food arrived, and it was really lovely. He was focused on his steak, and Allison was twirling her spaghetti. I leaned back just an inch to get a wider picture of them, and reminded myself this was just a first date.

The chef came over, touching Mitch's shoulder to get his attention. "You good, boss?"

"Excellent," he said. "This is Ruth and Allison."

"It's delicious," I said, quickly, like he had invented pasta alla Norma.

"Wonderful," he said, nodding at Mitch and moving away as quickly as he came.

"Boss?" I said.

"I have a lot of jobs," he said. "I'm a part owner of this place."

Now it made sense. The easiness of the staff around him, his sureness in ordering. "Well," I said.

"So, you're a model who doesn't model, we've established that," he said. "What else do you do?"

"I have a lot of jobs too," I said. "Well, not really. I work at Oaklawn, but the season's finishing up." I lowered my voice. "Her father, my ex-husband, passed away last September, so . . ." I trailed off. Let him think I'm comfortable. We were not looking for someone to come save us. "I mostly do, uh, volunteer work." *Oh, just tell him.* "Around AIDS."

He nodded. Just nodded. "Allison," he said, "have you ever had tiramisu?" We got two for the table. He and I shared one, and the violinist played on.

This is what a date is, I told myself.

Mitch asked if he could see me again on the following Saturday, and I said yes. He said I could bring Allison too, so I did. He took us to the Hibachi, a Japanese place I'd also never been to. This time I ordered what he got, the donburi, which I found out was sliced beef and green onions served over rice in a large bowl. It arrived with a lid, and the waiter took it off like it was a show.

Allison got the tempura, and it was so salty she couldn't eat it. *Here's where the other shoe drops*, I thought. We all tasted it and agreed.

"That's okay," he said. *Well.*

The next Saturday I had Bonnie watch Allison, but the thing with Bonnie was that she was more of a last-minute girl. If this was going to be a regular Saturday night thing, then she'd get antsy. Too much structure for her.

So I showed up at Allison's grandparents' house, unannounced, while she was at school. "I've got to have Saturday nights off," I said, "and Allison needs you." They stared at me, a bad debt they couldn't pay off and be done with. "You need to be grandparents, just for a few hours."

They relented. I had to drop her off at six o'clock Saturday evening, no earlier, and pick her up at eight Sunday morning, so they could go to church. That was the most they would do.

"If you die, we won't take her," said her grandfather. "You need to find someone else." I was certain they knew what I was doing with AIDS, and that clinched it. The first time I was in the paper, their friends must have brought it to them saying they'd been right all along. We never came that close to talking about my AIDS work again.

The third time I left Allison with them, I arrived to pick her up at a quarter past eight on Sunday morning. Fifteen minutes late. As I approached, I could see way down the street, and they were already backing their car out of the driveway. Allison was on the porch swing, locked out of the house. Alone. I was worried she'd be upset to be left alone, but no. She thought it was perfect timing.

"I knew you'd come," she said.

⋆ ⋆ ⋆

Mitch became Mr. Saturday Night, never wanting more. We mostly watched movies, because we were each so exhausted from the work of the week. It was nice to just have a warm, caring body next to me. He called me "Ruthie," which is how I knew somebody held me in their heart or at least close to it. And maybe I didn't want someone around twenty-four hours a day. I needed to be mobile for my guys, and I had enough trouble carting Allison around with me, eating her meals in hospital cafeterias. I didn't need to call some man to explain that dinner wouldn't be on the table because here's another patient.

Mitch wasn't the most sophisticated guy, but he could work situations and build anything with his hands. He'd designed and welded together the most beautiful docks out on Lake Hamilton and knew exactly how many cubic feet you would need to fill up a certain part of the lake. He was a man who could fix things, and I needed a man who could fix things. He would go to my guys' houses and could repair anything. And would do it for free.

I knew he loved that he flew during the week, back and forth to Mexico, getting parts for Jack Butcher and Wal-Mart. Sometimes he went to Asia, and it was in Hong Kong that he had his suits made. I think that's why he stayed so trim. They had his sizes on file and would send him fabric samples. But God, they were nice suits.

He was like me, in a way. He understood that the way you dress gets you into places that otherwise wouldn't even let you in the service entrance. He'd grown up behind the eight ball, living in a chicken shack that had been converted into a place to sleep. His mom was married five or six times, so he had a lot of dads, but he stayed an only child, because she wasn't making that mistake again. His real dad lived out in Mount Ida and looked just like him but wouldn't recognize him as his.

These details fell out as asides. Little things I collected because he was such a mystery to me. I had my mother's voice in my head still, saying I was only good enough for the tire-retread man. Mitch had a complex too, because he went to Cutter Morning Star High

School. It was the rural school, and people still assumed you got there every day by horse or on the back of a wagon. "Cutter" was code for the boonies, and if you went there you were dirt poor and had nothing. He was nice to look at, and he was industrious enough to wrangle a car even in high school, but when the Hot Springs girls asked, "Where do ya go to school?" the second he said, "Cutter," they'd laugh and head off.

He never thought he was good enough, and then his wife left him. I heard a lot about her, even though she'd been gone three years. She was still in Hot Springs, and I'd shopped in her store, a little lingerie shop. I liked her a lot. I remembered seeing him in there one time. He was just kind of a blur going by this once. "Oh, that's my husband," she'd said, dismissively. I had always noticed her wedding and engagement rings; they would slide down the side of her finger, the diamonds were so big. This was back in the mid-eighties, when women wore leather in different colors. She had these custom-made leather outfits that I now knew he'd had made with those suits in Hong Kong. I pictured her details still on file next to his somewhere.

He'd dressed her to the nines. Jewelry, diamonds, and furs. He bought her a brand-new Corvette for her birthday. But I wasn't going to see any of those things—not that I wanted them. I just thought it meant that he had loved her that much and maybe he could again. No one else would date me, because single men were terrified to be seen alone with me.

Mitch was honest that he'd slept around on his ex, to a point that I had to show him a picture of Sandy to make sure he hadn't stopped at her bedroom on one of his past side trips. My friendship with Sandy was no longer what it once was. We'd see each other around town, and she'd smile and do a pleasant, "How are you?" but she no longer called me to hang out. It took me a while to realize I had lost my best friend, but I would still stick to her code of girlfriend ethics.

Or at least consider it. I liked Mitch a lot and would miss him. The way he took me for rides in his sports car, a five-speed, going down dirt roads just to do it. Someone else to drive and pick the route for once. I was just a blond in the passenger seat, the wind in my hair.

He didn't want it to get deeper than that, and I was content.

On Mother's Day, I made sure to pick up Allison early at her grandparents'. Her grandfather always made a big deal about Mother's Day. Not about me or even Imogene, really, but the mothers at their church. Her grandfather, who I called the Old Man, had a greenhouse, and he spent months growing the most gorgeous orchids you've ever seen, coddled and placed in corsages for the mothers at church on Mother's Day. As he grew them, he pinched some off, sacrificing some to get the biggest ones to take in and show off. But I never got one. And Allison never got one.

The Old Man was already loading the orchids into the car when I got there. He was so intent on babying each one, he barely noticed Allison leaving.

"Wish Imogene a happy Mother's Day," I called to him, if only just to be acknowledged. The Old Man looked at me quickly and nodded, then returned to his bounty, stuffing a riot of flowers, white and pink and purple and red, into his car.

Chapter Thirteen

"I saw you on the television," the voice on the phone said. He was hoarse and sounded old. Even the words he said out loud sounded misspelled.

"Right?" I said.

"I got my son and a cousin," he said, punctuating it with a cough.

"Okay," I said, opening my datebook.

"They have that thing you talked about."

"AIDS."

"Uh, yeah."

He wanted me to come to them in Story, which was even farther out than Mount Ida. I drove up after doing the morning rounds, and as I got closer I started passing the crystal quarries and family-run rock shops along the highways. Something so beautiful making its way out of the ground in such a desolate place. I don't know what else people would do for work out there. It was different. People had run to the mountains of Arkansas during the Civil War, the ones that didn't want to talk to anybody or have anybody bother them. I found it was still true of the people there.

It wasn't quite a shotgun shack, but it was pretty close. The yard was full of kids and babies, all dirty. Five or six, moving so fast in and out of the house and wearing so little I couldn't tell them apart to count them. A dozen dogs, all skinny, some lying down, some

running with the kids. When I got out, the dogs barked furiously
and the kids stopped and stared. None of the dogs charged; they just
let out territorial screams. I waved in the kids' general direction as
I walked to the house. None waved back. They stared at me like I
was an alien.

The house was up on stilts, and I climbed the concrete blocks
they used to step up into the house. The washing machine was out
on the front porch, an electric one with an extension cord connecting it somewhere inside. No dryer, but a clothesline that had lots
of clothes. A truck was parked by a tree, the transmission hanging
from ropes and chains above it. Some group of guys had all pulled on
the ropes to get it out of the way to work on the truck. There were
leaves inside, so I wondered how long it had been left just hanging
up there. You had to have lunch, and then you had to have dinner.
Well, in the country, lunch was dinner, and dinner was supper. Then
someone had to do whatever. Might be two or three days before
someone could come back and help. Things happen. Jail.

I knocked on a screen door, metal and mesh. A dark brown
hound dog inside seemed to lose its mind, barking, jumping to snap
at the screen, and gnashing teeth like all it wanted to do was close
its jaws on me.

I held my date planner like armor. A teenager finally came to
the door. No shirt, just ratty blue jeans.

"*Daddy*," he yelled, as he pulled the dog off.

"She here?" came a voice.

"She is," I said.

"Come in," said the voice.

It was dark inside. I wasn't sure if this was a trap for the lady
on TV who loves those gays so much. An older man who may have
been in his forties or his sixties—who could tell?—sat at the table,
smoking a cigarette, tapping it just above the ashtray. Near him was
a picture window with a Confederate flag covering it. And beneath
that, on two couches, two very sick men. I was relieved to see them,

in a way—they were at least evidence I was invited here for a reason other than murder.

The older man didn't get up to greet me; he sat at the table leaning back in the chair with his legs crossed. He cocked his head at the two men.

I walked up to the couches. "Gentlemen," I said.

They said they were cousins, and I accepted that. They each had a rough buzz cut, one a muddy brown, the other jet black against skin so white it almost had the blue of skim milk.

"We got it from a blood transfusion," Jet Black said, and the other nodded. It was amazing to hear the quickness of the way he said "transfusion." Learned, then practiced with repetition. I saw a figure in the back, a woman, poke her head out a doorway to look at me, then retreat.

"Really," I said. "You were in the hospital some time?"

"Yeah," said Muddy.

"Where?" I asked.

Silence.

"Well," I said. "Do you have a doctor now?"

More silence. I looked around the room. There was a bumper sticker on the wall, crooked. It read: "If I'd a known all this, I woulda picked my own damn cotton."

The dad suddenly piped up. "We aren't all gonna get the AIDS, are we?"

"No," I said. "So, you get AIDS from HIV, which is a virus. It's spread through sexual contact and sharing needles. Or, uh, blood transfusions, though that doesn't happen anymore. So, without any of that stuff, you're good."

He stubbed out his cigarette as an answer.

"It's those faggots," said the muddy-haired guy.

That set off Jet Black, spewing stuff I don't want to repeat.

I held up a hand. "Look, this is the way it is. You are not better than they are. You are all in the same boat, and I don't care how you got it—in my mind you got it the same way everybody else got it, which is that it wasn't anybody's fault."

Jet Black only got madder, talking about the Klan cleansing Arkansas. It was ridiculous. Here I was trying to save the lives of two Klansmen who thought they had to talk sense to a blond white woman. These men with their robes and hoods in the closet.

"I don't have the same feelings about the KKK that you do," I said. I left it at that so I didn't get shot.

Muddy asked me if I condoned sin, probably showing off for Jet Black. If a question was ever a threat, it was that one. I wanted to call him a liar. Tell him the blood supply had been cleared of HIV since July of '85.

"I'm the only person doing this kind of work anywhere," I said flatly. "If you scare me off—or even just piss me off—I'll never come back. And then what are you gonna do?"

That shut them up. I talked to them about AZT and nutrition, opportunistic infections to watch out for. None of it was landing.

When I left, the dad still didn't move to get up. "When you need me, call me," I said. "But I'm not dropping by."

I drove past the crystal quarries again, hanging on to something beautiful so I'd stop thinking about the Klan. When I was in high school, there was a white woman over in Glenwood, where there were no black people. She said she'd been raped by a black man, because she didn't want her parents to know they were dating. They went and got a black man, some person living his life, and snatched him at random. Whichever one, they took him to the river. The story goes they nailed his penis to a stump and set it on fire and gave him a knife.

What was the answer to depravity? There were patients it was hard to help. I know how that sounds, but it was hard to help those guys. "You know what?" I said aloud. "They've been dying up here for hundreds of years and took care of it themselves. Up here you get a snakebite and suck it out and hope you live."

But I went back, twice. In August the dad called me and told me they were both dead. "You don't need to come back." He hung up before I could ask how or if it was in a hospital. I suspected it wasn't.

I didn't feel relief, but I did feel saved from the obligation of caring for them. And I wondered if this is what people who hated gay men told themselves when they died.

Louisa Simmons and Margaret Michaels were at an after-church dinner going on about gay people invading the town. They were really going at it.

"Why do those people need a place?" Louisa said. "I just think it attracts them."

"Flies to . . ." prim Margaret's voice dropped to a whisper. "Shit."

"What place are you talking about?" I asked.

"That disgusting bar," she said. "They just took over that place on Malvern and Convention."

"The gay bar?" I said. "Our House?"

"What kind of name for a bar is that?" said Margaret.

"Our House," spit Louisa. "Can you imagine?"

"It's probably code," I said. "If I invited you to meet at Our House, you would know what I mean but maybe someone else wouldn't."

"They speak in code because they know what they're doing is wrong," said Margaret. "I know you know that, Ruth."

They eyed me suspiciously, but they *always* eyed me suspiciously, even before I was the town pariah. I knew these women spread rumors about me, and I knew so many real truths about their lives. When I was walking in town as a child with my mother, she would say hi to some woman, then, as soon as they passed, tell me what that person thought she was hiding, filling me in on three generations' worth of adultery, murder, and thievery. "Her daddy bulldozed a graveyard to build that house she's so proud of," she'd whisper, smiling. Or, "She and her husband have an arrangement. I guess no one's being cheated on if they're both doing it."

I grew up steeped in these secrets from my mother's generation and was observant enough to see them repeating in mine. But I kept everything to myself. It just bothered me that people thought they could hide their own sins by inventing ones for others.

"Seems as though we should bring a gift basket to Our House," I said. "An apology. Say something like, 'You were the stranger, and we didn't welcome you.'"

Louisa didn't laugh. I was a tall snake in the short grass. But I was already moving on. *Our House*, I thought.

Chapter Fourteen

I sat in the car and rehearsed what I was going to say. Our House had just moved in to what was likely one of the rattiest buildings in town. It used to be a corner gas station, set catty-corner on the lot on Malvern and Convention, and probably needed to be torn down twenty years before. Even though it was August, all the windows were boarded up, so you couldn't see who was in there. Still, it hid in plain sight, just two doors down from the police station and next to the library. Right across from a median in the road, a patch of green where the Arkansas and American flags flew high. People just chose not to see Our House.

I had worn my nicest outfit, an ecru-linen sailor dress with embroidery, and I'd taken to carrying a datebook with me, covered in pink leather. I kept names of doctors and nurses in there. It was a talisman, something I could hold, as if I had some important business.

I walked in just after the bar opened at five that afternoon, but it could have been midnight inside, what with all the windows covered. I was hit with a wall of stale cigarette smoke and the sounds of Billy Idol singing "Eyes Without a Face."

A tall man about my age stood toward the front, wiping the wood of one of the tables to the left. He had his reddish-brown hair pushed back, thin and straight on top but curling down long in the back to his shoulders. He stared at me, then arched a perfect eyebrow at my datebook.

"Hello," I said, putting all the sugar I have in my voice. "I was hoping to talk to the owner."

He sat on the corner of the table, crossing his big arms with the rag balled in a fist. He was still eyeing my date planner.

"Nice to meet you," I said. "My name is Ruth Burks."

"Paul," he said, like it was an annoyance to give me even that. "I'm the manager."

"Paul . . ." I said. He wasn't giving me a last name. Okay, that was fine. "Listen, I wonder if you can help me."

"Depends."

"I guess it does," I said. "Yes, well . . ." My speech went out the window. "I am trying to help people. A lot of young men. They're getting AIDS, and they're dying, and I need to figure this out."

He looked confused.

"Do you know anything about AIDS?" I asked.

"That's people in San Francisco."

"I'm not saying it's in your bar," I said. "But it's in Arkansas. I've been helping a lot of people, so I know it's here in Hot Springs too."

"How many?"

"I've buried about two dozen men, maybe more. Sometimes the ashes came——"

"Buried."

"Yes, they all died."

"You buried them yourself?"

I smoothed my skirt. "Yes."

"How old?"

"Average? Twenty-two. Twenty-three. Young."

"Wineland."

"No, thank you," I said. "I don't really drink."

"Paul Wineland," he said, uncrossing his arms. "That's my name."

"Oh, I thought you were offering me a drink."

"Is that a hint?" he said.

"Is that an offer?" I said. "I'll take a club soda and bitters, and maybe we can sit and talk. With lime, please."

As he poured the drink, I sat at the small table he'd just wiped. Paul told me that none of the regulars at the bar had come down with it. "I would know," he said, coming over to the table. "We're a close group."

"You would know," I said. "The guys are gone so fast. But you can have it and not even know it for years. Then they're just gone. The trick is preventing them from getting it and spreading it by accident. I have a doctor I know who is willing to give AIDS tests—no grief or questions asked. I feel like nobody knows the most basic stuff."

"Which is?"

"You have to use condoms."

His eyebrows arched even higher. "Do you know many people like us?"

"Presbyterians?" I joked.

"Gay folks."

"Well, I do now. And I have a cousin in Hawaii. He's the one that turned me blond. And I had a friend growing up. I mean, he never told anyone, but Helen Keller could tell . . ."

Paul laughed.

"I'm sorry, was that rude?"

"I like rude," he said. "So, you're not a fag hag."

"A what?"

"A woman who just likes to hang around gay people."

"Are you calling me a hag?"

"No, ma'am," he said, laughing.

"Good, cause I may be a lot of things, but a hag is not one of them."

"I really thought you were coming in here to Bible thump," he said, pointing at my planner. "You look like a church lady."

"I'm a Methodist," I said. "So that makes me proud. But that's not what I'm here about." I opened the book to show him. "See? I'm taking notes on what's happening. I'm serious about this."

"Why?"

"What do you mean, why?"

"Why *are* you serious about this?"

I took a long sip of my drink. I hadn't stopped to ask myself that, and I wanted to give the answer the courtesy of real thought. "I just don't think it's right," I finally said. "I don't think it's right. You said I looked like a church lady. Well, I am, but I'm a real one. Jesus is tough. He calls you to do the right thing, and that's always the hard thing."

"Okay, but when you come back, don't mention Jesus."

"Oh, don't worry . . ."

"He's like an ex-boyfriend for a lot of people here."

"I get that," I said. "So, I can come back?"

"Come back Saturday night," he said. "We have a drag show twice a month. Brings in everyone and all the tourists."

When I left, my eyes had become so adjusted to the dark that now the world outside seemed too bright and too harsh.

I came back to Our House for the Saturday drag show, telling Mitch I was busy. I didn't want to worry about a plus-one when I felt like I was enough of an outsider as it was. I was surprised by how many cars were in the parking lot in back. I walked in, and it was burning up hot in there, like a steam room with no ventilation. They were playing Donna Summer's "She Works Hard for the Money," so loud I felt like I was in a music video. The blond surrounded by a roomful of men.

I spoke too soon. A woman who was shooting pool hopped over the corner of the pool table like she couldn't get to me fast enough to say hi.

"Ruth!" she said.

"Suzann," I said, smiling. She ran the flower shop and was also the local motorcycle cop. I'd known her since the sixth grade.

"I haven't seen you here before," she said.

"First time," I said, looking at the men dancing, kissing, laughing. It was the essence of fun.

Suzann was looking into my eyes. She was real cute, so I bet this worked on girls. "Honey, let me tell you, I'm just visiting," I said. "Men aren't that bad yet, but I promise you'll be the first to know."

She laughed. I looked right at her. "But I am really happy to see you." I made a show of looking around hopefully and crossing my fingers. "I have a feeling I'll meet a man tonight!" I joked.

We laughed. "Nice to see you, Ruth," she said, eyeing me up and down before she went back to playing pool. Other than that, it was like I was invisible. I was so used to men looking at me that it was weird. I'm not bragging—you and I know a straight man will size up any woman with or without a pulse.

I saw a drag queen at the bar and made my way over to get a drink. She was so tall, red hair for days falling all around her big shoulders.

"Can I put vodka in your soda and lime this time?" she asked.

"Paul?"

"Miss Cherry Fontaine," Paul said.

"You look amazing," I said.

"Thank you, Ruth. The show starts at ten," he said, pointing at a pair of double doors as he poured generously. It was top-shelf vodka he'd tucked away, the only bottle they had. "It's more of a suggested start time. The queens won't start until there are enough customers in the showroom to tip them, and people won't pay to go in until they know the queens are starting."

"That old story."

"Yes," he laughed, going off to tend to another customer. "That old story."

I turned and saw an empty seat and grabbed it. The two guys at the table looked at me for a moment, then turned back to each other with a "get her" face. I'd worn a little black dress and made my hair big enough to let the drag queens know I put effort in but not so much that I was competing. I looked at everyone, people in jeans and tees, definitely a beer crowd, and a lot of them didn't even have a drink in their hands. It was like the social halls my daddy and his veteran buddies would go to. It wasn't about getting drunk. It was about being together.

Just as I was beginning to worry I was overdressed, a man swanned in wearing a full-length mink coat. He walked toward me but didn't register my presence. In one fell swoop he threw his mink off onto the arm of a chair behind me. And then he laid a wallop of a kiss on a man, seeming intent on sticking his whole face down this other's guy throat.

I instinctively looked away, not because it was two men but because I knew him. It was my childhood classmate Greg. Growing up, other kids had teased him mercilessly and called him Liberace because he played piano. He was really so talented, but people couldn't see past his flamboyance.

Greg saw me only once he came up for air. Then he grabbed his fur and ran out. Couldn't run fast enough.

I tried to disappear. It was like, *Hi, everybody! Come meet me!* I felt so bad. I had known him since the fourth grade. I'd never said a bad word to him, but he felt like he had to run from me.

Thank God Paul rang a bell and yelled that the show was starting. People started walking to the double doors, and Paul was there to take the entrance fee. I reached into my purse.

"You're good," he said.

"I'm a little naughty," I said. "But thank you. I really appreciate the welcome."

I walked into the showroom, which looked like a legion hall rec room. It had the same low, tiled ceiling as the bar, but they'd hung red draping in the back to create a sense of a stage. The audience sat jam-packed at about forty metal foldaway tables, arranged with folding chairs that looked like they were pulled from the trash. Every once in a while, a face would peek out from a side door to see how the room was filling. It got to about 150 people, and the room got tighter and tighter. Standing room only, and people were still outside trying to get in. Finally, Paul took the stage to start introducing the performers one by one.

The first up was Miss Misty McCall, in a beautiful beaded gown that just looked expensive. She lip-synched "Take Me Home," looking more like Cher than Cher as she moved around the stage. Gradually, people would approach the stage and offer a dollar, which she would take in her hands during the instrumental portions of the song.

Next was Consuela, swinging her natural long blond hair as she did Paula Abdul's "Straight Up." She was as thin as Twiggy, and I kept thinking the word *willowy*. When people performed in our church, you sometimes smiled at them like you were the only thing keeping them from falling apart in the spotlight. There was none of that here. This was someone commanding the stage, with small movements designed for maximum impact.

Mother Superior was announced, and I expected a nun, but she was even better. A six-foot-five, three-hundred-pound person in a big dress with tassels and jeweled strings. She danced to Dolly Parton's "Why'd You Come in Here Looking Like That," at double the speed of the music. She was manic but light on her feet, twirling so that all her bangles and beads flew like some gorgeous taffeta car wash. There was a large support beam running across the ceiling, and Mother was taller even than the beam, so she had to duck her head as she moved to collect dollars. She spun and spun until I was dizzy, then she was hitting the floor and popping up like she was break-dancing. The crowd ate it up, screaming for more. She just scowled at us as she stalked around grabbing the money.

Miss Brown Sugar came out, leaning elegantly on her cane as she moved to center stage. She wore a brown sequined dress that hugged her wide hips, holding the mic with a shiny white glove, like a jazz singer from the sixties. I sat up as she began.

"Summertime, and the living is easy," she mouthed, seeming so languid about it that she made it seem true that nothing could harm any of us. She was so regal, briefly serenading people as they handed up offerings of dollars. The performers came and went, each trying to outdo the other with an even more glamorous gown. It was like *Dynasty*, but that was absurd because we were in Arkansas, which meant these people didn't have the means to have a fabulous life. But there they were in fabulous gowns. It wasn't clownish, it was elegance, a celebration of feminine beauty. They were goddesses. The idea that I could breeze by someone like this in Hot Springs, walking around in their boy drag, and not know it? I was in love with the whole scene.

And then the emcee introduced Miss Marilyn Morrell.

I swear everyone leaned forward before she even hit the stage. And when she did, people cheered.

Billy, aka Marilyn, made a classic drag queen entrance into my life. Just breathtaking. Fine-boned and broad-shouldered, wearing a shoulder-length, curly black wig that looked like God gave it to her. Marilyn sang Madonna's "Like a Virgin" in a beautiful long white dress that absorbed all the light in the room and shot it back at you. There were lesbians in the front row, and they sat up, giving her their full attention, holding their hands up to be ready to clap the loudest. You couldn't *not* look at her. I looked over and saw Paul staring in adoration. This was a star.

Midway through the song, I reached into my purse for a dollar and approached her. Marilyn turned to me and smiled, reaching out a hand like a queen accepting a tribute.

"Thank you, darling."

"You are so welcome," I said.

I turned and walked over to Paul, who was standing by the stage to watch. "Who is that?" I said. "She's amazing."

"She's my boyfriend," he said in a soft voice, touched with awe. "That's Billy."

Chapter Fifteen

On Sunday night Allison had trouble settling down. It was hot, which didn't help, but I knew it was because second grade was about to start and she was anxious. We both were. I was in her room, and she was all brushed and in her pajamas. The phone wasn't ringing, and there were no emergency visits to be had.

She looked at me with a conspiratorial smile. "You wanna go out on a midnight run?"

I smiled back. "Let's go."

We did these nighttime drives periodically, especially when it was hot. It fit my restless heart too. We drove out to the lake and then up North and West Mountains. It always worked for us. Allison wouldn't get sleepy in the car, but she knew that by the time we went home, it was time for bed. I've done my part, now you've got to do your part.

The lake was gorgeous, an expanse of black glass jeweled by lights across the way. The windows down, we breathed in great big gulps of air, summer leaving us soon. The roads up and down the mountains wind and wind; it's one-way now, but it used to be two-way or "however you want to get up or down."

We always stopped at the top of West Mountain to take in the view. In the sixties and seventies, this was Makeout Mountain. Everybody came up here with the excuse that they wanted to see "the duck." It was an outline of a duck shaped by the lights of Hot Springs, but you had to look for it. Kids would tell their parents, "We went up to see the duck."

"That's nice, dear." A lot of pregnancies started up here.

Hot Springs had grown out so much that the duck had disappeared, but Allison still tried to find it. We got out and sat on the front of the car, our feet perched on the fender. This was our spot, and sometimes we'd get doughnuts before school and watch the sun come up here. I reminded myself to try to do more of that this year—if there was time.

She pointed out Tim and Jim's building and figured out which was their light on the eleventh floor. "They are so funny," she said.

"I know," I said.

"I hope they can be okay for a long time."

I paused, not sure what to say. "Me too," I said. What was permanent to my little girl? Her father gone, dependent on the friendship of kids whose parents hadn't yet forbidden them to even play near her. Meeting these men, only to bury them. Sooner, later, but always the same end. At seven, her prayer was for time.

I held her with my right arm, my hand tucked under her leg to pull her toward me. With my other hand, I traced out the duck from memory. "It's still there," I told her. "You just have to look for it."

That weekend I invited Mitch to come with me to the drag show, telling him to dress up to show respect for the performers. Mitch wore one of his white Hong Kong shirts with the initials embroidered on the cuffs, open at the collar, gray slacks, and a black belt with a heavy gold buckle. I wore a red cocktail dress, which he complimented, so it must have looked good, because Mitch wasn't one for compliments. It's not that he was a jerk, it just didn't occur to him to point things out. The irony was that he was vain, which is partly why he enjoyed the show so much. He loved the attention he got from the guys at the bar, and when the performers made him a part of the show, serenading him at certain moments in songs, he seemed as mesmerized as I was. I guess a poor kid from Cutter dressed up in a hundred-dollar shirt felt a certain kinship with a drag queen.

Mitch and I were on the dance floor after the show, still enraptured from the performance. Between songs, I congratulated him on being so good and respectful about giving dollars to the performers. He laughed. "Well I give 'em to the strippers," he joked, "so why not your friends?"

I rolled my eyes but laughed. I put my arm around his neck, and I spotted Billy over Mitch's shoulder. His makeup washed off, he remained beautiful, with short hair, coal black. You'd now describe his cheekbones as chiseled, the flat angles of his chin as strong. He looked so young, probably just out of his teens.

I waved a hand at him as he walked by and simply said, "I loved the show."

He stopped. "You did?" he asked. His voice was deeper than I expected, with no country accent at all. There was a shyness to it that I also hadn't expected.

"Oh yes," I said, wanting to say so much more. "I loved your dress."

He let out a wonderful laugh, a hearty one that seemed like it would never be at anyone's expense. "I love yours," he said.

"Where are you from?" I asked. I could not place his voice at all. "Dardanelle."

"*Dardanelle*," I nearly shouted, unable to hide my shock.

He smiled, giving me a conspiratorial look before more fans came over to hug him. Dardanelle was an hour and a half north through the pines along Highway 7, right on the banks of the Arkansas River. A whole town just left on the shore, waiting for the barges of the 1800s to come back, bringing gin and cotton and news of the world out there. It was one of those places with all the cars putting out blue smoke because it's that poor of a town. The Great Depression never really left Arkansas, but I imagine when it came to shake down Dardanelle, there wasn't much to take.

We were drawn to each other, but for a long time it was just a mutual fascination. Me in my Junior League haircut, and him, the movie star from Dardanelle. I didn't see much of him at first, even though a couple of nights a week I would leave Allison with Bonnie for an hour or two so I could go to Our House when it opened at five. I sat at the bar, near Paul, drinking my club soda and chatting here and there with him. I didn't bother him while he was setting up. We were two cats getting to know each other, and this was his territory.

In Hot Springs, you learned who someone was by figuring out who their people were. That wasn't the case at Our House. Almost all the regulars had left their hometowns to create their own lives here in Hot Springs. Even Paul, who'd moved to Hot Springs as a sophomore in high school, seemed to have lived those fifteen years in a different world. If they'd had any skin in the straight world of Hot Springs, they couldn't just go to a gay bar. The family's reputation would be on the line too. But the men and women who went to Our House had already left all that behind.

Just by being a wallflower, I slowly began to break in to the community. I knew gay men from my AIDS work, but that was the language of T cells and symptoms. This was different. There was the interchanging of "he" and "she," depending on mood, and the passion for drag queens. People talked about pageants and of queens being robbed of crowns and trophies with such conviction that I worried real fights would break out. They dropped names like Miss Lena London and Miss Candace Kincaid and fought over who should have been last year's Miss Gay Arkansas if the score sheets were correct. "Those Little Rock queens . . ." someone would say, and people would shake their heads.

There was Marshall, who was Miss Brown Sugar out of drag. When he teased me, I felt anointed, because I could tell everyone liked to talk to Marshall. "Little Miss Muffet over here ears-droppin'," he said, his voice a dismissive slur that I loved. You had to work to understand him, and Paul explained the cane and slur in his voice were from having had a brain aneurysm.

Consuela told me I could call her Connie. She told me she liked me because I looked just like a Barbie doll. And Twyman, the bar's owner, would come in to keep an eye on his money. He was old, gray-headed, had a button-down short-sleeved shirt straining at his big potbelly. Even with shorts, he wore white dress shoes and tube socks pulled high, white with a green stripe around the top. Paul warned me he was "an old school, mean-as-hell queen" who'd been married with kids and talked like he was still a sergeant in the service.

Mother Superior was Larry, who ran hot and cold on everyone. He was a fry cook at the bowling alley, and the people loved him there because he had a photographic memory for their orders. Mother came in every night, manic and just off work. He was so big, charging in. "Ohhhh, it's so fun to be here," he'd tell Paul, his reedy voice booming. "So glad to be here. Get the music started, girl. Get me a large Dr. Pepper, light on the ice. Biggest one you got." Mother would dance until he was just dying and sweating all over the place, and Paul would play music to see how long he could keep him on the dance floor.

No matter who you talked to, somehow the person always managed to bring the subject back to Billy, the star of the bar. I collected information almost as a fan would. Marilyn Morell was in tribute to Morrell hot dogs, which they made up in Dardanelle. He turned twenty-one that December, and Paul, who was twenty-eight, got him a cake at the bar. Billy lived with Paul in a two-story house over on Oak Cliff, and Mother was their roommate upstairs. Billy had only been in Hot Springs a few years, stopping in Russellville for a bit on the way here. Russellville was a step up from Dardanelle, what with it having Arkansas Tech University. I pictured Billy walking to Russellville, anything to escape Dardanelle. Walking over that bridge with the Arkansas River flowing beneath him. He'd grown up Pentecostal, so I thought there must have been a lot to escape.

He'd had nothing when he got here, and Paul had felt bad for him. Paul told me that if you're even halfway decent-looking and you have half a personality when you came to Hot Springs, you'd have every suitor after you. So, of course, the whole town was just ready to date Billy. Not Paul, though. He thought Billy seemed like a lost soul, and he told him that he could use his spare room as long as he got a job. Slowly, they fell in love.

Billy got a job at the Miller's Outpost clothing store in the Hot Springs Mall, and I pictured all these men and women coming in for jeans and winter coats. Did they know they were in the presence of a star? How could they not?

I learned he was the bridge between the gay men and the lesbians in the bar, beloved by both. There was PJ, who had a wealthy closeted lover who had all the money in the world. Those two women loved Billy and would pick him up at the mall. "Come on, we're going shopping." It was nothing to them to buy him hundreds of dollars in looks, just so PJ could sit in the front row and say, "I bought that dress there." It made her feel like a patron of this great artist.

Mitch and I went back to the Saturday drag shows every two weeks, starting a routine where we would eat over at the Brick House Grill and then walk across the street to Our House. We would each get a ribeye sandwich, because you could get the steak cooked the way you wanted it; then you just took it off the bun and you'd have your steak and potatoes. They'd charge you twice as much for the regular steak. Even if he was paying, I wasn't going to waste anything.

Paul noticed I kept coming back, and after about five months, in January 1990, I'd hung around enough that I won his trust. He picked up on calling me "Ruthie" after overhearing Mitch do it. One weekday I went in at 5:15, and I caught his smile when I came in. He placed a photo album on the bar, right where I usually sat. I stood, lightly touching the band of gold that ran around the dark red cover. He nodded and I sat to open it.

"If you're going to be a fan, you need to know what drag is about," he said, opening to the first page. "From the beginning of time . . ." he said. There were four square photos from the Fotomat of a man walking a stage in drag, blond curly hair and a blue dress cut just above the knee. A long white kerchief and an eager smile gave her the look of an airline stewardess. "That's 1979, at the old Our House. I was Miss Dana Marie." He said it in a sweet, naive-sounding voice, which must have been how Dana talked. "We had a talent show once a year. You got in drag, and if you did good enough, you got in the Saturday shows. If you didn't, you got to wait another year." He paused for effect. "Dana got to wait another year."

"Well, I was pulling for her," I said.

"Miss Cherry Fontaine was born the next year," he said, pointing to himself in a red bouffant. "We dropped the blond hair, and she was a big hit. Tuna was the one who really decided if you were in the shows."

"Tuna?"

"Miss Tuna Starr," Paul said, pointing to a picture of a sharper-featured Lucille Ball. "She was almost like a Bob Hope, the emcee of every show. She would do a big monologue beforehand, and it was like a recap of everything that happened that month. Town gossip from the bar. The more scotch she had, the dirtier she got."

He leafed through pages of drag queens, saying each name like a baseball fan, reeling off stats and wins, only this was pageant crowns and trophies. Everything revolved around the pageants. The big one was Miss Gay America, but there were so many preliminaries. Miss Arkansas, Miss Hot Springs, Miss Little Rock.

I had arrived at Our House during a switch in eras. The "old queens," as Paul called them, were in their late twenties and called themselves drag queens and drag performers. They'd had set gowns for set numbers. But the new ones coming in called themselves "female impersonators."

"These new, young, 120-pound boys put on a woman's dress and wear street makeup, as we call it. They come out, and yes, they are gorgeous, but they do a show or two, and people are like. 'I've seen her. All she does is stand there and look pretty.' Now it's gotten more into the audience saying, 'We want a new song and a new dress and a new wig. Every week. We still wanna know it's you, but we want something new every week.'"

"My favorite is Marilyn," I said.

"Well, Billy has everything," he said. "The crowd automatically falls in love with him before he even starts the show. He can please the roughest drag queen who's been doing it for a hundred years, and the newest queen that just put on a dress that night."

Another man came in. "Hey, Tish," Paul said. "Miller Lite?"

I got to the last page on my own, a photo of Tuna in full drag next to an obituary from August, just before I came to the bar the first time. The man in the photo looked so sedate, handsome and smiling. He had just the smallest spark of the flame Tuna showed in the other photos. The obituary read at the bottom: "Memorials can be made to the American Cancer Society and the Leukemia Society of America."

I looked up to see Paul standing there. "I am so sorry," I said. "I didn't realize."

"Our history will always be Before Tuna," he said, "and After Tuna. She was the one who told us about AIDS, but it's been an outside thing. I remember the first time I met someone with AIDS, it was because of Tuna. She had told us, 'Someone from Dallas is coming up with AIDS, and they're gonna be my guest this weekend. I want you to meet 'im, and I want you to talk to 'im, and you might learn some more information. And these are condoms.'"

"Oh, that's wonderful," I said. "Tuna gave out condoms?"

"'Condroms,' she called them. I remember she had a meeting before the show, which was very bad timing 'cause everybody was waiting for a show, and she asked for a meeting on safe sex. She'd had too many scotches, and she had 'condroms' for everyone. She was very explicit, trying to be technical but using a lot of street words. She had a catchphrase—"

Paul stopped himself. "I'm going on here."

"I'm pretty unshockable," I said. "What was the catchphrase?"

"Tuna said: 'Spit it out, it wasn't yours to begin with.' Which is self-explanatory."

"Self-explanatory."

"But she was, you know," he said. "She was Tuna." Paul changed the subject by taking the book. "Anyway, I just thought you'd like to know about the history."

"Paul, I'm just wondering, did people take the condoms? The 'condroms'?"

"I didn't watch, but I think so," he said. "We actually had a basket over the cigarette machine. Not a big thing, just a little one. Someone came down and made the comment that they had been in the bar and 'You just wouldn't believe it. They're down there having sex all the time. You can't even walk in there, there's condoms sittin' all over the place. It's like a big orgy house.'"

"Oh dear," was all I could say.

"Any time someone from the outside comes in, a lot of times it's, 'Let me see what's going on in here so I can close this place down.' There's a lot of people who would like to see us gone."

I wasn't sure if he meant the bar or all gay people. Both, probably.

"Like when you came in, I knew you had a good story and you looked nice, but I was looking for my name in the newspaper for days. 'This is the ringleader, Paul Wineland. He's the main bartender, and the one everybody looks to . . .'"

"Oh, never." I said. "Never, never, never."

"You can't be too careful."

"Paul, if I got you a lot of condoms, would you put them out?"

He paused.

"I know you said nobody here is sick, but they might *get* sick. But the main thing is that you have people coming in here from all over. You're across from the Hilton, and guys from out of town come right from the Convention Center auditorium. I'm not saying people have to stop doing what they're doing, no. Lord, no. I just want everyone to be able to keep doing it. So let's give them something to keep in their pocket for later."

He thought about it for a minute. "Okay."

The next morning, I drove to Little Rock to the health department and went in through the back like usual. Everyone was used to me by then.

"I need condoms," I said. "To give out."

"Well, who signed off on it?"

"What do you mean?"

"I need a name," she said. "Someone who ordered it."

"Uh, he's on the third floor, I think. What's his name . . . ?"

"Okay, third floor," she said, typing it in. "Got it."

"Yes," I said. "Third floor."

People don't care. Just long as somebody gives them a name that they don't have to come up with so they can pass it on, they don't care. And that's how you get stuff done.

The condoms were a breakthrough. If anyone asked who brought them, the answer was "Ruth." Since I talked to everyone, it wasn't a sign if someone said to me, "Can I call you next week?"

"Yeah, give me a call. Great show tonight, wasn't it?"

If I'd have come in and had a special meeting before a show, that would never have worked. "Hello, I'm Ruth Coker Burks. Everyone that has AIDS and needs help, please come to the front of the stage, and I'll help you."

I did more and more testing with the Doctor, and I broke more and more bad news. But at least they knew. Or they would tell me about a friend that needed help, and soon I'd be driving out to take them to a doctor's appointment. And I helped people all over the state plan their funerals. I learned that some people had suddenly left Hot Springs with no explanation, and then someone at Our House would hear they passed. "Cancer or something." Maybe they had returned to their hometowns, just like so many of the men I saw coming home to their families in Hot Springs. Only to find there was only me.

As the circle of people I needed to care for expanded, I needed medicine. It took time to get people onto Medicaid, and they wanted to get medication right away. I often had a small share of AZT or other meds left over from people who died. Dave, Wally, Steve . . . As people got closer, they would give me their keys, and I would go get it. I learned that we all have treasures, usually kept in a sock drawer or on top of a dresser where it could be seen. So along with the medicines, they would tell me to mail a note to someone, with an old school ID or a family photo. Something to leave to their people, even the ones that rejected them.

I stockpiled medicines that otherwise would have cost thousands and thousands of dollars a year. Sulfamethoxazole for pneumonia, clarithromycin to prevent tuberculosis, acyclovir for herpes outbreaks, inhalers of pentamidine for pneumocystis carinii, ganciclovir and the fancy foscarnet for CMV retinitis . . . My kitchen pantry began to look like a pharmacy, because I would take anything just to store. What if Arkansas just plain decided they weren't going to let people distribute AIDS medication? Nothing was off the table.

When someone needed AZT and couldn't get it because of money or access, I would go around to my guys, spare-changing for pills to get people started. There were guys that I knew had six weeks to live and they had eight weeks' worth of pills. But I would never say that. If I took away those two weeks, they would know. They'd think, *She doesn't think I'm gonna live.*

So I'd ask them to spare three or four doses here and there. Whoever needed the most hope, I'd ask for the fewest pills from.

From the trials I read about in the medical journals, I didn't think AZT did much. It still wasn't proven to even postpone the onset of AIDS, and there was already talk in the journals about viral resistance. HIV could maybe mutate in your body to outwit AZT. The only real benefit I saw myself was that taking medicine gave them hope. And that was what they needed, because that was all they had.

I hadn't forgotten Marc, my New York Yankee, showing me that first bottle. He died—yet another person I buried in Files—but I remember the label on that bottle had power, like a talisman. So when I would go to people who were doing well, like Tim and Jim, I would say, "Here, you keep the rest of the pills, but I need the bottle too." I had to give the person getting the pills *proof*. Proof that I was giving them something that might help them save their own lives.

My guys craved information and wanted to know what the end might look like. "When *people* die . . ." They never said, "When *I* die . . ." Nobody said out loud that they thought they were gonna die. Because the day after tomorrow the vaccine would come out. Maybe tomorrow, but more likely the day after. And that's how they lived months and, sometimes, years. It was hope.

Chapter Sixteen

I had a new patient who was dying on me, and I couldn't shake my surprise. Keith was a friend of a couple who had called me for help, Bob and Phil. They had come down together from New York and were the first mixed-race couple, gay or straight, I'd ever met. Hot Springs was still very segregated, from the cradle to the grave. Even the cemeteries were kept separate. When Bob called me, he made it clear that if I had a problem with Phil being black, then they wouldn't be needing my help. It took me a minute to understand, because I was so used to being on the side of the underdog. People were hated because they were gay, but I forgot people were capable of hating people for other stupid reasons.

Bob was bald, and his face was just a blank canvas colored with the purple and red lesions of Kaposi's sarcoma, one large one on his right side and a spray of them on the other. It was the first time I'd seen the lesions, because my guys never had them. But that was the face of AIDS on TV and in magazines. Phil was very handsome, his hair cut short and his smile bigger for his becoming gaunt. They had picked up Keith on the way from New York. He was a little guy with a mop of sandy, curly hair. He had AIDS too but seemed healthier than Bob and Phil. He was smiley and always pushing his mop of curly hair back from his eyes as he took a deep breath.

So when Phil called me from a hospital pay phone, I assumed it was to tell me that Bob was sick. I started pulling his file from my mind when Phil said it was Keith.

It was a fever. Keith had been in his room alone, and Bob had checked on him when he didn't get up in the morning and found him unresponsive. They rushed him to AMI hospital. He was in the intensive-care unit.

One look at Keith, and I knew he had about a day. Phil and Bob looked stunned. Bob's health had been starting to decline further, and I think they had rehearsed for him to be in that bed. "Do you guys want to take a break?" I asked. They looked at each other, neither wanting to be the one who said yes. I told them I thought Keith had time but not much, so this would be a good moment to rest themselves. "Go for a walk."

They did, leaving me alone with Keith. I sat down and held his hand. "You snuck up on me," I said. "You have to watch the quiet ones." Char, a new nurse at AMI, saw me through the glass and came in. She had quickly become my favorite nurse at any of the hospitals. We nodded at each other, and I could tell she also knew Keith didn't have much time, but she had the decency not to say it in front of him.

She was older than me, her brown hair lightened to hide the gray. She accepted all the patients as they were, and she was also kind to me. If I was with someone all night, she would bring me a coffee. We had bonded when we were checking in on this Serbian gentleman who had shown up out of nowhere. He was beyond talking when he got dumped at the ER, but his ID said he was fifty-five, when almost everyone else I dealt with was in his twenties. Char and I were checking his vitals and taking his rings off. She was telling me this beautiful story about when her husband died and all the trouble she had gone through to take his wedding ring off herself. We were deep in conversation, and then this man just died right in front of us. And we didn't realize it at first. It was like he'd pulled something on us.

I was right that Keith had a day. Phil and Bob were there when he passed, and I was grateful he went easy for them. They didn't need to see any nasty coming attractions. They wanted to honor him with a funeral, and I thought Hot Springs Funeral Home would help now. My friend Dub Townsend, one of the kindest people I knew, had become the general manager there. I went over and explained it, assuring them they wouldn't need to embalm the body, because I knew that scared funeral directors. I could help arrange the cremation, but the funeral would be there.

Dub said yes, and I gave him a big hug. I told him I knew I could count on him, which I hoped was true. But good people do sometimes let you down. The thing about being a pariah in my church and town was that when people like Char and Dub were kind, it stood out.

I could help Phil and Bob do Keith's funeral at a low cost, but I would need an urn. I couldn't just stop by Dryden Pottery to get a cookie jar and then put Keith up at the funeral home in that. I needed forty dollars for an urn, and I didn't have it. Phil and Bob were tapped out too. I sat with that a minute, thinking about the elders in town I could go to. If my church was worth a darn, I could go to my fellow parishioners. Do a special collection and have it in a minute. We did that to get the new hymnals to replace the perfectly good ones we had.

I went to Our House that night, to be around some life.

"Water for me," I told Paul. "I'm here for the company." I told him about Keith, explaining that Dub was willing to bury him, but I couldn't afford the actual urn to put him in.

"Well, how much is it?"

"Forty dollars."

He seemed surprised. "That's it?"

"Yes," I said. "I have everything else covered. And I just need to figure this out."

He paused. "It's really just forty?"

I felt embarrassed. I didn't have a spare forty dollars that wasn't earmarked for a bill or gas to drive people around. It was all spoken for. "Yes," I said.

"Ruthie," he said slowly. "I'll talk to some people, and maybe, if you can stop by tomorrow, we can take care of it."

"I didn't mean to ask—"

"I know you didn't," he said. "I want to do this."

The next day I went back, and I was ready to pretend the offer had never been made. But Paul pulled a little tackle box from under the bar. "I told people what you needed," he said. "And why."

Inside was a wad of singles and quarters and one five. "We got to forty-seven fifty. I just wanted you to see it all."

"Thank you so much," I said. "Thank you *so much*." I started to cry, and I didn't want to. Paul was nice, but he didn't seem the type to handle big emotions. I grabbed a cocktail napkin and tried to stop the tears, but they wouldn't stop.

"He was just a really sweet guy, Keith was," I said. "He even died not wanting to make a fuss. Just got away from me."

"Ruthie, you're so thankful, and this is something so small." Paul put the money in the register, and placed two twenties and the rest in a neat pile in front of me. "It's something anyone would do for anyone. I would do that for someone's *dog* if they died."

"That's the thing," I said. "Nobody has wanted to do that for these guys." I tilted my head back and blinked to dry the tears.

"Oh, my mascara," I said.

"It's on the run," he said.

"I'll never catch it at this rate," I said. I picked up the money, holding it up like the blessed offering from the collection plate. "I cannot thank you enough. You know you and anyone else are welcome to come to Keith's service. It's Friday at ten."

"No," he said. "I don't like hospitals or funerals."

"Me neither," I said. "I just keep meeting people that way."

*   *   *

They had passed a hat for me to help Keith. I thought about that for weeks. Even later, when I buried Bob and Phil at Files Cemetery within a few months of each other, that kindness was a balm. It gave me an even greater appreciation of Our House as a place of community. I knew I was hearing only from people who were already diagnosed or suspected they'd been infected. So I asked Paul if I could come some night and just have information available about AIDS. Actively give out condoms and lubricant. I promised not to be a downer.

"I know people come here for fun," I said.

"It's such a relief for people to go down to the bar, let your hair down, and let the week go," he said. "Have a few drinks and tell a few stories. And the occasional spat between queens, and nobody really gets hurt."

"I know that," I said. "I can keep it light and fun." I promised to do it once, and then if they thought I should do it again, then I'd come in. I would wait to be invited. I didn't ask to be part of an act or get up onstage. I knew well enough that drag queens don't share a stage.

The first night I went in and just tucked myself in a little vestibule with a lot of condoms and pamphlets I'd picked up from the health department. The response was okay, but my sales pitch tendencies weren't satisfied. A couple of months later, I asked Paul if I could do it again, this time with props.

"Props?"

"Nothing crazy," I said. "You'll see."

Well, cut to me using a can of spray-air to blow up different-size condoms and pinning them to a pegboard. I had regular ones, plus an extra-large one, but the biggest one was a pony condom, which they use on farms to gather semen from animals. They're real big, the size of your arm almost. And then I had a little finger cot I blew up with the last of the air in the can and tied off. I had them all up, smallest to largest.

Guys approached, and I acted like a saleslady. So many would see the pony condom and say, "That's me! That's me right there." Just a conversation starter that wasn't depressing and celebrated sex. I asked true-or-false questions, with the prize being condoms. I tried to keep my language very street, mimicking what I'd overheard here and there at the bar.

"Is Crisco a safe lubricant?" I'd ask.

"How do you know about Crisco?" a guy asked me.

"Well, is it?"

"Yes?" he answered, tentatively.

"No! Oil-based lubricants like Crisco, Vaseline, and baby oil break down condoms! And so does suntan lotion so be careful on the beach." I'd hand him two condoms. "Thanks for playing!"

They were laughing, but they were learning. I had to be careful and not turn the crowd off to what I was saying. Walk a very fine line and switch it up at a moment's notice so I wouldn't offend people. It reminded me of selling the time-shares, saying whatever I needed to in order to put people at ease so they'd listen. I surprised myself, getting more used to listing off sex acts that were safe or at least safer. I wanted them to reduce their chances of getting infected, not tell them to stop having sex. But I was still shocked by how little people knew. These were the people most at risk, and they'd been left to die.

When I came back, it got to be a fun thing for people to do, watch other guys guess and get the wrong answers. And they would know about the pony condom before anyone else did. There were people bringing friends over to learn about it. Everybody was trying to save everybody else's life.

I also saw tourists, their wedding rings tucked in their pockets. I don't know what the guys at the bar thought of them, but as a woman, you're trained to look for the "waistline" a ring leaves. If some guy is coming on to you, and you see that waistline, he'll probably lie and tell you a sob story about his wife just dying. But at least you'll know what you're getting into. I had a drunk guy stagger over, and when I offered a condom, he said he didn't need it.

"I'm not gay," he said, keeping one eye closed so there would only be one of me.

"That's nice. You ever have sex with men?"

"Well, sure."

"There you go," I said, handing him a condom. "Here, take another."

It was those guys, the tourists who kept what they did in Hot Springs secret, that I worried about. People take risks when they're afraid of being found out. They weren't going to learn about safe sex because they thought that didn't apply to them.

Billy never came over, but one night he walked by as I told everyone to tell their friends to come to me if they wanted to get tested.

"It's anonymous," I said. "It's Mickey or Minnie Mouse. Your pick."

"I got tested," he said, loud, so people could hear. "I'm good."

I was so relieved. Both that he'd said he knew his status so people could hear him, since he was such a role model, and also, of course, that he was negative.

Billy always told me he'd been tested. Nobody needed to worry.

Chapter Seventeen

The Pancake Shop on Central is right across from the Arlington Hotel, and even on weekday mornings it was smart to get there right when it opened at six thirty or a little after. Otherwise you'd have to wait in line forever.

I took Allison as a treat before school, smiling at the owner, Ruth Ardman, as we walked in. She was there every day behind that register, an old Southern woman who liked me okay. She ran that place like a machine, watching the whole show, arms crossed, shoulders back. It was a cash business, so she didn't want to let any money walk out that door unattended.

I ordered ham, which you had to have there, because it would be a sin to miss out on it. I was surprised to see Clay Farrar in the back at the business table. The table was a square, one corner set against the wall, and you knew not to go up and bother anybody sitting at that table. Clay was a true Southern gentleman lawyer in town, a couple of years older than me, and we shared a real love of Hot Springs.

Whatever it was ended with a handshake, and we nodded at each other as he passed. He paid the bill, and I was surprised when he came back to my table.

"Good morning, Ruth."

"Hello, Clay."

"I was wondering," he said. "I read about what you've been doing."

"I hope it wasn't in the police blotter."

"No, no," he said. "But listen, we need a speaker at Rotary. Would you be interested in coming in and talking about, uh—"

"My AIDS work?"

He nodded, looking around quickly. I jumped on it before the offer was rescinded. "Clay, I would be truly honored. That would mean the world to me."

"Wednesday."

"It's a date."

As he walked out, I sat up a little straighter, hoping someone overheard me. "Allison, I was just asked to speak at Rotary."

My eye went over to Ruth Ardman, who was looking at me a little differently now. The Rotary Club of Hot Springs was the old guard. They met every Wednesday, upstairs at the Arlington's grand ballroom. It was all men, and it's where all the bigwigs in town were. The Rotarians were all the people who could help me help people. *If I sound the alarm*, I again thought, *the cavalry will come.*

Clay was a former president of the club, so him inviting me was him vouching for me. I prepared statistics about HIV in Arkansas and figured I had to do the most basic information about how you get it. Other than that, I wanted to wing it. I had to be able to read the crowd to make sure they weren't turning on me at any point, just like at Our House. To know just how far I could take it. To sugarcoat some of it, but they would know I was sugarcoating it. Mainly because I was a lady presenting it to men.

I got there early, wanting to shake everyone's hand as they came in. Smile a lot and let them know they weren't going to be lectured at. The room just looked important, with gilded wallpaper and chandeliers. I sat at a long table at the front, right next to the Arkansas flag.

Clay introduced me, and I started out thanking them for letting me speak to them about this important issue. I told them the men in this room had the power to keep our community safe. It was buttering them up, but I was sincere.

I think I was about a minute into talking about the people with AIDS that I had cared for in Hot Springs when it happened. A man stood up, this real blowhard who owned a housecleaning business.

"We don't want that here!" he yelled.

A shock went through the room. You just did not do that at Rotary. The men next to him touched his arm to get him to stop, but I wasn't about to be rescued.

"None of us want it, but it's here. Or I wouldn't be up here." I waited a beat. "Heckled at Rotary, can you imagine?" I smiled, and the men laughed. Now I had them.

I explained why they didn't need to be afraid of people with HIV, laying out the basics about how it was not contagious through the air or skin to skin contact. It was spread through the sharing of bodily fluids, mainly through sexual contact and the sharing of needles. The only way it was like the flu was that whoever got it hadn't done something to deserve it, they were just exposed to it.

A guy I knew from church, a landscaper, shook his head, rolling his eyes.

I stopped. "Did you have a question?"

He looked down. I noticed Roger Giddings, superintendent of Hot Springs National Park, giving me an encouraging nod. I talked about the people with AIDS in town, how they needed food and access to care, but what we mainly needed was education. We couldn't ignore that it was here, and we had a duty to help each other.

There was a man who sneered the whole time. He went to my church, and he was one of the older men who gave me the dirtiest looks every Sunday since I had asked Dr. Hays for a room for a support group before the finance committee meeting. Not long after I spoke at Rotary, I saw him as I was crossing the railroad tracks in my car. He was right there, picking up a little black boy. From where I was stopped, I watched him help the child, a young teenager, put his bicycle in the back of a van. The old man seemed nervous but excited, smiling like a clown at this young man he'd clearly just met.

The car behind me tooted the horn, a polite, "Get moving."

The old man turned at the sound of the horn and looked right at me. We didn't wave. I showed no sign of recognition. He looked caught.

At church the next Sunday, he made a beeline for me. Like it was all he had thought about since he saw me.

"Where I was picking up that boy," he stammered. "He does my yard work." For the last year, this man wouldn't have said "excuse me" to me if he'd knocked me down the stairs. Not a word until now.

"Uh, I didn't ask you why you were down there picking up that little black boy."

"I was giving him a ride," he said.

"I do know that young people need to be safe and looked after."

"I wanted us to be clear," he said. It was poker. Would I ruin him? Could I? Of course, I wouldn't. But guilty people think everyone else is too.

If being on TV and in the paper hadn't made me the AIDS lady, talking about it at Rotary did. The Rotary Club in Arkadelphia heard about me and invited me, then the Lions Club. After I started doing those talks, word got around, and I got calls from married men who felt they could confide their concerns about their own exposure. It turned out people were so busy having affairs and getting blow jobs from strippers that it was amazing any work was getting done in town.

About a month after speaking at Rotary, I got a call from someone I'd known almost my whole life. He'd done real well for himself, but there was panic in his voice.

"Oh my God, what are you doing right now?" went the call. "You've gotta come up to my office. Something horrible's happened."

"Ryan, what are you . . . I've gotta be in Arkadelphia at the Rotary Club. I can't just come up there right now, but I can stop by on the way back."

"No, no, no. You've gotta come here right now. This is awful. This is just terrible."

I got up there to his office, and all the ladies in the secretarial pool stared at me. Apparently, Ryan had been making calls in the conference room, not realizing the secretaries could hear everything through a grate. They were so weird that when I walked in to see Ryan, I asked him, "What's up with them?"

"I don't know, but shut the door. I think I gave Sara AIDS! I think I gave her AIDS!"

"Ryan! What's wrong?" He looked like he hadn't slept in days. He clearly hadn't shaved, and from the looks of his suit, I think there was a good chance he'd spent the night at the office.

"I'm gonna have her tested."

"Why don't you start with you?"

"Oh God, that would mean I have it."

"Well, that would be how it works, if you think you gave it to her."

"Well, last month I went to a conference in Michigan," he said.

"Yeah, so what's wrong with Michigan?"

"I got a hooker. I am just connecting the dots here and— *oh shit*."

"Ryan, you gotta tell me what you did with that hooker so I can tell you if you're at risk or not. Just come on, you can tell me anything."

Ryan closed his eyes and yelled, in the most plaintive, confessional voice he could muster, "We did the Jimmy Swaggart thing."

Oh. "You got a blow job?" I asked, deadpan.

He looked shocked. "Yes, yes, I did."

"Oh my God, Ryan, you're infected all right," I said.

"I knew it! I knew it!"

"You're infected with the Guilts, is what you got. You got a massive case of the Guilts," I said. "Ryan, there's no way you got AIDS from a blow job."

He looked like I'd freed him. "I can come back and test you, and what you tell her is your business," I said. "But if you go to any more *conferences*, just remember you need to use a new condom for every sex act, okay? Now, I have to go."

When I walked out, the secretaries made no attempt to hide that they had been listening. One was sitting on a rolling chair by the grate, about a mile from her desk, palms on her knees and mouth still wide open in shock.

"Ladies," I said in my sweetest voice.

I tested a lot of straight people myself, because I was worried that if I brought them to the Doctor, his involvement would get out. In the beginning, I would go to their offices, but when you go into a man's office, and he closes the door, the secretaries think something's going on in there. I didn't want the men coming to my house, because I knew how that would look, so I had to get creative. I tested a lot of people at Hollywood Cemetery, sitting on memorial benches under the oak trees. It was hilly, and there were many places to hide out. Nobody's going to bother you at a grave, because it was very natural in Hot Springs to stop off after work and visit your relatives. And if someone is crying, you can comfort them. The irony was that Hollywood Cemetery was so well-to-do that they would never have let me bury someone with AIDS there.

Then, when I saw the men in town, they would nod at me with a guilty look I didn't return, but the wives would see there was something secret between us. I know a lot of rumors started from those glances. I even had some women ask me point-blank how I knew their husbands, and I would act like I didn't know anything about it. Nope, I never talked to your husband about AIDS *or* running off with me, thank you very much.

The hate calls got more specific. "I can't believe you brought those faggots here. They're gonna kill us all." I had a woman at church get me in the basement and lay me out in lavender about AIDS and how sinful I was to help *those* people. "Your daughter will never be a debutante," she said. "It will only happen over my dead body."

I wanted to tell her that I knew her son was gay. He was "those people" too, but that was his story to tell, not mine. I looked at her and sighed. "She is seven," was all I said.

I set aside time to call Sandy, because I needed a break. I asked if she wanted to go canoeing. She said yes, but there was a catch in her voice. We met and floated out to the Dragover spot on the Ouachita, where the river snakes back on itself and some people get out and take a shortcut. I tried to talk about what I was doing, just state it plainly, because I knew she knew what was going on.

"Ruthie," she said quietly, "I told you to quit going around those people."

"Sandy, I can't," I said. "They really need someone."

"So you'll ruin *your* life because they ruined theirs? And you'll ruin Allison's life?"

"I'm not trying to ruin her life," I said quietly.

"You are," she said. "You know you are."

I wanted to dive into the water. To let it fill my ears so I couldn't hear her. And at the same time, I wanted my friend.

"Stop going around those people," she said. "I can't for the life of me figure out why you're being so nice to them."

"If you met them—"

"No. I see enough of them."

I felt a door closing. The same feeling I had when I went to someone for help and they refused. I never asked them why or yelled at them or tried to convince them that they should care when they didn't. I didn't waste time. I just went to the next person.

Only I didn't have another best friend.

I had to put my car in the shop, so Mitch let me borrow his van while he was out of town. He was doing more of that, because he had sold his share of the restaurant and was focusing on his work.

While he was gone, I drove his mother, Donnie, out to Wal-Mart, and she acted like that was the least I could do, considering I was taking advantage of her son's generosity. I wanted to remind her of all the other times I looked in on her and took her to the store, but I held my tongue.

I'd been holding my tongue since we met, but Donnie was mostly harmless. She made it known that no one was good enough for her Mitch, and in case she wasn't clear, that meant me. She settled into her seat on the passenger side and looked at me for a second.

"You know, Ruthie," she said in her drawl, "my biggest fear when Mitch got divorced was that he would end up with some old hussy." She pronounced it "huzzy," drawing out the z's long to fill them with disdain.

I waited for the "but." No, she let it drop. I chuckled, because it was so mean, which is probably how Donnie went through life. Saying things so cutting you were more surprised than mad that someone could be so mean.

"Well, thank God that didn't happen," I said, making a right turn on to the highway. "I mean, I'm not *old*."

Now she chuckled. I knew deep down Donnie liked me. She'd probably rather deal with me than some shrinking violet. Donnie had had a hard life, and I'd lost track of how many husbands she'd gone through—five or six. I'd had the one, and that almost did me in.

She shifted in her seat, trying to get comfortable, and that reminded me why I always gave her a break. She had lost her right leg because of a blood clot. It made her talk a lot about death, like her ride would be here at any moment. Donnie liked a deal, and she knew that I had all these cemetery plots "up for grabs," as she said. I said that would be fine.

"Naw," she said. "I don't want to be buried in that cemetery with all that AIDS juice running down over me."

"Well, you'll be dead, so what would it matter?"

"Still," she said.

Donnie talked like that, but she also cooked for my guys from time to time. I sometimes took her around with me to deliver the food, so she could see what it meant to them. She knew what I cooked for them, so she would say, "Now try *this*."

We pulled into the Wal-Mart parking lot, and she pointed to a handicapped spot right near the front. Like I wouldn't see it. We had just gotten out when someone walking by stopped to give us a disapproving look.

"You know that spot is for handicapped people," he said. He was a little pip-squeak, someone who should have had something better to do than heckle two ladies.

"Oh, you're just who I need," Donnie said in a sweet voice. "Can you come over here and help me with something?" She pointed to the inside of the van.

He softened, maybe remembering his Southern manners. "Well, sure," he said. "I can help you."

Oh boy, I thought.

He ambled over as she leaned on the side of the van. When he went to look in the window, she took off her right leg in one fell swoop and started beating him with it.

"*This* is why I park in the handicapped," she said, hopping on her good leg. He ran away, ditching whatever he was going in to Wal-Mart for. I didn't say a word, and I looked away as she hiked up her dress to reattach her leg. I acted like this happened all day, every day.

"Give *me* a hard time," she muttered to herself.

"Well, you showed him, Donnie."

"Well, sometimes," she said, straightening her posture to walk in with me, "you have to let people know what's what."

Later that day, after I dropped her off, I was driving through Hot Springs when I saw the house I had been dreaming of. I only found it because I was in Mitch's van, and the carriage made me sit up higher. I was up on the hill, and I could see over the tree line to this

Sears cottage–style house on a pie-shaped lot at the intersection of three streets. You used to be able to order a house from a catalog. The house was worse for wear on the outside, fifty-some years later, but they always had beautiful woodworking in them. It looked exactly like the dream house I had torn out of the magazine and pinned on the pegboard in my kitchen.

The house was in a part of town that was once the neighborhood you wanted to live in before everything moved out to the lake. From the landscaping, I knew the owner had given up. Some couple had probably built it after the war when they were twenty-three or twenty-four—picked the floor plan from a catalog and planned on never leaving. I left a note on the door, saying if they ever wanted to sell this beautiful house, let me know.

The owner called me the next day. Her husband had recently died, and she wanted to move out to Mount Ida. "This house was his dream," she said.

"It would be mine too." I said.

She said she would let me have it for two thousand dollars up front, then three hundred dollars a month mortgage. It seemed like fate, because social security had just given me a check for two thousand dollars in back payments.

"I can do that," I said.

"It's a deal, then."

Allison loved it too. I felt good providing this for her. The neighborhood we were living in was only getting worse. Someone recently got stabbed on the street, and we came home to find blood all over the sidewalk and the yard. The police had left a note on the door saying there was a stabbing. "No need to worry," it said. I got out the hose and sprayed the blood away.

When Mitch came home, I told him I needed him to build a pergola. "Where?" he asked.

"My new house," I said. He looked at me like I was crazy. But, as usual, he didn't ask a single question.

I wanted to marry Mitch and be a woman who has to check with someone before she buys a house, but I wasn't. My birthday was in March, and it turned out his ex's was the day before. I had to hear about all the gifts he'd wasted on her, and all I got was flowers. I finally told him I didn't want to hear about her anymore. I didn't think he was going to propose on my birthday, but I realized I would have said yes if he'd asked. So I broached the subject of marriage.

"Yeah, we'll get engaged someday," he said. "But I figure it's cheaper by the piece." He'd invested in buying the whole cow before and wasn't interested. I was hurt, but I didn't show him. It was enough, I told myself, that he was Mr. Saturday Night. I knew how men were, though.

"Don't you go out there and get you any strange," I warned, "and tell me it didn't mean anything to you, because it better mean losing me."

He chuckled, but he started working on the pergola. I moved my pegboard of dreams into the new kitchen, and I felt like I had checked something off with the house. I had provided that for Allison and me, just not a man who would take up for us. That would still be me.

Chapter Eighteen

May 19, 1990, had seemed like a very ordinary Saturday night until we had to pull over on the side of the road because of the downpour. Mitch and I were driving out to dinner at Bohemia, which was our favorite German restaurant downtown. It had rained throughout the day, but now it felt like three thunderstorms had settled right over us, battling for the right to rain on Hot Springs.

Even Mitch, who generally preferred to ignore the world around him, had conceded defeat and pulled over. We were still high up.

"The lake is gonna flood," he said, matter-of-fact. He'd built enough docks out on the lakes to know what they could take and what they couldn't. I was worried about my house, which I had barely moved into.

We turned around, and he inched back to my house, then said he needed to leave to be ready. He knew he'd be getting calls about the docks. My house was fine, and I called Bonnie, who was safe and dry, with Allison beside her, watching TV. "ABC's showing *The Ryan White Story* again," she said. "I thought you'd like that."

They'd run it last year but were rerunning it because he had died in April. Ryan was a kid with hemophilia in Kokomo, Indiana, who got HIV from a plasma product. He had just turned thirteen when he was diagnosed in 1984, and Kokomo reacted so horribly. They got out a petition instead of pitchforks and banned him from school. He was a great kid, and I admired his family, but the media loved an AIDS "innocent victim." Where were my guys in that story?

"Well, tell her I love her and I'm okay too," I said, drying my hair with a towel. I called around, checking on my guys and the elderly people I kept track of, like Melba and Miss McKissek. Some didn't answer, so I got in the car.

There'd been a slight lessening in the downpour after ten, but what I saw was so much worse than I'd anticipated. We'd had a flash flood, and I couldn't even get to Central Avenue, which was a river. Water rushed by like the Colorado rapids, going up to lick the second floor of buildings I grew up with. Water was rushing by, so loud I couldn't hear myself say, "Oh my God." There were mannequins floating by, then cars. Later, Paul told me that the guys in the bar had to do a human chain to get two people who were stuck in a taxi, the water moving so fast it would take them all with one slip.

I wasn't able to get to everybody until the next day, after all the downed trees were cleared. People were in shock, and so, later, when I passed a house that had a lot of life about it, it stood out to me. A banner hanging between the two columns of the building read "Psychic Fun Fair."

I went in and was relieved to be among people who weren't shell-shocked. It was sort of like the sales room at the resort, with people giving you free readings to get you to get hooked on them, so you'd keep coming back.

This one smarmy guy called to me right away, sitting at a table with what looked like a pile of crystals in front of him. He was from out of town, because anyone who'd been in Hot Springs a week could tell that was just a pile of milky quartz. But I sat down, and he made a show of gathering the "crystals," huffing them like Scarface with a pile of cocaine. I tried not to laugh and did a sympathetic nod when he exhaled.

"What do you come here to know?"

"How's the relationship between my daughter and her father?"
I asked. That would be a good test of legitimacy.

"It will get better," he said.

I grabbed my purse. "Thank you for your time," I said. He didn't
seem surprised, so maybe he saw *that* coming at least. I walked around
and noted a sandy-blond-haired man, a big bear of a guy with a long
walrus mustache, doing a reading. His eyes kept drifting past the
person he was reading to and falling on me. I could see he started
to rush through the reading with this poor guy, turning the cards
quicker. I was distracting him so much he finally said to the guy,
"Okay, so, like . . . be careful." He gathered the cards up, the reading abruptly over.

"Careful of what?" said the guy. It was like getting to the climax
of the story and then not hearing the rest of it.

"Just stuff," he said, motioning to me. "Thanks." The guy looked
back at me, blinking. I smiled. He didn't.

When I sat down, the reader sat back and put down the cards
and rested his hands on the crest of his belly. He leaned back like he
was trying to get a wide angle on me. "I see a lot of death around
you," he said. "Or something. It's weird. What do you *do*?"

"Well, you tell me," I said. "You asked me to sit down."

He picked up the cards in his hand, then put them down again.
"Uh, are you a chaplain? No . . . What *are* you?"

I smiled. He put the cards down. "I gotta smoke," he said. He
got up quick and pulled out a pack. I noticed they were Mores. I
followed him out to the front porch. He offered me a cigarette, and
I took it because it had been that kind of day. He lit us both with a
pretty lighter and exhaled with a knowing nod at me.

"You're doing something that I gotta know about," he said. "I
think I can help you."

It was a game, in a way. I wanted him to guess the unfathomable.

"You're not a doctor," he said.

"No, not really," I said.

He cocked his hip, aiming his cigarette at me. I raised one eyebrow, some unspoken conversation between us telling him he was getting warmer. "I help people with AIDS," I finally said.

His whole body melted. "Okay," he said. Then to himself, in some confirmation of what he'd seen. "Okay."

"It's a lot, I guess," I said.

"Yes."

"I don't even need the cards," he said. "It makes people think it's real. I'm Owen."

"Ruth."

"I'm actually a home health aide," he said. "I live up in Memphis. My boyfriend, Bill, and I, we had a friend."

"Did you help him?"

"Yes."

"Good for you," I said. "I'm glad he had you."

"Who's got you?" he asked.

"Excuse me?"

"Sorry, I was just thinking of this scene in *Superman*," he said. "Christopher Reeve catches Margot Kidder when she's falling off the top of a skyscraper. He says 'I've got you,' and she looks down and says, 'You've got me? Who's got *you*?'"

I smiled. "You're a movie buff."

"No, I just like people," he said.

I stubbed out the cigarette. "So, what do your psychic powers tell you about my future? Are we going to be okay?"

He didn't smile. I gave him my number, telling him if he had any more friends in need, they could call me.

Owen did call me, some months later, but it wasn't about a friend. He'd taken an elderly patient to dialysis at a hospital, where he saw a flyer about the American Psychological Association hosting a conference about AIDS care and mental health, up there in Memphis, Tennessee.

My family cemetery in Hot Springs, Arkansas.

I buried Jimmy at my father's grave.

My daddy and me on a trip down his beloved Peace River in Florida.

My mother was held at a TB sanatorium from the time I was six months old to when I was five. This was my one visit, and they had to spank me to sit on her lap.

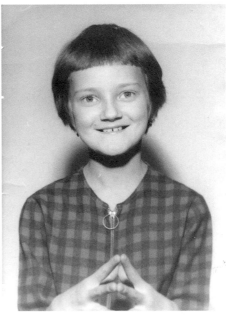

The last picture of me and Daddy, taken a few weeks before he died. He angled himself to hide his tracheotomy.

My second grade school photo. My mother cut off all my hair in one of her episodes.

Me in 1986, when I began
my AIDS work.

My daughter Allison at age five.

My home at that time in Hot Springs.

Allison and I would bring a picnic breakfast to watch the horses doing their morning workout at Oaklawn Park Race Track.

I buried the ashes of my men in these cookie jars.

My church, First United Methodist, where God was every Sunday morning. And where I was not welcome.

On a dock my boyfriend Mitch built.
I wore that just because I could.

Miss Marilyn Morrell and Paul Wineland,
manager of Our House lounge.
A love for the ages.

In Little Rock with the lovely Miss Sookie Simone (left) and
the lovely Miss Lena London, the reigning Miss Gay Arkansas 1991.

Billy was always a star, even when he wasn't performing as Marilyn.
He left me that red Victor Costa dress.

Allison right after her daddy died.
I had to fight to make our church let her be an acolyte.

Paul, Billy, and Mother Superior
at home.

Billy and me.

One of Marilyn's last performances at Our House.

Billy near the end.

Returning to the hospital where
I met Jimmy, three decades gone by.

"I'm not a psychologist or a psychiatrist or even a counselor," I said. "How am I going to get there?"

"Can you get a ride to Memphis?"

"Well, sure," I said.

"You could stay with me and Bill," he said.

"I don't think I can just show up, though."

"You'll figure it out."

"Owen, I don't think you're much of a psychic, because you clearly don't know what all I've got going here. I'm trying to do school with Allison, volunteer for church, and I've got like ninety-five thousand AIDS patients across the state, and they're all dying."

"Call them and ask," he said. "I *am* psychic. I know you'll figure it out."

Figure it out, Ruth. Memphis was right across the river. If they were doing AIDS stuff there, I could get them to come here. I went to the library and wrote down a bunch of numbers for the American Psychological Association, and I eventually got to an events coordinator. "It's two hundred fifty dollars for nonmembers," he told me.

"Well, I don't have that," I said. "I can pay in information, though. What I've seen here. My patients are living longer than—"

"I'm afraid not," he said.

"Who again is organizing this? I had it written down but I seem to have misplaced it."

"Dr. John Anderson," he said.

"Do you have his number?" He gave me a number with a 202 area code—Washington, DC—to get rid of me, and I called it right away and left a message.

"I would love to come, but I need a scholarship," I said. "I don't have two hundred fifty dollars to come to this meeting. If you waive the entrance fee, I can handle getting there and a place to stay."

I called four more times, and when Dr. Anderson finally picked up, he sounded caught. He did not understand why I couldn't afford the two-hundred-fifty-dollar registration.

I set aside all pride. "Do you have a hardship thing?" I asked. "I promise I will be no bother. I can stand if I have to, and I won't use more oxygen than anyone else. I'd like the chance to talk to people about coming to Arkansas. We need you."

He sighed. "I have to go in to a meeting."

"It's just my name on a list," I said.

"Okay," he said.

I closed my eyes. "Ruth Coker Burks."

"I have it," he said. "You've left several messages."

"Thank you, Dr. Anderson."

He softened slightly, like a pressure was lifted. "See you there."

"I will look for you!"

"Uh-hmm," was all he said.

I called Owen, and I told him it was a go. I mentioned that I needed a sitter for Allison, and he said he and Bill would be happy to look after her. "She's safe with us." I knew he was right when we walked in. Bill was a slight guy who looked like the country singer George Jones, and he seemed so kind. They'd never babysat before, and I could tell they would have been great parents if they'd only been given the chance.

When I got to the conference, it was like angels singing. I had felt so alone doing my work, and here were people who cared. Still, I didn't meet anybody like me. There were people who had cared for one or two people on a professional basis. The deaths happened off-screen, somewhere else.

When I met Dr. Anderson, I saw why he was so reluctant to make a wave by bringing me on. He was already twisting so many arms to get a conference on AIDS and mental health. He was tall and completely bald—not a hair on him because of alopecia. He said we could all call him Dr. Smooth and joked about how he lost it suddenly while in school in Texas. He used to have long, luxurious hair, and the rednecks would drive by and yell, "Boy, when you gonna cut that hair?" And then one day, it fell out. "My hair, my eyebrows, my eyelashes, just gone," he said. "And then the rednecks drove by and yelled, 'Boy, when you gonna grow you some hair?'"

Dr. Anderson was a clinical psychologist looking to train health professionals and educators to show compassion for people with HIV. He called it the AIDS Community Training Project. I cornered him at lunch and gave him the same speech I gave to everyone: "Please come to Arkansas. There's plenty to help. Y'all can each have ten patients, just please come over."

He was sitting there trying to figure out how to get away from me, but I had wrapped my ankle around his chair leg, and he didn't know that he was not moving until I got him to commit to coming to Arkansas. I was desperate.

"Well, we need funding," he said.

"Who gives you that?"'

He explained it was the Arkansas Department of Health. "Can I take your info to them?" If I could get testing kits and condoms from them, why not try?

As soon as I got back to Arkansas, I drove to Little Rock with the packet, along with a long letter that Bonnie had proofread for me twice. I wanted it to matter if I had to leave it.

I went in through the loading dock, like always. The head of the Arkansas Department of Health was Dr. Joycelyn Elders, so I had to get to her. I knew the floor she was on, so I got on with a group, looking like I knew where I was going. I rehearsed a speech for her secretary. People slowly got off, floor after floor, until it was only me.

When I emerged on her floor, I looked around, still trying to look like I belonged there.

"Hello," said a voice. I turned to see a man with close-cropped, neat, dark hair. He was wearing a white shirt and suspenders. "I guess you're looking for Dr. Elders's office."

"Yes, yes, I am."

He had folders and papers in his hand and looked like he was headed somewhere important. But he smiled. "Come this way," he said.

I followed. It was nice to be led. It was what I had done so many times for people. He brought me right to the receptionist. "She's here for a meeting with Dr. Elders."

The receptionist was flustered. "I don't think she has an appointment."

"I'm sure it's a mix-up," he said, more to her than to me. I held my packet of paper. I knew that if I said, "I can just leave this . . ." then it would be over. *Let this play out*, I thought.

"What is it?" called Dr. Elders.

The man turned and smiled at me, then went through a door. His work was done. The receptionist grimaced, like she was going to hear about this.

"Hi, I'm Ruth Coker Burks," I said, handing Dr. Elders the packet. She looked like she wanted no part of me. She brushed past my letter to the data in Dr. Anderson's material. She had been the health director since 1987, and I'd read an article saying even she was shocked that Arkansas had the second-highest teenage pregnancy rate in the *world*. She was hated by politicians and church folk in Arkansas, who fought her at every turn on sex education in schools. "We've taught them what to do in the front seat of the car but not the back seat," she famously said. Trying to teach heterosexuals was bad enough, and here I was looking to get her to help my guys.

She was reading as I talked, and I realized I should probably be quiet, but I was afraid to miss the opportunity. "Should I be quiet?" I asked. "Can you read and listen too?"

She stiffened but did not look up. "How do you think I got to where I am today?" she asked. "Certainly, I can."

"I'm sorry I didn't mean it that way." I paused. "Of course you can."

She read through the packet and set it aside. I started to speak, and she cut me off.

"Thank you," she said, blunt and abrupt. That must have been the signal to the receptionist, who was now at the door.

"Thank *you*, Dr. Elders. I appreciate what you are doing for Arkansas."

When I left her office, I figured I should pop my head into the door the suspendered man had gone into and say my thanks for his guidance. But I couldn't find the door. I could have sworn it was right there.

"Do you know where that man went?" I asked.

"What man?" the receptionist asked, in a tone that said if I asked for one more thing she would send me to my car by way of the window. *What man?* I said to myself. I don't know what happened, but I was grateful to that angel.

Dr. Anderson's program got funding. And the American Psychological Association would eventually have a team touring hospitals in Arkansas, offering advice on how to treat people with HIV with the only things I had actually seen work so far: compassion and hope.

Chapter Nineteen

My dedication made an impression on Dr. Anderson, and he invited me and Allison to come up and use his town house in Washington, DC, for six weeks that summer. He told me his roommate was a photographer for CNN and would be on assignment. "We need to find you a job up here in DC," he said. "Some place where you could do some good nationally."

I made a bunch of copies of my résumé, packed all my professional clothes, and tried to line up as many meetings as possible. Nonprofits and bureaucracies had already started to answer the coming gold rush from the Ryan White Comprehensive AIDS Resources Emergency Act that Congress would pass in August 1990. The CARE Act was set to give money not only to states but to public or private entities that said they helped people with AIDS. I hoped to get a position where I could bring what I knew to bear on real policy. I decided that while I looked for a job, I would volunteer at Food & Friends, a wonderful organization started in the basement of the Westminster Presbyterian Church in southwestern DC. They had a volunteer army delivering meals to people with AIDS all over the district. I liked that they kept a lean staff, with about six people in the kitchen. I did this kind of thing myself anyway, so Allison and I got right in there, peeling vegetables, cooking food, sorting the meals, and packing everything. Then all these great people came in on their lunch hour to grab the bags of food and deliver it.

The first day, I kept hearing one of the dispatchers ask, "Is any-body delivering to Anacostia today? Anacostia? Will anybody deliver to Anacostia?"

We were done cooking, so I said, "I'll deliver."

"Oh, okay. And your daughter too?"

"Well, yeah."

"Oh, okay."

I didn't know Anacostia was considered the most dangerous neighborhood in DC. But I didn't see any of that when we went. It was a predominantly black neighborhood, and everyone was kind to us. Elsewhere in DC, when I nodded and said "hello" to pass-ersby, people looked at me like I was crazy. But in Anacostia they smiled back at us, even if they looked a little puzzled as to what we were doing there. Delivering there became our routine, and I liked it because I found a lot of people in the neighborhood who were in the same shape as the men and women I delivered food to—but who didn't have any connections to call Food & Friends or realize that they even qualified for help. There was nothing better than delivering food to someone you'd met by chance.

I spent afternoons that summer focusing on getting a job. When I applied to work in positions with any kind of authority or salary, however, I would get the runaround. I didn't have a college diploma, and my experience meant nothing. "If you only had a degree, we could hire you," was what I heard over and over. It was true that I left college when I got married. I was just shy of graduating, and back then I had time but no money. Now that I had a little bit of my own money, I had no time. I was too busy taking care of people.

One prospect seemed promising after the administrator put my résumé in his top drawer. He said my work sounded very valuable. I thanked him, but the only time I ever saw him again was at a lobby-ist meeting about what should go into the Ryan White CARE Act.

"You know it really surprised me that I never heard from you," I said. "I thought you were going to hire me."

"Oh, no," he said casually. "I knew that I would want to sleep with you, and then I would lose my job."

"Oh, no," I said, echoing his tone. "You would have been perfectly safe with me."

There were other indignities to the meetings of advocacy groups and lobbyists deciding what to push for when putting the bill together. There were some activists from New York who interrupted me when I spoke about the importance of social security to families of people with AIDS. "That way these men and their kids are taken of—"

"Honey, gay men don't have kids," one huffed at me. "Are you out of your *mind*?"

They dismissed me—and the lives of so many men in the South who had complicated lives. Who didn't have the luxury of living out of the closet safely. Who were pressured as teens to have sex to prove their manliness, in areas where the teenage pregnancy rate was astronomical. Or who didn't fit into the pigeonholes of gay or straight. No, *I* was the crazy one not worth listening to. What did I know about the lives of gay men?

I went back to Hot Springs a little broken. I'd prayed for the cavalry to come for so long, and now they were starting to show up with Executive Director titles and six-figure salaries. Meanwhile, the people they were supposedly helping couldn't afford a week's worth of AZT.

It was even happening in Arkansas. There was money in AIDS patients now, or at least saying you did something for people with AIDS. I got a nice letter from a woman asking if I could get her into churches. At first I was excited, because I'd been so overwhelmed. But then she went in with sob stories about what she'd "seen"— "innocent victims" who'd been infected by dastardly villains. Then she'd pass the collection plate. I knew a con artist when I saw one.

An organization started that was on a constant search for "speakers" to go to churches and schools. They marched in with

some poor sap, saying, "Don't end up like this." They stressed absti-
nence education and didn't mention condoms. When the speaker
died, they just got another one. People sitting behind desks getting
paychecks sent AIDS patients out to do their bidding on a volunteer
basis.

I had poured my rage into a letter to Governor Clinton, telling
him how upset I was about the rampant mismanagement of funds.
He wrote me back a letter telling me I was wrong. There were good
people working through the system. I tore it up in anger. But later,
when one of the main offenders I complained about suddenly went
on leave, I wondered if maybe he was listening to me after all.

In October, I got a call from one of the people with letters behind
his name. He wouldn't hire me, but he was happy to put me to work
on their behalf in the field, dealing with the "complicated cases."

"It's a girl," he said. "She sounds like one of yours."

I didn't know what that meant, so I cleared my throat. "What's
her name?"

"Dolly," the man said. "Teenage hooker in Little Rock. Pregnant." She'd been getting treatment and stopped showing up at the
hospital. She was already in a downward spiral, so now she was either
dead or knocking on the door. They gave me an address in Little
Rock, where she might or might not be. It was an awful neighborhood, so I knew that's why they called me. "Call Ruth."

When I got to the apartment complex, I saw it was worse than
I'd remembered it. Crack had really gotten a hold of the area. But I
had to find her. I went and knocked on the door of the apartment I
was told to try. There was no answer.

I knocked again, more insistent this time. The door swung open,
and a great big huge man stood in front of me.

"What the fuck do you want?" he yelled, mustering every cell
of his body to intimidate me. My heart skipped a little half a beat.
That was all I was giving him. I kept a smile on my face.

"Well, I'm looking for Dolly."

He tried to hide the flicker of recognition going across his face. "If she's alive, she's in big trouble with her health," I said. "If she's not, then——"

"She's alive." He went to close the door on me, but I stuck my left foot forward and leaned back on my heel to create a wedge. He was so surprised he looked down, but he didn't force it.

"She's gonna die," I said, still smiling. "She's gonna die if I don't take her to the hospital right now. And then the police are gonna come here, and I don't want that to be big trouble for you. So if you would help me get Dolly's things together and put her in my car, I haven't seen anything. I don't know anything. I've never seen or met you. I'll forget the whole thing."

He stood there, looking at me, but I wouldn't back down. I finally whispered, "I know she's here. Come on."

He stepped aside, letting me in. "I'm Ruth Coker Burks," I said.

"Name's Tank," he said.

"Well, that suits you fine," I said. The place was a mess, but I only had eyes for a closed bedroom door. I knew she was in there. I marched to it.

Dolly was in bed, very sick. She had strawberry-blond hair, a pixie cut, but there were patches of hair missing from her scalp. She had the freckled face of a little girl, but her frail body had this enormous bump, probably about five months. She had a fever and seemed not to know where she was.

"Okay," I said, more to calm myself than Tank, who couldn't look at me. "Let's get her to the car." It was almost rush hour, and my brain was already on to wondering whether I should take Interstate 30 to 630 and take it across, or 430 and then 630. Because she and this baby needed help right away.

Tank lifted her up as I threw her belongings into a suitcase. There were clothes all over the floor, and I grabbed them all. As we raced to the car, I repeated my name to Tank. "I don't know who Dolly was to you," I said, "but if you ever come across this type of thing again, find me. You'll see I am trustworthy." He nodded, laying her across the back seat.

I raced to the hospital, parking right at the ER entrance in the back. I lifted her myself and carried her in. Dolly had Hepatitis B and C, herpes, syphilis, and HIV. Thankfully, she responded to treatment quickly, and when I went to check on her a couple of days later, she was already out of the ICU and in a regular room.

There was life in her again. Tomboyish, with her strawberry-blond hair brighter for being washed. Her cheeks were starting to fill out, and she had light eyes, hazel in the sunlight making it through the windows.

"How long have you been positive?" I asked.

She shrugged. "Dunno," she said. "Well, I was diagnosed when I was fifteen."

"Wow," I said. "How old are you now?"

"Nineteen," she said. "I only found out I was positive 'cause I got stabbed."

I nodded, like this was a common form of detection. "How'd you get stabbed?"

"A guy," she said. "He didn't want to pay me, so I guess he thought he'd just kill me." She pulled down her gown to show a big long scar down her chest. "Stabbed me in the heart and in my head," she said, waiting a beat. "Nothing I needed."

I smiled. She'd used that line before, I could tell. "I'm sorry."

"Left me in a dumpster," she said. "That was San Antonio. They tested me at the hospital and told me I was a miracle for surviving, but I was gonna die anyway on account of the AIDS."

I pictured how people would treat a fifteen-year-old prostitute with HIV in San Antonio. "So, I came back here. My mom is here."

"I live in Hot Springs," I said.

"Oh, I've danced there," she said. "I was at the Black Orchid the night of the flood. The water was going through, and the fire truck came through with the . . . what's that called?"

"Hook and ladder."

"Yeah," she said. "Us and the firemen were all drinking champagne. It was great."

There was an innocence to her that made you want to help her.

"So now what?" I said, looking at her belly.

"The doctor said the AZT might help him."

"It's a boy."

"Yeah," she said. "It's funny because my mom just had a girl a few months ago. That makes her his cousin. No, his aunt."

"Can you stay with her?"

"No."

"Do you have someone you can stay with?"

"I think so," she said.

"Besides Tank."

"Then, no."

I held back a sigh. I knew what I had to do. "Okay, well, how about you come and stay with me?"

She shrugged. "Okay." This was a girl who went where the wind blew her.

"Just for a little while," I said. "I can get you in the system with housing assistance and that will get you and the baby a place. But listen, I have an eight-year-old girl. No men, no drugs, no none of that stuff."

She nodded, and I walked out of there planning for a new roommate.

Dolly came to live with us right before Halloween, and FooFoo eyed her suspiciously. She took Allison's room, because Allison would always end up in my room anyway. Allison had a trundle bed, and it held a second mattress that we called the "guest mattress." I would switch them out for the people who came to stay with me in emergencies, as they sometimes would have issues with holding their bowels or urine.

When Dolly got to the house, Allison and I were trying to get a Halloween costume together.

"Oh, I have costumes!" Dolly said. She ran to her suitcase and started pulling out these spangly, barely there strips of clothes. She held up a pair of devil horns and beamed when Allison took them. "Or wait!" She pulled out a black bustier with white ruffle. "You could be a pirate!"

"Okay, Dolly," I said, before Allison could even consider it. "We're going to have to think on this one."

I told KARK-TV about Dolly, and Doug Krile agreed to do a story on her about teen pregnancy and access to information about safer sex. I wanted people to make that connection. I also hadn't had many women, and I knew there were more out there than what I was seeing. I wanted them to feel less alone. Also, the women I'd seen with HIV in the media pushed a victim agenda that somehow made gay men seem like they had it coming. I liked that Dolly didn't talk like that, even if it was more about Dolly not reflecting on anything long enough to really form an opinion.

I had to get her some clothes to wear for the TV interview, because her wardrobe consisted of feathers and sequins. I went to see Rebecca Hanke, this lovely woman who went to my hairdresser's. She'd recently had a baby, so I knew she would have nice maternity clothes. I took Dolly with me to pick up the clothes, and she eyed the baby with a mix of terror and uncertainty. I remembered how lonely I'd felt when I first had Allison. How unprepared I was. I recognized that look of fear.

For the TV interview, Dolly chose a white linen blouse with a sailor neck and sleeves. Rebecca had told her she'd bought it in Dallas, and it had matching pants. When Dolly put it on, she kept touching the fabric, running her hands over the material.

"I love it," she said, surprise in her voice. "I never really had something this nice."

Allison and Dolly got along because Dolly was so childlike, and it really was like having another kid in the house. She wanted to be waited on hand and foot, and she was always hungry. I found these little pieces of meat I could get for a dollar a pound. They had a little bone in them, but you could take that out, put some flour on them, and fry them. Throw in some potatoes and onions and make a gravy—Dolly loved that dish. The one time she tried to help clean up after a meal, she took the iron skillet, missed the sink, and broke one of the tiles by the counter.

When Mitch met her, he put two and two together and realized that one of the guys he had helping him build a dock, Mike, was always talking about this stripper, Dolly, who he was obsessed with. Mike was a real shy guy but a good worker, so we arranged for Dolly to surprise him and say hi.

I drove her out to the dock they were working on, and she came out of the car pregnant, in stripper heels.

"Hi, Mike," she said. And he about fainted. I might've too. I saw why he loved her, right there. There was a sweetness to her, even with the scars on her mind and heart. She thanked him for being a fan, and if she didn't remember him, she did a damned good job of pretending. She held his hand as they caught up and hugged him when she said goodbye.

A lot of people wrote off people like Dolly, the same way they discarded the men at Our House. I knew what I had to do next: I had to start with the strippers in town.

There were so many different strip clubs in Hot Springs. Well, "titty bar" was the official term. You put any kind of a name in front of it—Tom's, Dick's, or Harry's—we had 'em. I knew all the owners from living around town, but there was one guy, Claude, who owned a bunch of them. Claude and the other owners were all pretty accepted, because it was really a boys' club in Hot Springs. Most of them weren't married, so they didn't get invited to the social parties, but they didn't really want to go.

The clubs were all out on 70 East, one-floor numbers with no windows. The clientele was mostly men visiting from out of town, because the locals went out to Little Rock, where they wouldn't be seen. The only one Hot Springs men went to was Centerfold, because it was so far out that no wives would drive by looking for a car in the parking lot.

I saw Claude out while I was walking with Tim and Jim in the park. I'd met them near their apartment with Allison, and we brought four mugs and packets of hot cocoa mix. We did this every now and again in late fall and wintertime, getting hot, hot water from a fountain and sipping as we walked, until we ended up on the wraparound porch of the Arlington. It was November, and the temperature never really got below forty-five, but it still felt cozy to have a warm mug of tea or cocoa as you watched the world go by.

When I saw Claude, I knew it was my chance. Anything to do with smut, Claude was your guy, but there was something charming about him. "Just the man I was looking for," I said.

"My lucky day," he said. "It's nice when a blond is looking for you."

"Role reversal, I guess."

"How can I he'p you?"

"Well, Claude, I've been doing a lot of work with HIV, and I gotta say it's something the heterosexual community needs to know about."

He smiled politely. Tim and Jim were walking a little bit ahead now, and Allison was showing them cartwheels. I lowered my voice to a slight whisper. "I know you want to make sure your girls are safe," I said. "I'm not saying anything about the clubs, but we all know people have after-work jobs and side gigs."

He nodded quickly, enough to acknowledge that we both knew what that might be. "Okay, so what are you talking about doing exactly?"

"I could come in, talk to the girls, offer free testing. All voluntary. Nobody knows, and in a couple weeks we all have a nice Thanksgiving knowing we did a good thing."

"Where would you do this?"

"Well, you gotta fish where they're biting, so the club, right?" I'd been thinking about this. I wanted to go when the most girls were there, and I figured if I declared I had drop-in hours at my place, nobody would come for fear of gossip. Just like at Our House.

When Claude didn't say anything, I leaned in. "Come on," I whispered. "It's a real thing we need to worry about."

He nodded. I said, "Great," before he could change his mind.

That week I asked Bonnie if she could babysit Allison on Thursday. "I need to hit the strip club."

"It's come to that, huh?" she joked.

"Yep," I said. "It's come to that."

Chapter Twenty

"No unaccompanied women," the bouncer said. "You need to come back with a guy."

He was big and doing his best to look bigger. Behind him, I could see a red-haired woman dancing on a bar to Bon Jovi's "You Give Love a Bad Name." There was a purple spotlight on her, and the bouncer shifted his weight to block the view.

"Well, my guy is Claude," I said, switching a heavy tote of test kits and boxes of condoms from one hand to another. "I mean, Claude told me I could come by."

"Oh," he said, stepping aside to let me in. "Sorry."

"Thank you. Is Claude here now?" When he nodded, I took a few steps into the club, and turned back to ask him, "Why is it 'No girls allowed,' anyway?"

"Some come in looking for, \uh, clients, ma'am."

"Got it," I said, turning to casually take in the whole place without looking like I was gawking. I'd dressed in nice blue jeans, a simple top, and my highest black heels to avoid the church lady look. Just something I thought the women might wear. The club had a big rectangle of a bar, and the redhead, dancing expertly, stepped over glasses and beer bottles. Men stared at her as she moved in her red bra and panties, some transfixed, some standoffish, clearly saving their dollars for someone else.

Claude spotted me first and brought me to the dressing room. I walked in holding the tote behind my back. It was like a long-hair salon back there, full of women getting ready in various states of undress. There was a bulletin board right at the door, next to rows of lockers. The board had pictures of kids and pets, smiling shots of the strippers at birthday parties at the club, the flash harsh on them, all made up in the dark of the bar. Touches of home.

The women looked me over. I picked out the alpha immediately, a leggy blond with a skeptical look on her face. She had her arms crossed across her white nightie.

"I'm guessing Claude told you why I asked to come here," I said. "I've been helping a woman, a dancer. She has HIV, she's going to be a mom, like some of you probably are, and she has a chance at staying healthy longer because she knows her status."

I paused. "It's all voluntary and anonymous," I said. "If you want, I take your blood now, real quick, and either you give me your number or I give you mine so I can give you the results. It's nobody's business but yours." The alpha shifted her weight from one hip to the next but kept her arms crossed.

"Claude," I said, "can you give us a minute?" He turned, reluctantly, and left.

"I'm not going to tell Claude anything, not even yes or no if he asks if anyone tests positive. But *you* need to know. You can keep working, but you'd know you have to start taking care of yourself, make sure you have safe sex every time."

I paused, seeing Alpha soften. She looked over at a woman, maybe in her early forties, a motherly type in a black bustier.

"I'm a friend," I said.

"Okay," said Alpha, and she and the motherly one came toward me as I reached my hand out to shake theirs.

"I'm Ruth," I said, then pointed to a little card table. "Okay, can we set up over there?" I turned to Alpha. "I love that shade of lipstick. What is it?"

"Covergirl. Cherries in the Snow."

"It suits you," I said. "Hey, do you think you could tell the girls out on the floor that I'm okay? Tell them to come on in when they have a minute. That's all it takes." I turned to the motherly one. "Would you like to start?"

She did. If somebody wanted to get tested they did, and if they didn't they didn't. No one was looking over their shoulder or anything. It reminded me of those GI movies from the 1940s, with the recruits lining up for exams. I gave each one the same speech. "I'll take the test home tonight, but if something happens between now and when I get the test results back, it could say you're negative but you're not. I can come back and test you again in six weeks, then six months, then a year. You're good as long as you use protection. If you meet someone, and they don't want to use protection, you have to decide if that's something you want to risk your life on. It's nobody's fault, but there are things you can do to protect yourself. It's your body, and you have to live in it."

Alpha came back with more girls, and I thanked her. A lot of them made nervous chitchat while I prepped their arms with alcohol, asking what type of work I did. Some suggested that I could make a lot of money dancing, and I thanked each one profusely. "I'll have to think on that," I lied each time. "I get shy."

No one believed *that*, but many would invite me to watch their show. I felt bad saying no, so I moved the samples to a cooler in my car, then came back in and watched. A lot of them had real pride in their acts, usually two songs. A fast song where they danced quickly and got the lay of the land in the audience, and then a slower one, with fewer clothes, when they could focus on the men who seemed enraptured.

Some would put on a good show up there, but the truth is, I'd been spoiled by drag queens. Now, *that* was a performance. A lot of these girls, you could hear them thinking, "Okay, to the left. Now, to the right." A glob of goo up on that bar. If they only had Miss

Cherry Fontaine and Mother Superior to mentor them. "Girl, get out there and work it, and you can get more tips." I was imagining a stripper-training seminar at Our House, when Claude came over.

"Everything okay?" he asked.

"Oh sure," I said. "The girls are lovely." I explained my testing schedule. How I would like to come back in periodically. He nodded, but I could tell he had thought this was a one-shot deal and I'd give him everybody's report card.

"One thing," I said. "I have all these condoms I brought with me, and I would love to give them a home here. Do you think the dressing room is good? By the front door?"

"Uh, dressing room, I guess," he said.

"I just want people to have access to information and protection. I don't need to know what people do."

After that night, I was in. I could go to the owners of other clubs and say that Claude would vouch for me. Then it was, "I was just at Tom's." I saw men from my church there, so it was no wonder I was starting to get more and more looks on Sunday mornings, but we were all so practiced at keeping secrets. They gave me a look that said, "I'll keep yours if you keep mine."

So many of the strippers tested positive. Some were already looking sick when I tested them, that wearing away of the body. I kept my promise to tell the women privately, away from the club. A lot of them were angry, and it was different than telling men. They felt they had been unfairly put at risk, and I would gently tell them that it was unfair to anyone who got it, gay or straight. I would teach them the intricacies of safer sex, based on what we knew, and get them into medical care. I talked about IV drug use, which was always a flash point.

"I don't do 'em," they'd say.

"Well, I know you don't, but others do. And sharing needles is a very efficient way to transmit HIV, so tell anyone you know not to do that."

There was a secondary wave of testing, after the strippers, that I did not anticipate but maybe should have. I was in my car outside of town looking at a map to figure out the best way to get to Jasper, up north, where I had a new patient. There was a knock on the glass.

"Hello, Officer," I said.

"Good morning," he said. "You're Ruth Burks."

"Yes," I said, tentative and a little concerned.

His girlfriend was a stripper, and he wanted me to test him. He also asked if he should get his wife tested. "I think everybody should get tested," I said. "That's my motto." I tested him over at Hollywood Cemetery, and he was negative. Then it turned out there were a lot of police officers in Arkansas dating strippers, so I spent more than a few afternoons sitting in the front seats of squad cars taking blood.

I told all this to Mitch, not naming names. He listened, impassive, and I sometimes wondered what it would take for him to be a real partner in my life. I had helped Dolly move into her own apartment, and I watched her pregnancy progress with a little bit of envy. I pictured having a child with Mitch, and the four of us—me, Mitch, Allison, and our baby—being a family. I had a fantasy world, where my guys would hold the baby while I sorted their meds or helped them fill out forms. And another world, where there was a cure, and we could all go back to our normally scheduled programming.

Mitch took me to see *Dances with Wolves* one Saturday in December. The Union Army's First Lieutenant John Dunbar requests to be stationed at the furthermost outpost on the western frontier so he can see it before it's gone. When he gets there, he finds the fort abandoned but dutifully restocks and fortifies the outpost. He's convinced the cavalry is going to come. They'll be there any day, and he keeps looking for them through his binoculars. And they never come. He is completely alone but convinced he has to keep at it.

There was one tear, then another, finally a flood. Mitch kept looking at me, and I slunk down in my seat. I wanted to hold someone and be held, but I was alone amongst all these people in the theater. And with Mitch, my boyfriend, who was still Mr. Saturday Night.

As the movie played on, I got sadder. It felt like I went to two funerals a week throughout the state. It got so I was so sick of hearing "Wind beneath My Wings" playing at every funeral. I would get hopeful when there wouldn't be any for a week or two. But there were always more. Some of them were in Little Rock, and some were in other places, and I had only talked to them over the phone when I told them to bring home whatever medications and medical records they needed from wherever it was they were coming from. Some of those guys didn't even live long enough for me to drive over to see them. Or sometimes they would simply show up, ashes in a box.

I was coming up on five years of manning the fort. Naively thinking I was just keeping the fort going until the cavalry came.

Dolly gave birth, and the baby tested positive for an alphabet soup of acronyms. As far as I knew, he was born with antibodies for HIV but then tested negative at six months. It was a miracle. The baby ended up living with Dolly's mother and her sister, who was only about six months older than him. His grandmother was able to breastfeed him to keep his immunity up.

I lost touch with Dolly, but I knew she would borrow the baby, because an organization was taking her around to the churches for a dog and pony show. They bought a sundress for her and a sailor suit for the innocent baby. She would tell her story, and the organization would get tons of money thrown at them, helping this poor, infected woman and her baby.

Then she started hooking again, so they dumped her. Can't have an active hooker going to churches. She might recognize a john in the pews, I guess.

The last time I saw Dolly was at the mall, the same one where Billy worked at the clothing store. She was walking slowly with some other women and was dressed in a catsuit.

"Hi, Dolly," I said. Up close, she was skeletal. So far gone she blinked at me to figure out who I was.

"Ruth," she said, like she was pinning a name to something almost forgotten. There was a sparkle for a second in her hazel eyes, which looked even bigger for the gauntness of her face.

I wanted to help her.

"How's your little boy?" I said. She looked over my shoulder at a man who slowed as he walked by.

"Not sure right now," she said. "You have a nice night."

"You too," I said. "You know where I am, okay?"

"Okay."

I never saw her again.

Chapter Twenty-One

I had to park a little down the street from Billy and Paul's house because there were so many cars. As Allison and I got out, I was again shocked that such a movie star could live in a cute little house on Oak Cliff. Paul had invited me to their 1990 Christmas party, and it was just a few days short of the actual holiday. It had snowed an inch, and Allison crunched a design with her shoes along the path to the house. I'd made a sweet potato pie they could either keep or put out. It was still warm. I wasn't sure what kind of party it was, but I'd said yes as soon as Paul asked me.

There were so many people inside, mostly men, and I went straight to the kitchen and left the pie next to a tray of cookies and chips. I handed Allison a couple of Oreos and then went to find Paul. He was in the living room getting the music going on the record player. He had a whole stack of records in a crate ready to play for everyone. "The soundtrack to the night," I said.

"Something like that," he said. "I'm so glad you could come."

"Thank you for inviting me," I said. "This is Allison."

"Merry Christmas, Allison," he said.

"I like your tree," she said.

He turned to look at it, charmed by her. Their Christmas tree was sweet, positioned in the front window for all to see. It had the collected ornaments of a relationship, red bows tied to the ends of branches, and a red angel on top smiling down at us. There were presents under the tree, which I caught Allison eyeing. I looked around and saw butterflies above the window, little gold sculptures or drawings of them in small frames.

I heard a laugh and knew it was Billy before I even turned around. He wore a light blue sweatshirt with an ornate white snow-flake edged in gold. He was holding court, people all around him. Mother Superior was across the room, watching some sort of Christmas on Ice special on TV, and I remembered that he lived upstairs. He was wearing a dark blue turtleneck that stretched across his frame. It was exciting for me to see everyone outside the bar. Allison gravitated to the TV, lured in by the skaters in their short princess dresses.

We watched, but the real draw was Mother's running commentary. Allison loved it, and Mother loved a new audience. After a while, I turned to look back at Billy and saw him slipping out the front door.

"I'll be right back, okay?" I told Allison.

"Okay," she said, entranced by the TV.

Billy was smoking on the porch out front, looking up at the stars. I didn't realize how loud it was inside. "Am I interrupting a quiet moment?" I asked. I could hear Wham!'s "Last Christmas" starting inside.

He blew out a puff of smoke. "I don't like quiet moments," he said, offering me a cigarette from his pack.

"No, thank you," I said. "I only came out for some air."

"Do you believe this sky?" he said. Even with just a crescent moon, the snow on the ground reflected light back into the night sky, a dark purple blue with the detailed brushwork of white clouds. I could make out the details of every last branch on the sweetgum tree in the front yard and every angle of Billy's face in profile. He'd turned twenty-two a couple of weeks before.

"Imagine if it was a full moon," I said.

He took a drag on his cigarette and exhaled. "Why ask for the moon?" he said dreamily, in a voice lighter than his own. "We have the stars."

"Is that—"

"Bette Davis," he said. "*Now, Voyager.*"

"Oh," I said.

"I've loved movies since I was a kid. I could go whole days repeating dialogue, and nobody really noticed I was living in a black-and-white movie."

"I picture you running from Dardanelle," I said.

He exhaled smoke, and his answer was that laugh of his, sent up to that bright sky. It echoed in the cold, and he covered his mouth quick. I tried to imagine him in Dardanelle, going to the one barbershop in its tiny downtown. I remembered all the times I'd escaped my mother. "When I was little, my place was the woods," I said. "I had a bike, and I was the queen of the woods."

"I'd take my bike to the sandbar," he said. "Take off on my banana seat, with the little wheels, right to the edge of the river to look out as whoever I was that minute: Grace Kelly, Marilyn Monroe . . ."

"Your family Pentecostal?"

"Yeah," he said.

"Most of the guys I help were raised Pentecostal," I said. "I don't know why. Pentecostals, you're just out the door, so maybe that's why. I'm where they land."

"What got you into this?"

"Well, Paul invited me to this party."

"You're funny," he said. "No, helping people with AIDS."

I told him about Jimmy and about those first thirteen hours. "I don't know," I said. "There was a need. They kept coming. Now I'm trying to focus on people getting tested so we can at least put off people getting to that point."

He was quiet for a minute—so long, I almost filled the space with some compliment about his last show. I had them to give. He asked quietly, "What's it like when they die?"

"We all die different," I said. "Yet the same. You know, this is gonna sound weird: I can see Death. It's like she's a human but an angel, who comes and waits with me. She's become a friend." I stopped myself, embarrassed I'd been so open. "I've never told anyone that, but it's true. I know I sound crazy."

"I don't think you sound crazy," he said, looking right at me. I could tell he wanted to say something. Instead, he stubbed out his cigarette and hugged me. It was a surprise. I felt a quickening in my heart, then an ease. Like falling into the same rhythm.

We went back inside, and Allison and I stayed past her bedtime, listening to all the men swapping stories. The subject always returned to Billy. How he'd shown up in Hot Springs and jumped the line in the drag circuit, winning Miss Hot Springs and then Miss Discovery in Little Rock. He had been heading for the Miss Arkansas crown.

Paul took over: "Then Steve and Violet—" He turned to me and Allison. "Violet was my ex-boyfriend Kenneth, a beautiful queen. Anyways, they had moved to Texarkana, and Steve was managing a Twelve-Dollar Store. You know, where everything cost twelve dollars."

"He called Paul," said Billy, "and told him, 'I've got perfect sportswear for Billy. The Contemporary Fashion category. You've gotta see it.'"

Paul took the conversation like a relay baton. "I said, 'At the Twelve-Dollar Store?' He said. 'Yes, it's color-blocked, a new thing that came in.' They got clothes from overstock places, so a lot of the stuff was expensive, but they sold it cheap."

"I was skeptical," said Billy.

"But we went down there, and we loved it," said Paul. "This black-and-white, color-blocked dress that was so beyond what everyone else was wearing."

"I ordered a dark black wig and had a little whalebone thing in the back, so it kind of poofed up here," Billy said.

Paul beamed. "He came out, and he just looked like a million dollars. All the Little Rock queens that were, like, stuck on themselves —'I'm gonna win Miss Arkansas and be Miss America'—they were all stunned. You could hear them *inhale*."

Billy made it to Miss Arkansas, "and no Hot Springs queen had won in twenty years," said Paul. "And the crowd loved him, of course."

"Of course," said Billy, looking right at Allison, who grinned back at him.

Paul put his hand on Billy's knee. "I remember we were sittin' there, and they called out the preliminary winners of the awards. And we knew he'd do good, but we didn't realize how good." His voice took on that of the pageant announcer. "'The winner of Male Interview: Marilyn Morrell.' Everybody was screaming and hollering, because it shows the audience, not only is this a pretty queen, but he's smart. Then they're like, 'Contemporary Fashion: Marilyn Morrell.' And 'Evening Gown: Marilyn Morrell.' He won every category except for Talent."

Billy frowned, and we pretended to be shocked. Paul continued: "And the judge that judged the queen that won higher in talent did it just enough to knock Billy down to first runner-up? Well he was the show director from the bar in Louisiana where the winner was from before she moved to Little Rock."

We leaned back and shook our heads. Even Allison seemed to know what it meant.

Paul continued: "Which, I'm not saying it was rigged, but I'm just saying. The cards didn't fall right."

Billy lifted his chin. "I carried on."

"Miss Congeniality," I said.

He smiled. "Always."

After that night, Billy would tell me when he was going to be at the bar and ask me to bring Allison by. I couldn't bring her inside, for fear Our House would lose its license, and I would lose her, but I would drive around back to the stage door. Billy would come out, sometimes half in drag, sometimes fully, to say hi to her. Allison would open the car door, and Billy would kiss her cheek, ask how school was. The other queens would follow Billy out, and soon everyone treated Allison and me as family. If Our House was closed, I could bring Allison by to see Paul. Even Twyman, the owner, who could be so crusty, was nice to her. If he wasn't there, Paul would give the claw arcade machine a shake so Allison could get a prize.

There wasn't a Mrs. Doubtfire nanny type among them, but they would come through when I needed them to. If I was at a hospital holding someone's hand and couldn't get away to pick up Allison at school, I could call around until someone was free to run over and pick her up. I had gay men and lesbians lining up with all the stay-at-home moms in station wagons at St. John the Baptist Catholic School, and I can only imagine what people thought.

Billy and I began meeting at the Wyatt's Cafeteria in the mall during his lunch hour. Not so routine that it was an everyday thing, but enough that it became our thing. Hot Springs Mall was close to everything, so I could just stop in, and the food at Wyatt's was really good. Billy and I went down the line with our trays, and these bored people would dish out the offerings. "Chicken-fried steak," they'd say. "A dollar ten." We'd both get that and the mashed potatoes, so their next question was about the gravy: "Brown or white?" The right choice was brown, and that's what we got. Billy always gave the person an encouraging smile as they first dipped the ladle in the potatoes to make a bird's nest, then filled it with the gravy. Where we diverged was that I went for the green beans, while he chose corn. Billy would say his requests as if this was a play the audience was seeing for the first time, an actor repeating the same lines with a spontaneity that contrasted with the listless delivery of the servers.

We'd try to sit in the window that looked out on the mall so Billy could see and be seen. It was fun to look at the people with bags and guess what they bought.

"This one, Ruthie," he said, admiring a woman carrying two huge Dillard's bags. "Sisters *are* doin' it for themselves."

"Working girl," I said. "She got that promotion, and now she's gonna show them how it's done."

When a man turned to look at the woman's rear end, Billy and I were mad for her. "Acting sly like you even have a chance, sir," he said. "All that Just for Men seeping into your brain."

We'd laugh right on the edge of loud, enough that people looked at us. Billy and I never ran out of things to talk about, but the routine at Wyatt's did get boring. Work gave him an hour for lunch, so I asked him if he ever wanted to break out of the mall and go eat someplace else. You couldn't beat the prices at Wyatt's, and we didn't have the money to eat at nice places. That left McDonald's, which didn't seem worth the trip. The next time I was planning to make a lot of food for my guys, I offered to make us a picnic lunch to have at the lake. It was so close that I could pick Billy up and take him back after we ate.

I packed my fried chicken, along with some rolls and potato salad. I brought my favorite quilt, an old family one on the edge of being raggedy. He was outside waiting for me and ran up to my car before I could even park. I remember the graceful way he looked both ways and how he jumped in like I was driving a getaway car.

With the windows down, we drove out to the point on Lake Hamilton. This had once been the property of my mother's family, before she sold it to a resort. It was my playground before my daddy died and the place I would escape to after. Now the resort had taken the wildness out of it, and a grouping of teenage pines was what was left of my forest. They'd built a lovely dock, and I led Billy out to the very edge to set down our picnic. He kept looking back, because it felt sneaky to Billy, going out on a dock where he didn't think we were supposed to be. He was waiting for someone to yell at us.

He calmed down once I unfurled the quilt for us. Billy gasped at its beauty, and I smiled. It was my mother's and had a three-inch Tiffany-blue turquoise border, bright red X's, and hand-stitched triangles and squares of fabric scraps—dishrags and worn dresses given an elegant new life. I had so many quilts folded up at home, but this was my favorite one to use outside.

"I take this to the beach, and people scold me because it's too nice," I said.

"It's too nice not to use," Billy said.

"Right?" I answered.

"I'd be mad if I had to spend my life in some cupboard."

We sat down and started our feast, and I stole a look at him as he swooned at the first bite of the fried chicken. Boats floated by as we did our usual thing, talking about absolutely everything and nothing in the same conversation. At one point some fish broke water; I had the muscle memory my daddy left me with—the urge to grab a fishing pole with a spoon lure to get the bigger, smarter fish that were always swimming deep beneath that frenzy splashing on the surface. But they left as quick as they came.

When we ran out of things to talk about, Billy traced the outline of square after square on the quilt, smoothing his hand over each one. I'd look down and tell him whose it was. I was there at its creation and remembered my mother and a group of women with the big quilting hoop in the middle of our old living room.

"And now here we are," I said, "all these years later."

"Here we are."

Other than that, we didn't talk about our childhoods. I think we much preferred our shared present to our pasts. We talked about Mitch and Paul, and Billy spoke with such pride in his voice. Twice he mentioned that Paul was so busy because he managed the bar, and I realized Billy felt that being the bar manager's main squeeze gave him a lot of clout. As if he needed any more. But really what he loved was the sureness of Paul. "If he says he's going to do something," Billy said, "he does it."

"They still make men like that?" I joked. "Well."

We met like this again and again, getting to know each other more each time we hung out. Sometimes we didn't even need to talk much, just feel the warm sun on our faces. Billy always thought he needed a little color, and so did I. If I had a pen handy, and I always did, he would draw a self-portrait for me. They were beautiful pictures of him in drag, his face half-covered by a hat, a dark veil, or a cascade of long hair. Just enough mystery that he didn't fully commit himself to being captured there on paper. I kept them, sometimes putting one up on the fridge for Allison to see too.

But where I got to truly know Billy was watching him create his looks for the shows. He'd invite me over days before, and we'd go into his and Paul's bedroom, where he had a sizable walk-in closet. They kept their home immaculate; it was an older house, but it had a freshness to it. I'd sit on a chair in his room, and he would come in and out of the closet wearing different dresses and wigs. He'd raid Paul's record collection but only selected the newer songs to test out. There was always a vision he had in mind, so he didn't ask what I thought of the looks. It was enough for him to do a quick reading of my expression at the reveal. He could see what had a wow factor.

There were sheer curtains on the back windows over the bed, and the sunlight would stream in on the maybes he laid out on the bed. Eventually one of those dresses would graduate to the living room, along with the perfect heel and wig. The only times he outright asked for my opinion was about earrings, and even that felt like politeness. I usually had the same answer, which was the truth: "I like the chandelier ones."

"Me too," he'd say, with a quick nod. I imagined it was what it must have been like to have a sister growing up, and then I realized Billy and I had become best friends.

At Allison's ninth birthday, the Memorial Day weekend of 1991, I invited a bunch of people to come to the house to celebrate her. Tim and Jim, Billy and Paul, and some more people from the bar. By then I'd opened up to Billy about how hard things were for Allison, and he understood what that felt like, to be lonely. They started to form a friendship that was almost independent of me, and he led everyone in making a big deal of her birthday.

Allison turned nine surrounded by the love of these men singing "Happy Birthday" to her. I stepped back to see her in the light of those nine candles and pretended to fuss with the camera so nobody would see my eyes welling.

With their help, she blew out the candles. I looked at them all smiling and made my own wish.

Chapter Twenty-Two

Glenwood was one county over from Hot Springs and about forty years behind. It had a beautiful little view of the Caddo River and a sawmill where everybody worked for generations. And not much else. If you came from Glenwood, people guessed you were just another idiot from Glenwood.

Chip was anything but.

He got out, made it all the way to Washington, DC, and now here he was on my doorstep. "Thank you," he said, when I opened the door to welcome him. But his face betrayed him. There was such a sadness to it, to be stuck counting only on me. It was a beautiful face, though: Roman, with a long nose, full mustache, strong jaw and chin. All beneath a full head of sandy hair with a sharp part up the side. Aside from his sorrowful expression, he looked like he was here to ask for my vote.

He was down to one lonely box of his earthly possessions, having sold what he could as he got sicker. He kept the books that mattered to him and left behind the suits he wore as a rising star in the Democratic Party in DC. That's where he wanted to be, with his friends. Not standing in my house, awkwardly, trying to make this seem normal.

He'd gone to his mother's house first, but she'd rejected him: "See what you get? I told you so. Look what you've done to me." His dad was already gone, dead by the time Chip was eleven. When he called me for guidance, and I offered him a place to stay until we got him an apartment, he sounded so reluctant that I asked if there wasn't a friend he could stay with.

"No," he said, quiet and matter-of-fact. "They're all dead."

So, now, here he was. My house seemed so small, and I could feel that he would give up if we stayed here too long. "Would you like me to give you a tour of Hot Springs?" I asked.

He said yes, always polite, though I quickly realized he'd already been here. We went for a walk along Central, up through the promenade along the brick path. Right at the start of the path, I stopped at the bush of wild honeysuckle. I took one of the long, tubular flowers and pulled the end off to reveal the nectar inside.

"Here," I said, handing it to him, "taste it."

He did. He had to have grown up doing this. We all did in Arkansas. I wanted to remind him of what was beautiful about this place too. Maybe I thought I could see his smile.

We walked along the path, and in the distance, a girl was having her graduation photo taken with her family. They stood at the crest of a little hill, with the art deco buildings of Central Avenue behind them. Just ahead of us, an older man sat on a bench, the sleeves of his white button-down rolled up his arms. His eyes were closed, taking in the sun. I knew what he would do when we got close. He rolled one sleeve down to his wrist until we passed.

"There's a Jewish arthritis hospital nearby," I said quietly to Chip. "We have a lot of Holocaust survivors who come here to take the baths. Mostly men. They never want you to see their tattoos."

"The spas here were modeled after the ones in Europe from the 1900s," he said. "Maybe it reminds them of home."

I looked at him for a second, because I was so used to being the tour guide. I turned my head to see the man on the bench, his sleeve again up and his eyes closed. I wondered what country he imagined himself back in, the sun there falling on his skin once again.

"So, what's *your* history, then?" I asked. "I can tell you went to school."

"Henderson State," he said. "I was in the Young Democrats and stayed political."

"I bet you were great at it."

"I was," he said. We kept walking.

"You look the part," I said. "Do you think Governor Clinton's going to run?"

"I hope so," he said, showing a little more life. "The Democratic Party needs a Southern leader again. It's him." I thought about all the letters I'd sent to Clinton. I knew he could never play dumb about AIDS like Reagan and Bush. Chip went through scenarios of potential nominees and then suddenly stopped. November 1992 seemed a lifetime away from May 1991.

Tourists were gathered at the Cascade, the only place where you can see hot water from the spring coming down the rock of the mountain. People seemed to make Chip nervous, so we moved on, all the way to Central and Whittington Avenues. I knew a place he might like: a set of stairs up to a little grotto next to St. Mary of the Springs. There's a statue of the Virgin Mary there in a red-brick shrine, hidden from the street. She's on a pedestal, so she looks down on you, but there's kindness in the stone of her eyes. Beneath her, on the ground, was a large metal heart with a sword piercing it.

"Whatever their religion, or lack thereof, my guys often like to visit her," I said.

Chip nodded, noncommittal, as we climbed the steps. "Do you smell the gardenias?" I asked, breathing in the scent. That's what I really loved about the grotto. But the guys all came, even Tim and Jim, who told me, "We don't believe in that shit. We'll go up there anyway. Just in case."

"Yeah, be nice to her, just in case," I said. "You don't know. She might be up there checking your ticket or something. She might be at the door."

My guys would sit on the brick and talk to her. They'd cross themselves out of respect for the statue, and I'd slip away down the stairs to the middle level to give them space. Wait until they got antsy or turned back to be sure I was there.

Chip bowed his head, and I left him there like my other guys. As I watched the traffic go by, I could just hear the hum of him speaking softly.

Then, louder, "Ruth."

I turned, shaking my shoulders, making like I'd just been preoccupied with the cars.

He was holding a religious flyer he'd picked up from the ground. He read aloud the words, "Our Lady of Fátima requested: Pray the Rosary." He looked at me. "You ever hear of Fátima?"

"No," I said.

"It's this little parish in Portugal," he said. "In 1917 or so, Mary supposedly appeared to three little shepherd kids, a girl named Lucia and her two cousins." He looked away, like he was remembering something for a test. "Mary told them three secrets. Prophecies. The first one was something about hell, and the second one was about World War I ending and World War II starting."

"And the third?"

"Nobody knows," he said. "The cousins died soon after of flu, and Lucia wrote the third secret down in a sealed envelope and gave it to the Vatican. She said not to open it until 1960 or so. So the time comes, Pope John XXIII reads it, and he has it sealed up again. People say he cried. Whatever it was, he thought the world wasn't ready."

I had a little shiver. "What do you think it said?" I asked.

"Probably the end of the world," he said.

"Sometimes that feels about right," I said.

He finally smiled.

Chip stayed a few weeks with us, watching television at night with Allison. He was not someone who liked kids, but he liked her. FooFoo got used to him and would sometimes sit in his lap. By the time we got Chip his own apartment, he was already so weak. With each day, I could see his body getting weaker, though his mind remained sharp. The day he left, he took his extra pair of shoes from the box of his belongings.

"Maybe you can find a home for these," he said.

"But they're brand new," I said. "They look like you've never even worn them."

"These are too heavy for me to walk in."

I picked them up, Rockports, that felt so light to me. "What do you mean, 'too heavy'?"

"Too heavy."

I nodded. His world was getting smaller and smaller. "Well," I said. "I know I can bring them to the bar and let people play Cinderella."

"Send my regards."

"I'll tell them Prince Charming sent me," I said. "I can bring you to the bar, you know. It might be nice to see people."

"We'll see," he said, and I knew he wouldn't take me up on it. He was humiliated to be in this state.

Allison and I moved Chip into the apartment, and I promised to come back daily to help him bathe and bring him food. After two weeks, we had a routine going, where I would bring the newspaper and read to him until he fell asleep in a chair in the living room.

I noticed that he'd managed to shave himself over the past week and seemed to not need as much cleaning up. I wanted to tell him I was impressed, but I was afraid he would find it condescending.

I was reading something to him about Mikhail Gorbachev when I heard a key fitting into the front door. I tensed, worried it was the landlord and there was a mix-up. I stood up quick as the door flew open.

"Hello—" said the man who walked in, so happy, ready to see someone he cared for.

It was the Doctor.

He looked caught, and he looked at the door as if he could some-how undo this moment. The three of us said nothing at first. *He had a key*, I thought. *Chip had been bathed, shaved. Cared for by someone. The Doctor.*

"I am so glad you're here," I said. "I was just getting ready to go."

Chip used his first name. There was love in his voice, an old love. The Doctor put down his bag but would not look at me.

I left. I was terrified of losing the Doctor as a resource, and also ashamed for him that he had to hide whatever it was he felt for Chip. Even if it was friendship. They'd known each other years back, I was sure of it. Before the Doctor was married and had a family.

Chip never mentioned the Doctor to me, but told me he had someone coming every day. "I'm glad," I said. I continued to bring food, and as Chip got even weaker and skinnier, we switched to bone broth. I knew it was the Doctor carrying him to the bathtub.

When I next brought someone to the Doctor for testing, there *was* a difference. He was more formal with me, and at first his eyes darted about, not meeting mine. I was worried the door would close, and I would lose him. His advice, his prescriptions, just his presence as an ally in all this.

"This is completely anonymous," I said to the man we were testing. "I would never betray your trust." I said it too loud, too desperate.

Chip was down to eighty pounds when he told me he was mov-ing to his mother's house. She was taking him in after all, now that it was ending. I asked if he needed me to keep bringing him the broth.

"She wants to do that now," I said.

"Okay," I said. I wanted to ask if the Doctor would be visiting. I hoped so.

At the end of July, a man called me, some relation of Chip, who didn't give me a name. Chip had died. The man told me Chip had asked that I be notified.

"Thank you," I said. "Do you need help with the burial? I would be happy to—"

"It's taken care of," he said. "He had a plan."

"May I . . . May I come and pay my respects?"

"Okay," he said. The burial would be at Mount Tabor Cemetery near Glenwood, the place he tried as hard as hell to get out of. The irony of it being Mount Tabor would not have been lost on Chip—so smart, he would appreciate that. In the Bible, Mount Tabor was the site of the transfiguration of Jesus, where we hear God's voice say, "This is my beloved Son, with whom I am well pleased." How many sons had longed to hear those words?

The graveyard was full of funeral plots that were sinking. That's what happened to an old country cemetery with poor people returned to the ground without burial vaults. You have to be careful where you step in a place like that. I saw that the Doctor was there, quiet, standing apart from the family.

The hearse drove around, and Chip's family stood back like a herd of cattle. If you've ever watched cattle when they're watching something, like if somebody just had a baby, they're all standing back in a semicircle. Even the preacher and funeral director stood back. Afraid.

I stepped forward, and then the Doctor came from behind the family. We nodded at each other and went to pick up Chip's casket and carry it to his grave. The casket was nothing more than a cardboard box with light baby-blue cloth draped over it. The cheapest one they could do. For a second, I almost had Chip put back in the hearse so I could get something decent to bury him in. I knew he was probably down to sixty pounds, but even if he was two hundred, I would have found a way to carry him.

We set him on the boards and stepped back. The Doctor and I looked at each other, and I knew he knew that, where I was concerned, whatever he had with Chip would stay between them. The preacher said words, but nothing about Chip. "As long as people do not fear the truth, there is hope," he said. I knew the preacher's idea of truth—the damnation of sin—was not mine or Chip's. It was the last-ditch hope that Chip's soul would be welcomed in heaven. A sinner in the hands of an angry God, showing just enough fear to warrant some kind of mercy.

"The deceased asked that a song be played as we leave him," said the preacher. There was an awkward fumbling as a male relative with Chip's same sandy hair stepped forward with a boom box. He placed it to the side of the casket, pressed play, and moved away quickly.

As soon as I heard the opening, the aggressive beating of piano keys, I recognized it. Billy Joel's "Only the Good Die Young" filled the air at Mount Tabor Cemetery. The family looked shocked, as Chip sang to us all through Billy Joel, a last condemnation about choosing religion over love.

There are sad funerals, and sometimes there are funerals full of relief. This was a "Screw you" funeral. He drew back that bow and aimed that arrow straight into the heart of anyone who hadn't loved him enough.

Part Three

Chapter Twenty-Three

It was easy to overlook Billy's cough. He was a performer first, so it almost became an added affectation. He would laugh at something uproarious, because there was always something to laugh at, and the cough would take over at the tail end. Ladylike even out of drag, he would make a show of covering his mouth and then wave his other hand in front of his face, as if he were dismissing whatever craziness was before him. It was almost a badge of honor for people to have sent Billy into such fits.

There was no shortage of reasons. He smoked, and there was always some Hot Springs flower in bloom to cause allergies. And we *all* coughed at Our House, a boarded-up hotbox of cigarette smoke.

Billy developed a stiffness in his neck and shoulders. The tightening was in his chest too, but he didn't tell me that. I sent him to Bill Reilly, a chiropractor who attended First United. Dr. Reilly was a kind man, whom I had gone to for care, but the doctors at church never let him into "the club," because they didn't think he practiced real medicine.

Once Billy was disrobed on the table, I heard later, Dr. Reilly immediately saw a stripe of painful blisters running from his side to his back. Shingles. Some chicken pox virus left over from Billy's childhood, lying dormant for years around the spine, sprang into action once his immunity had been compromised, apparently. Dr.

Reilly advised Billy to get tested for AIDS. Knowing Dr. Reilly's kindness, I could hear him adding, "to rule it out."

So, finally, Billy got an HIV test. But without telling me. I don't know where he went, I just know they called him first at home. When Paul answered, they said, "Never mind," and called Billy at the work number he gave them, Miller's Outpost, at the mall. I only know that they told him, "You have AIDS," and hung up on him.

He called Paul from the mall. "I'm coming home," he said.

My answering machine had about seventeen messages from Billy when I got home. I drove right over, and Paul answered the door, ashen. Billy was devastated, his almond eyes red from crying. I sat with him and explained that while they said he had AIDS, they had only tested him for HIV. He needed to go to a doctor to get a sense of where his T cells were at. I made an appointment for the next day in Little Rock, at Doctors Hospital, and the best I could do on short notice was Dr. Rhein. He was always mildly nasty. But not nasty enough that you could call him out on it, because he kept his disgust on a slow simmer.

It was only going to be me and Billy, because Paul couldn't come. I knew Paul well enough that I believed he meant it when he said he didn't do hospitals, but he was also working two jobs already, and I could see him calculating how he was going to cover Billy if he could no longer work. Billy understood, knowing Paul was a provider first.

Billy sat on the couch, and he leaned in to me as he cried. I had no words for him, except the promise I would be there, no matter what. Once we were in the car, we reverted to our lunchtime selves as a sort of defense mechanism to get through this. We talked the whole way on the hour drive out to Little Rock, nervous chatter to fill the space—what drag queen did this or who stole whose act. As we got closer to Doctors Hospital, I talked Billy through what would happen at the appointment and why an actual diagnosis would help him get services and care. I was reading everything I could, I assured him, and people were working on a medication, maybe even a cure, right at that moment. Someone we would never meet was going to save us all.

Dr. Rhein came in, dismissive as ever. As he talked, I stopped him. "Can you slow down and explain things a little bit more?"

"Well, you've been through this before," he said, already exasperated with me. "Haven't you?"

Had I? "Yes, I've been through this before, but you need to tell Billy. He's your patient." I tried so hard to be nice, but I always hated when doctors spoke past their patients. And he hated that I kept *bringing* him patients.

We drove back to Hot Springs on a long stretch of four-lane blacktop. On the road, I drove by a sign that had been up all my life, reading "PREPARE TO MEET GOD." I sped up to get by it quickly. Billy was silent on the passenger side, staring out the window. How many times had I been in this exact space, helping someone in the minutes after they were told they were going to die? All those rehearsals and here we were, with me forgetting all my lines.

We passed a place with a giant billboard advertising elephant rides, a big tourist thing. Billy suddenly put his hand up to his beautiful face.

"I had always wanted to ride an elephant," he said.

I pursed my lips, nodding. I checked my rearview for cops. "Well, Billy. Guess what?"

I jerked the wheel hard to the left, doing a complete one-eighty on the road. Billy screamed, half in shock and half in delight. I roared into the parking lot. A sign said the elephant ride was five dollars, and we had barely any money between us. I fished in the ashtray for pennies and the hope of quarters. When we got to five dollars, Billy jumped out of the car and ran to the elephant, yelling that he was coming, as I ran behind him. The attendant on the raised platform saw this wild-eyed duo coming for him. God knows what he thought.

I handed him our pile of singles and change for a ticket. They let two people on the elephant at a time, and Billy took my hand.

"We're doing this," he said.

"Yes, we are," I said.

I was wearing these fancy culottes and tall heels in the hopes they'd convince Dr. Rhein to take me seriously. I looked a sight getting up on the blanket on top of the elephant, but I hurried because Billy was so excited. It was like he was rushing through a door about to slam shut.

Billy sat in front of me, and when the elephant started to walk, he reached back to grab my hand and gave me a huge smile.

"Whatever you want to do from here on out, Billy," I said. "If you want to ride an elephant, we'll ride the elephant together."

The attendant held up a Polaroid camera. "Say 'Dumbo'!"

"Dumbo!" Billy and I shouted in unison, real smiles on our faces.

Once we were back on the road, we quickly returned to our new reality. As we drove past a bean field, the tension had built up so much that I had to crack a window to get the pressure out of the car, just so we were able to breathe.

"Billy?" I said. "What are you in such a deep thought about over there?"

"Well, I'm thinking I want you to have my red Victor Costa dress."

I knew the one. It was the kind of red dress Rhett makes Scarlett wear in *Gone with the Wind* so people would know what she's done. "Nothing modest or matronly will do for this occasion," Rhett tells Scarlett. One of *those* dresses.

"Billy, that's so sweet," I said. "But tell me the truth. Do you want me to have your red Victor Costa because you want me to have it or because you don't want your mother to find it when she comes to clean out your stuff?"

"No, because I want you to have it."

"Well," I said, "I'm not sure I can pull that off."

"Why not?" he asked.

"I'm not sure I have the balls for it."

We laughed. We had to.

When we got back to his house, Billy paused at the threshold and placed his hand on the doorknob. He took a breath, an actor preparing to go onstage. Paul was waiting, and it felt like the whole bar was there. Everyone knew Billy, and he was the first person at Our House to get diagnosed and let people know.

Billy's T-cell count was so low it was dangerous for him even to keep working at the mall, with all these people coming in with their germs. We agreed that he would need to give his notice at Miller's Outpost. I went with him, because he wanted to tell them why, and I was grateful. More people needed to know that HIV was here in Hot Springs. He told his manager. She cried, and so did he. The staff loved him, and they didn't have the hope I had to have in order to keep going. To them, this was a death sentence.

We walked out of the store, holding hands and looking down at the drab floor. The carpet muffled the sound of our steps, so there wasn't even that to drown out our thoughts. Billy squeezed my left hand so tight my skin went white, and when he suddenly stopped walking I felt the pull all the way up to my shoulder. I turned to look at him as he broke down, and I put my arms around him as he shook.

Billy let out a sob, a sharp, loud noise he'd held in who knows how long. People turned to look, then to watch, as I held him. One woman was staring so intently, I spoke to her as you would a child or a dog. "Just move along," I said. "Go on." Billy could not hear me; he was somewhere else in space or in time. Caught in this now, he couldn't escape, but the details of the "before" were still so fresh in his mind that if he could only catch his breath for a moment he could go back there.

He shook like the patients I'd had with end-stage pneumonia, shivering from an internal chill no blanket or hug could get close to warming. But I couldn't let him go. Until he turned loose, I wouldn't turn him loose. I didn't care if he needed me forever.

*   *   *

There were tangible things I could do, and I seized upon them. Instead of Billy having to wait for his prescription to kick in, I supplied AZT from my pantry in the set dosage. I assured Paul that I could get housing assistance to help them, at least with Billy's part of the rent. Plus, I would get them social security disability benefits. "I will get them this month," I said, a promise I kept.

Paul wasn't used to being helped. He had been an outsider so long that he assumed he would have a life of making do. He wanted to do something in return for me, and I couldn't imagine what.

"Well, what if I helped you organize your house?" he asked. "I like that sort of thing."

I took him up on it, more to ease his conscience than to get my house in order, though I did need it. He walked in, and his eyes went everywhere.

"Should we start in the kitchen?" he asked.

"You're driving," I said.

Paul went in, looking at the cereal boxes left out. I had a lot of stuff on the counters, and when he opened the doors of the long walk-in pantry, he saw why.

"Oh my God, it's like a pharmacy in here," he said, overwhelmed.

"Well, it's not for me, so don't worry," I said.

"What would you ever need all this for?"

"Honey, there's people everywhere," I said. "I'm getting calls from the whole state. Men, women. I'm all that people have."

It shocked him. He was the first to say his world revolved around Our House and his home. He couldn't fathom how many people I was helping. "Let me make us some coffee," I said. We sat down, and I explained that people died and left me things, so I could have medication for others who needed it. "Remember how I had it for Billy right away? So he could start that night?"

We talked for an hour about what I'd seen and how many pharmacists had chased me out. I explained just a touch of what Billy would need to know, because I didn't want to further overwhelm

Paul. The importance of staying on his medication schedule and not living in denial about symptoms. Any infection, we had to get in front of it.

I wanted Paul to get tested, but I also knew not to push it. I made it clear that he should, and people don't need to hear that more than once. But Billy coming forward had encouraged other people—some who only I knew had tested positive—to share their status. It created a small community, the one I had hoped I could create at church. As it formed, Paul said he wanted to introduce me to Norman Jones, who was a legend in the area's gay community. He was in Little Rock but a native of Hot Springs. Norman started Norma Kristie's, Hot Springs' first gay bar, giving it his drag name. He owned Discovery, the big gay bar in Little Rock, and basically ran what we knew of as the drag pageant circuit. He had started an organization, Helping People with AIDS, a few years before, and seemed like someone I needed to meet. Immediately.

Soon after, I went to Discovery. It was a giant box of sheet metal and yellow-beige stucco with a rock fascia on it to make it pretty. It was in the middle of nowhere in Little Rock, and Norman ran it with a velvet glove that covered a steel fist. When I went to meet him the first time, this slight but formidable man—with a perfectly tight face and painted-on eyebrows—eyed me suspiciously. He sat behind a desk in his corporate office, and I felt like I was at a job interview. The bar's doorman, Ken Brown, was in and out, as well as drag queens in their boy drag. Some knew me from Hot Springs and said hi. Norman looked at me like I was a puzzle.

As I talked about my work, he softened and began to share what he had been doing. He had quietly paid for funerals and medicines out of his own pocket, holding yearly drag fundraisers and events as needed to create a fund. They'd twirl up a drag show on a Friday night, and here would come the money. One hundred percent of the proceeds went direct to people. "That's how we buy their medicine, that's how we pay their rent."

So, we trusted each other. Norman began giving me a small monthly stipend to help with gas, and he eventually agreed to give me a title in the organization, even if it was just to give me the clout to scare doctors into doing stuff. The fact was that Norman was tremendously powerful in the gay world but not in the straight world. He told me he had trouble getting people to come to Discovery to fix an air conditioner. Nobody wanted to be around gay people. So here I was, not fully welcome in both worlds but not a stranger to either. When I had to press it with people, out came, "I am the Executive Director of Helping People with AIDS."

I would use the title in the endless letters I sent to people, trying to get my guys help, and Bonnie would chuckle at "Executive Director" when she proofread them. But I could tell she was proud of me. She knew I was still diving in dumpsters to get food for people, but these folks didn't need to know that.

In the letters I would offer to do training and information programs at hospitals and clinics, all the stuff I was doing on a day-to-day, person-to-person level. Some said yes, if only to get me to stop writing, and while I was there I would always make a pitch for my dream: starting a hospice in Hot Springs or Little Rock. We had a hospice in Hot Springs, but it wouldn't take AIDS patients. We also had a medical facility that was going broke, and this initiative would have saved it, with all that Medicaid.

"I'm not gonna make this an AIDS hospital," an administrator at the facility told me. "I don't want them here."

"I worry you're saying you'd rather throw your hospital off a cliff than help someone with AIDS," I said.

"Watch me," he said.

"I will," I said.

Chapter Twenty-Four

I was in bed, so I didn't see the flames. It was only when Dr. Biel, my neighbor across the street, called me at four o'clock in the morning that I went to the front window. Someone had burned a cross in my front yard. It was about four feet high. A lazy man's cross burning.

"Did you know?" he asked. "Oh my God." I could see him parked outside, talking to me on his car phone. He was one of the doctors who lived on the well-to-do side of the street. When he saw me at the front door, that was his cue. "I'm just on my way home from the hospital," he said. "An emergency."

He wanted me to know the cross was burning, but he didn't want to help me. I'd woken Allison up when I ran to the front door. I saw fear in her eyes, but I was just mad.

"It's okay, honey," I said. "I'll be right back." I went out to get the hose, and it occurred to me that maybe the cross was so small because it was a diversion. Something to draw me out so they could get me. But it was a fleeting thought—whoever did this was just a coward. I took the hose and held the nozzle with one hand like a gun. They'd used treated lumber, hoping it would burn a long time, I guess. Or maybe it's just what they had handy.

It was probably someone who'd made hate calls, and they weren't that smart. "Hi, this is Larry with the Klan," one said, before saying, "Oh shoot," and hanging up. Another time someone didn't realize I had caller ID. "Harold, does your wife know you're calling me at midnight?" It had become easy to laugh off the hate calls. I was relieved I could just stay in bed and not race to some hospital.

Enough water from the hose finally put out the flames, and I doused the area around the fire in case I missed a spark and then kicked the cross over with my foot. Without the fire, I was alone in the dark, the sun not yet peeping out. I looked up and saw Allison watching, a silhouette with the light behind her. I loved this house, but I knew the neighbors didn't exactly love me, on this street where all the doctors lived, making calls on their car phones. A doctor at the hospital had hit on me, offering to come over for a cup of coffee some time.

"That'd be fine," I said. "But I think all the doctors who live across the street will recognize you, and they're going to start a rumor you have AIDS. That might cause a problem for you around town."

I was sure the neighbors were all watching the early morning show in my front yard, and maybe the person who burned the cross was still watching too. What's the fun in setting a fire if you don't watch it burn?

When I saw Mitch that weekend, I told him about it, maybe thinking he would, oh, I don't know, care. "They used lumber?" he asked, leaning back on the bed.

"Yeah."

"Well, that's just weird," he said. He seemed more annoyed they were wasting good processed wood than that they set it afire on his girlfriend's lawn.

"Maybe the cross store was sold out," I said. "Anyways . . ."

"Oh, hey," he said, "Cotton Cordell is looking for people to make fishing lures." Cotton had an office next to Mitch's. "I was wondering if any of your guys would need some cash. They can just do it at home if they—"

"Uh, yes," I said, sitting up. My guys couldn't find work anyplace else. "Yes. Tell him yes."

"Okay, okay," he said, laughing at my enthusiasm. "I mean, if I knew I'd get this reaction, I'd have 'em work for me too." Mitch had people putting together lamps for Wal-Mart. At his office, every person had a job: the putting-it-together part, the getting-it-in-boxes part, and the getting-it-out-the-door part. He also had people who drove trucks to Little Rock to deliver them. All those jobs . . .

"Mitch," I said quietly. "Don't say that if you don't mean that."

"I don't say stuff I don't mean," he said. "I just need people that are gonna show up."

"I will pick them up and drive them there if I have to."

Mitch put a lot of my guys to work, paying them cash each and every day, because he knew they needed it. He always made it clear to them he didn't give them work because they were sick, he just needed people who'd come back and know how to assemble, pack, and ship. If they needed a little extra money and asked for an advance, Mitch would always give it to them. They worked it off every time, right alongside the rough guys he also had at the office. These men, the ones who might have beat the hell out of my guys at the 7-11, became friends with them. Mitch told me they would bring stuff in to eat, and they would share it.

I brought Cotton's parts for fishing lures around to the people who had a hard time leaving their homes. They were able to sit and put the little BB in each one, and glue it together. Sometimes I would bring someone to the house to divide up the job and spread the wealth. Neuropathy was a big side effect of the medicines, so someone who had lost feeling in their fingers couldn't grip a BB, but they could glue. It was a short assembly line, but it was also a way to get them out of their loneliness. There were all kinds of lures, and some people hadn't really fished, so I got to explain what each one was, so they'd have pride in it. A lure is a lure, if you ask me, but Cotton had a business, so he convinced a legion of customers that they needed all kinds. What lure you chose depended on the time of year, water clarity, and of course who you were fishing for. Were you after crappie or bass? The lures would be different colors, and the ball bearing was inside to rattle, because you want it to make a little noise. Make it say to the fish you were after, "Hey, come over here. Look, my fin's broken. I'm not swimming like a normal fish, and I'm making noise so something's wrong. Come eat me, come eat me." It was just like dating.

With so much hate in the world, it made me feel good to know that all these people were out there fishing, not knowing their lures had been made by someone with AIDS.

That June a bunch of us went to the Arlington Hotel to see who would be crowned Miss Arkansas of 1991. This was the straight pageant, and Billy had no use for that, so he stayed home. I was excited, but once I was there, I saw why he skipped it. Once you've gone to a drag show, a so-called regular pageant is a letdown.

I sat with Norman and a bunch of the Little Rock queens who came over for it, including Misty McCall. Misty and I were next to each other, and she just picked those poor girls to death. "The earrings don't go with that dress." "Oh honey, the first rule of the Talent portion is you're supposed to have one." It was miserable watching these poor little country girls, and Misty told me most of them only did it to find a husband. "I like the husband-getting dresses," she explained. "Like Miss Texarkana, she's not going anywhere, but that gown was lovely. She'll be looking to unload it, so maybe I'll call her."

"You buy dresses from beauty queens?"

"The losers' dresses go *cheap*," she said, and mimed a call. "'Meet me at the Wal-Mart.' They sell them for nothing. The Miss Texas pageant used to be where it was at. We'd bring the U-Haul and sit through the show, and it was like the Paris runway, 'Okay, Miss Austin, like the shoes. Miss El Paso, where'd you get those earrings?'"

"Pageant shopping."

"Oh sure," she said. "Because Daddy was an oilman or cattleman, and he was gonna buy his baby girl that pageant, so these dresses

would be thousands of dollars. And in the parking lot, the girl is crying, and they'll practically pay you to take the dress so they never
have to see it again."

"Well, I know who to go to if I need a dress," I said.

"My drag closet is open for business."

During a break, Norman and I talked about a guy named Corbin
that we saw in the pageant audience. I knew of his family because they
were rich, and he certainly did nothing to hide his wealth. Whenever
he clapped during the show, he raised his hands up like he was trying
to catch every bit of light in the diamonds on his many bracelets and
rings. I said something to Norman about Corbin's bracelet, and he
scoffed. "Cora? Oh honey, those are his summer diamonds."

"Oh my God, I knew he was rich," I said. "But he's rich enough
to have seasonal diamonds? What are summer diamonds?"

"Well," said Norman, "some are diamonds, and some aren't."

I laughed, filing it away to use again and again. It was fun to
laugh with Norman and Misty, to lose myself in a world of husband-
getting dresses and summer diamonds. But I also had an agenda
that night with Norman. I had to formally ask him if I could maybe
come by and do some of the safer-sex education at Discovery that I
was doing at Our House in Hot Springs. I knew there was a mostly
friendly rivalry between the bars, but there was also a divide between
me and the Little Rock queens. They were sometimes leery of me,
like I was the health inspector. Norman agreed to let me do education there, but I know there was a general feeling in Little Rock that
I was drawing too much attention to AIDS. Also, I was a straight
woman, and they thought this was a family matter. I couldn't dis-
agree more.

Later in the summer, I was doing my rounds at a hospital in Hot
Springs, when there was a commotion at the nurses' station. A doctor had just been brought in to the ER, dead on arrival of a heart
attack. When I realized they were talking about the Doctor, I looked

for a place to sit down, fearing I might pass out. I felt as if the person who was holding the other end of the rope had let go, and I was plummeting.

I learned that it had happened on a running path. He'd driven to it alone. I thought about his car and what he might have in there. A little black book, something from Chip, anything.

His wife came to the hospital, and I waited a long time to approach her. I offered my sincere condolences. I said I had seen the Doctor sometimes at hospitals and that I could tell he was a good man who cared about his patients.

She thanked me.

"You know," I said, "why don't you let me bring his car over to your house, so you don't have that burden."

I knew it was forward, but I was desperate. She looked at me a moment. There was a slight turn to her head. Who was I to him?

"No, thank you," she said. "It's taken care of." The conversation was over.

"Good," I said. "That's good to know. Again, I am so sorry for your loss."

She turned away.

Driving to the next hospital, I remembered something from months back. I had been complaining to the Doctor about all the people lying about the cause of death in obituaries. "Donations can be made to the American Cancer Society," I said. "Don't ask any questions."

"Doctors used to not even tell people they *had* cancer," he said. "Doctors have all kinds of secrets." He told me about the pressure. How so many of them were dealing with addiction. "A much higher rate than other professions," he told me. "And the suicide rate is likely double that of other professions."

"Why?" I asked.

"Well, there's the pressure of being God, right? But also, we know exactly how to do it. We even know how to do it so it doesn't look like a suicide. Shoot yourself up with enough epinephrine. Then do something strenuous—that's just a heart attack. Who's going to check?"

He'd said the last part like a joke, so I dismissed it. "People don't do that."

"You'd be surprised what people do," he said.

I went to his funeral. I tried to be discreet, but I sobbed throughout it, feeling alone. Women looked at me, and I saw them whispering. I knew they thought I slept with everyone's husband and probably only hung around hospitals trying to marry a doctor. This was just one more on my checklist. "Was she after him too?"

I wanted to stand up and tell everyone what the Doctor had done—the risks he had taken to help me these three years. He allowed so many people to have the last months or years of their lives to sort out what had happened to them and what they were going to do now.

He was a hero, and no one would ever know. I hoped he was not in pain when he died. But I knew he was.

Chapter Twenty-Five

In September, KARK-TV had me in the news studio in Little Rock at five o'clock in the morning talking about my AIDS work. Once I got back to Hot Springs, my plan was to maybe take a nap with Allison in the hour we had before I had to take her to school. I didn't think many people would be up that early to see it, but my phone was ringing when I walked in the door. The caller was a soft-voiced woman, and I don't know how many times she called and didn't leave a message, because she sounded surprised when I picked up.

"I'm calling for the cousin of a cousin—"

"Of a cousin," I said. "It's okay, I understand. What can I help you with?" She tried to explain, something about someone being in Texas, and then she finally ended up asking if her sister could call me. "It's her son."

"Of course," I said.

"She's very upset," she said.

"Tell her to call me," I said. "See if I can help." I hung up, lay back, and closed my eyes.

The phone rang five minutes later. "My son Luke is at Peter Smith Hospital in Fort Worth," she said. "He has AIDS and a brain tumor. He's thirty-seven. They can't, or won't, operate, and he is almost completely paralyzed. He can eat . . ."—she paused—". . . if I spoon-feed him. He can't talk anymore."

"I'm so sorry."

"We live in Hot Springs, and we'd like to take him back home to take care of him."

"That's a wonderful thing," I said. "I can't tell you how rare that is."

"We just don't know how to get him home," she said. "They're saying we need to fly him, because, uh, the ambulance ride could kill him."

"Right, they call that an air ambulance."

"Okay," she said. "We have money, but they said it's very expensive. They're making it seem so complicated, and I just don't know how to get him home."

I thought about powerful people who get things done. "Do you mind me asking who you bank with in Hot Springs?"

She said the name of the bank. The president was one of the town elders who helped me from time to time.

"Let me see if he can give us some guidance," I said. "He's a good man."

I promised to call her back either way. I put on my nicest outfit, a flowing beige A-line skirt with a beige top, and brought Allison to school before heading straight to the bank. I knew the president would be there first thing in the morning. His blond hair was now all white; he was at least sixty-five but showed no interest in retiring.

"Well," I told him, "I have a family that banks at your bank, and they have for a long time, and this is the situation . . ." I reeled off the facts I knew, expressing their wish to bring Luke home from Fort Worth.

He paused for just a few seconds. "There'll be one waiting at the airport," he said.

"Well, listen for a second, they need an air ambulance, not just a helicopter."

"I understand you," he said. "It will be at the airport."

"I cannot thank you enough," I said.

He just had to pick up a phone. He was so certain this was a done deal, he didn't even have to make the call in front of me. I wondered what having that kind of power must be like. To have so many favors everywhere that the cost of this wasn't even something to consider. What I could do with that power.

I called Luke's mother right from the bank. "Tell them it's a go," I said. I figured it was an hour-and-a-half flight to Fort Worth, and I'd ride over in the air ambulance and meet the family and help out. I could be there and back and still get Allison after school. While I was in the air, Luke's mother arranged to have a hospital bed and the supplies brought to her house in Hot Springs, to set up a care facility in their living room. Again, I marveled at what money could do.

They were waiting for us when the air ambulance landed at John Peter Smith Hospital in Fort Worth. I stepped right out, the wind of the propellers lifting my hair and making my skirt billow. Luke's mother later told me I looked like an angel coming to take her son home. Luke's father was there, a burly but gentle man. And there was Luke, six foot five and so skinny, looking almost completely paralyzed, and unable to speak. He was curled on the stretcher, probably down to ninety pounds. From his eyes, I could tell he understood everything. There was a man there too, saying goodbye to Luke. Todd was twenty-eight and blond, and moved so gracefully, like an actor in a movie. He looked haunted. I gave him my number and told him he could call me anytime.

Luke's parents were deeply religious and belonged to this Pentecostal church. I knew the one—the church elders supposedly once walked a dead preacher around inside the church for three days because he was supposed to come back to life. I might have assumed Luke's family was backwards, but they weren't. They just didn't have words to talk about their son being gay. So they didn't.

Todd called me that first night. They'd been together five years, and Todd was a principal dancer at the Fort Worth Ballet. He'd met Luke while he was studying at the School of American Ballet in New

York City. "I'd just done an audition for Twyla Tharp, and I was in Union Square," Todd told me. "This six-foot-five guy goes by on a bike and just kind of stopped. We looked at each other and I said, 'Nice day for a ride.' After that, we were together." Luke worked construction, and in the summers, he got Todd jobs working on buildings too. "If we were doing a building in the Village, we'd take our lunch breaks outside."

The nine-year age difference didn't matter, Todd said, because Luke was just a giant kid. They had a friend, a pianist. He was the first of the three to be diagnosed with HIV, in 1986. Then they both were. They traveled around. Florida. Dallas. Landlords would rent a one-bedroom apartment to two guys, unclear about what was going on. "I guess they realized we were gay, but we didn't talk about it," Todd said. "It's a nonissue for us, so it should be a nonissue for other people too."

In Texas, Todd joined the Fort Worth Ballet. "I did *Apollo*," he said. "Luke got to see that." His voice trailed off. "We just . . . uh, we just bought a house. We were going to renovate it together. We had a lot of plans."

Their pianist friend had died at the end of May. On June 25, Luke had had a seizure. Todd took him to Dallas to get an MRI. Within a week, he'd had another one. "And then he couldn't move. He was paralyzed, starting on his left side, then spreading to everything but his eyes."

Luke's mother moved from Hot Springs to Forth Worth to help care for him in the hospital. When he was discharged, they arranged to have a hospital bed in the living room of their one-bedroom apartment. Luke's mother stayed with them, insisting on sleeping on the couch by her son, though Todd offered to let her have the bedroom. Todd worked six days a week at the ballet, and she cared for Luke while he was away.

"His mother is wonderful," he said. They didn't discuss the relationship. It was something that never came up. "There isn't much to talk about," he said. "It just is what it is, and I think that's beyond their understanding."

Luke had a great doctor, Patti Wetzel, who had finally leveled with Todd that he was taking on too much and couldn't give Luke everything that he needed on his own. Their current system wasn't sustainable. She advised him that if Luke's family was willing to take him, then at least he could have a network of support in his family and church.

"So, this wasn't a kidnapping?" I said.

"No," he said. "Well, yes and no. Luke has been taken from me, but it's not the family's fault."

I breathed easier. The next day I told Luke I'd talked to Todd, and his pupils dilated from pinpoints. "I promised to keep him updated, so he can be close to you."

I squeezed his hand. "I'm giving you this hug from Todd, okay?"

He blinked twice.

"Okay," I said.

Todd was going to try to get time off to come visit. I promised to keep him updated, and I did. Allison and I were there every day, and they were kind to her. Luke's father would always make sure there were cookies for Allison. He was successful in his business, and he wore that well. He had a huge parcel of land, complete with a big house and a hot tub. But he didn't lord his wealth over you. Luke's mother was smart but presented a meekness that made her big husband seem even bigger.

Luke's brother was a looker, just gorgeous, and I imagined that Luke must have looked like him. He was very accepting of his brother, but there was a sister who was a zealot. She ran roughshod over all of her other family members, her faith stronger than theirs. She made it clear that because Luke was gay, he was in danger of going to hell. But she lived in Texas and came by only occasionally, so I didn't think I'd have to deal with her too often. Still, his sister's presence was felt even miles away. This is something I had learned:

the boss is never who you think it is—never who they say or who they pretend it to be. In this family, his sister was the boss.

His mother spoon-fed Luke to keep him alive, and he was her baby again. A couple of weeks into our time together, Luke's mother told me she had been in touch with a funeral home. *We have time*, I thought, but I was glad that she was able to do that. She was a planner, and seeing to things helped her.

"They said that they could take him," she said, "but they have to soak the body in bleach."

I bit my lower lip to keep from yelling.

She continued, "I just . . . I'm just afraid it will bleach his hair."

I touched her arm. "They told you something that is not true," I said, almost shaking. "What they told you is wrong, and they are wrong to say it. Can you just tell me who told you that?"

She named the funeral home and the owner she'd spoken to. I knew him. If you were anybody in Hot Springs, he did your funeral.

I grabbed my purse.

"I'm just going to go have a chat with him," I said. "Clear this up."

I drove up to the funeral home, a huge place made to look like a Southern plantation at the end of tree-lined driveway. I marched into that place and noted its grand foyer, with a staircase built to look just like a smaller version of the one at the Arlington Hotel. I saw him.

"Hi," I said politely. "There aren't any funerals going on right now, are there?"

"No," he said.

"Good," I said. And then I yelled, "*How dare you?*"

I told him who I had just spoken to. "*Bleach?* You told a mother that you had to soak her dead son in *bleach?* Do you know what she is going through?"

"It would be a precaution," he said.

"You know what? You've had AIDS patients before. A car wreck, and you're picking glass out of his face? He could have AIDS. HIV isn't gonna walk in and say, 'Hi!'"

"Well—"

"If you are going to be in business, then you better change your way of thinking and of talking. This is bigger than anybody knows, so you better get ready for it."

I turned to walk out but realized I wasn't done. "And if you don't do better by people, I will be your public relations *nightmare*. Do you know how much an ad on the front page of the *Sentinel-Record* would cost you? Well, I can get you an article about your funeral home on the front page for *free*. But you won't like it one bit."

I drove back to the house and for the first time really looked at the mimosa tree in their yard. It stood alone among all those oak trees. Now that it was October, there were so many pods hanging off it. Six-inch seedpods that look like brown desiccated beans. A tree never looked sadder, but in June it must have been the most beautiful sight. Draped in beautiful, soft flowers, the pink powder puffs of summer.

That night I was home in bed when the phone rang at eleven o'clock. If you get a call after ten, it's probably not a good phone call. I reached for it, resigned to dealing with whatever came my way.

"Ruth, it's Bill," said a voice that was familiar.

Bill . . . ? I thought. This wasn't Billy. "What do you need?"

"Nothing, I just . . . Ruthie it's *Bill*."

I couldn't place him and felt awful. I didn't have a single Bill. Was this the hospital? "I'm sorry, who is this?"

"*Bill*."

"Oh," I said. "Ohhhh. Oh. Governor Clinton, yes. Hello."

"Is something wrong?" he asked.

"Well, I'm sorry, but I was going over my mental Rolodex about who would be calling me at this time, and you were not in it. Which is lucky for you, considering the calls I get."

He chuckled. "Ruthie, I just wanted you to know that tomorrow I'm announcing that I am going to run for president."

"Oh, that's fabulous," I said. "We need you."

I was mystified that he'd called me. "I'm letting some people know, and I wanted you to be one of them. I'm doing it tomorrow at the Old State House. Will you come?"

"Of course," I said, and paused. "Do you remember all those times on the porch at your Uncle Raymond's house?" I asked.

"I do," he said. "I think about that time an awful lot." He started talking, naming the men of the GI reform movement who gathered at that house on Lake Hamilton to map out how they were going to run Hot Springs now that they'd taken it from the gangsters. All the small details that made them stand out to us kids, me a toddler and Bill a teenager. "I was no bigger than a minute," I said, "but I remember it all."

All of those men were leaving us, and it was almost down to just us now. Raymond was in his eighties and still in Hot Springs, but I knew he couldn't have much time left.

"Well, thank you, Governor. Bill."

"And thank you for all the work you've been doing," he said. "I want you to know how proud I am of you. I know all the work you're doing, and I've learned a lot from you."

I had felt so alone, a nobody, and here he was calling me.

"Well," he said, "I have a few more people to call. Good night, Ruthie."

"Good night, Bill."

The next day, I watched him announce on the steps of the Old State House Museum in Little Rock. I stood over to the side and thought that maybe having a president who cared about AIDS could make a difference. It gave me hope.

Todd came to visit for a week in mid-October. He stayed with Luke's family and slept in a chair next to his bed. I gave him a lot of space to be with Luke. Todd cleaned him, and later he told me that while he was cleaning his toenails, Luke had an involuntary reflex, his paralyzed body pulling his foot back.

"I thought he was coming back," he said quietly.

Allison was there, and I told her this was love. Luke was so skinny, his skin tight on his six-five frame. She stared at him, and I worried for the millionth time what this was doing to her. On the way home, she told me she could see his insides moving. I saw it too—the organs of his body working hard to keep him alive.

Todd went home, and Luke's mother promised to call him when it was time. I knew she would.

By late October, the cold was setting in. I arrived one afternoon at the house to find Luke's father pacing the living room. There was something strange. I found myself holding my breath. Luke's brother was there, and so were a bunch of Luke's nephews, ranging in age from three to about twelve.

"You know, we have a real problem," Luke's father said. He had a metal tape measure, and he kept pulling it out and letting it snap back, making a *snik* sound again and again.

"Well, what is it?" I said.

"Luke needs to be baptized, he said. *Snik.* "His sister . . ."

Oh, I thought. I'd thought this was about Luke. It was about them. The sister, really.

He said they were going to immerse Luke in the hot tub. "He says that would have worked." He pointed to the corner, and I realized I hadn't even seen their preacher. He was standing in the corner, his back to us, reading a Bible.

"Hi there," I said, loudly.

The preacher flinched, looking like he was going to walk through the wall. He was so afraid of being around a gay person. I knew he didn't have even a clue about AIDS. The gay was enough. But I figured he had to be nice to these people because he had to be nice to these people's money. Without them, the church would go out of business.

"What do you mean *would have* worked?" I said. *Snik.*

"The heater's broken," said Luke's father.

Snik.

"You know," I said, putting my hand on his arm to stop the tape measure sound. "My God is very forgiving, and He is very nurturing, and He likes to see you think of different ways to serve Him and do things. Why don't you immerse him under the shower? Stand there and hold him under the showerhead. Whatever sin you think he has will wash off him and down the drain."

"We thought that too," he said. "We ran it by his sister."

I sighed. Something was escalating in the room, but I didn't know what. Luke's father was moving around faster, like he was wrestling with something. He threw the tape measure down and looked out on the creek. "Well, we've got to do something."

I realized what was about to happen, and I quietly said, "No."

"Boys!" he yelled. "Go on down there and dam up that creek."

This was late October. The water would be cold. "You don't have to do this," I said. But this was family, and this was their belief.

They moved quickly, rolling rocks into the creek. His father and his brother carried skeletal Luke down to the water, the preacher and his mother trailing behind. I gave his mother a beseeching look. She closed her eyes and kept walking down to the water. The boys got right in the creek, waist-high in the ice-cold water, to finish the job of damming the flow.

"I can't be here," I said to them. Above us, the Arkansas crows were cawing in the trees. "I can't." But I stood, watching. I felt I had to.

"Luke, because you have repented of your sins," the preacher said, "and because you now desire to be baptized in Jesus's name, I now baptize you in the name of Jesus Christ for the remission of those sins, and you shall receive the gift of the Holy Ghost."

Luke's nose was held as he was immersed. I turned away, unable to watch him, alive in the river, with the cold, dark water covering him.

I had to leave. I turned to go back to the car. Behind me, I heard the preacher shout up to heaven, "In Jesus's name!"

These were good people. And good people can sometimes do things we can't understand. I drove past the mimosa tree. It was completely brown, the leaves all dropped, with nothing left but the gnarled seedpods that would persist all winter.

I got a call late on the following Sunday that Luke was at the hospital. I walked in and knew it was close. His mother had a bowl of oatmeal, and she was trying to get him to eat, as she had done so many times in the past six weeks.

"Here, Luke," she said, "take a bite. Eat, Luke." I walked around to where she was standing, and she began to get louder: "EAT, LUKE. EAT. EAT." She was always so stoic, but now she began to cry silent tears that were only for Luke. There are some people who cry for others to see, but these tears were only for her baby. I gently took the spoon and bowl out of her hands and put a gentle hand on her back. She snapped back into my arms.

She called Todd at four o'clock in the morning to tell him it was time, just as she had promised. He drove up, but Luke died just before he got there. He missed him by such a short amount of time.

"He was still warm," he told me.

I had put Luke's mother in touch with Hot Springs Funeral Home, to replace the one she had talked to. There would be no bleach. Only sweet Dub, the manager, to help the family. When I stopped by the house the day after Luke died, I went straight to his mother, breezing past the women from their church. They were up on ladders, their skirts down to their mid-calves, with aprons and yellow Playtex gloves at the end of their long sleeves. They were wiping down the blades of the ceiling fan with bleached towels. They were a sight, older long-dress ladies exorcising whatever had been there. I didn't know how much they knew.

The family didn't believe in cremation, so this was one of the few times that a funeral would be complete, with a wake and a service, the casket brought to the front. Todd came with his own mother, but he didn't get to sit with the family. I think it just didn't occur to them that he should be included.

He looked so young, only twenty-eight. The seats left were in the front row, to the left, so he and his mother took them. My eye kept falling on him throughout the service. I was not alone. Some of my guys were there, and another gay man happened to be there, Harry. Todd was so handsome, this ballet dancer who seemed so out of place and of a different class than the Hot Springs guys. There were a lot of them cruising the widower, and Harry was especially ready to pack his bags to move to Fort Worth.

"Oh, man, I have got to get that number," Harry said.

"The love of his life just died," I said.

"I could come out to the house, help him get everything arranged," he said. "Now, what's his name?"

"Harry, no," I said. "This is a funeral." I successfully blocked Harry from cornering Todd, and later I asked Todd how Luke's family had treated him.

"Cordial," he said. I nodded. I wished that wasn't the height of what we could expect. But he loved Luke's family deeply and was grateful that he'd died surrounded by love. I couldn't bear to tell him about the baptism. I only wanted him to remember the warmth of Luke's body.

Todd called me a few weeks later. He'd hosted a memorial at the home he'd bought with Luke, still unfinished. "I'd put in floors and some Sheetrock," he said. He'd gathered some carpet remnants and arranged them to make the place look closer to the home he and Luke would have made. "We had an early freeze, and that day it was so cold. Down to the teens, with no heat in the house. People were holding each other to stay warm."

Todd told me he gave a speech and promised Luke that he would always be there in his heart. I wanted to tell him what I had learned: that love doesn't go away, and neither does grief. You just keep going, living with both of them. And maybe you get to hold someone to stay warm.

Chapter Twenty-Six

"Oh, thank God, you're here."

Tim opened the door wide to his apartment, wearing just blue jeans and waving a cigarette to say "come in." It was January, so I hopped in to keep the heat inside. I had just thought to stop by and say hi.

"Jimmy ran off and took her!" he said, his eyes red-rimmed from crying.

"Who?" I asked.

"Furball!"

"Furball . . ." I said. "Your hamster."

"Yes, she's the mama," he said. "She's got six kids who need milk, and he's run off with her to Little Rock."

"I see," I said, walking to the cage he was pointing to. "They're, what, like three weeks old?"

"Four."

I looked at Tim. He was looking so skinny, his tight jeans getting looser. I should have thought to bring food for them. The FDA had just allowed the second AIDS medicine onto the market, DDI. I'd finally gotten it for Tim and Jim and the other people who needed a Hail Mary pass. Tim called it a horse pill because it was so big, and made a neigh sound whenever I asked him how it was making him feel.

I sat down. "It's gonna be okay," I said. "We'll figure something out." Their brown and white cocker spaniel, Nelly, came to sit by me, and I stroked the fur on her head. "At least Daddy didn't run off with you, pretty thing."

Tim and Jim were always having these harmless little crises. Any kind of diversion to get their minds off of dying. Sometimes they were both getting so sick that I wasn't sure who would go first. I don't think they knew either. They were in and out of hospitals, and I know they would stockpile painkillers when they could and then steal them from each other and sometimes end up at the hospital sleeping off a pill high. The hospital would call me to wake them up, but as long as their coloring was good, I wasn't that concerned. I'd caution them against this routine, but I didn't want to be a jerk about it. "Oh, no, I'm not taking Timmy's medicine," Jim would tell me. "I'm trying to be a good example for Allison." And then "Oh, no, I'm not taking Jimmy's pills," Tim would tell me. "I'm trying to give Allison a good example." They were the sweetest trouble sometimes. At times, it felt like I was juggling chainsaws and kittens, but if you'd told me in April 1987 that I would be refereeing a fight between Jim Kelly and Tim Gentry over hamsters in January 1991 . . . Well, I knew when to count my blessings. They were here. Squabbling and still crazy but here.

"You know where Jim goes in Little Rock?" I said.

"Oh, do I," he said, stubbing out the cigarette.

"Well, call him and explain," I said. "This is about the children. I'm gonna call the vet, okay?" It was funny to call the veterinarian instead of a hospital, and I knew Tim was listening, so I spoke like it was a matter of grave concern. "Thank you, doctor," I said.

I turned to Tim. "Baby formula does in a pinch for hamster milk," I said. "You wanna go with me? Your food stamps will cover it."

He raced to get his coat, a shearling sheepskin Mitch had stopped wearing because he got grease on one of the cuffs. "Aren't you going to wear a shirt?"

"I like how it feels," he said, gathering the collar to his chin like it was a fine mink.

Walking to my car, we passed a few of the elderly residents who lived in the building. They all smiled at Tim, and he greeted them by name. There was a real fondness for him around here, and I was happy to see it.

Once we were in the car, I asked what the fight was about this time. "I don't know," he said. "I know he was drunk, and maybe I picked on him a bit about God knows what. But you don't just run off with our hamster."

"No, no, you don't," I said stopping at a light. I looked over at Tim, so tall and lanky in my car. "You know, Helping People with AIDS is working on something, and maybe you can give me some advice."

I reached to the back seat to grab my enormous purse, pulled out my journal, and opened to a page where I'd taken notes.

"We're coming up with guidelines for safer sex," I said, as I kept driving. "We want to make little cards, business cards, that list things that are 'Safest, Safer, Not Safe'—not just 'Safe,' because I think that turns people off. We want to give them real information."

"'Safest,'" he read. "'Massage, beating off together . . .'"

"Yes," I said. "Check out 'Safer.'"

"Whoa," he said, with a laugh. The words were what gay friends said to each other when they could be themselves, talking about what they did and liked.

"I want the language to be really real, so people pay attention," I said, "I got the money from the Department of Health, but this is an HPWA thing, so we can make something that actually *helps* people. The language seems right?"

"I'll say," he said.

"Good," I said. "That's settled, so let's get your babies some formula."

Jim came back with Furball, the mama hamster, as soon as he sobered up the next day. And our safer sex campaign was a huge success. We called it "Challenge '92, a Helping People with AIDS initiative." I had two thousand business cards made. On the front they read: "As part of the Challenge '92 campaign, I agree to follow the guidelines for safer sex." There was a little place to sign, and we gave the toll-free HPWA number for more information. On the back, the card had the current guidelines, written in a way that showed the reader that the people who came up with them were either gay or at least cared about them. It talked about oral sex in a frank way, how to use sex toys safely, fetishes, mutual masturbation . . . It wasn't some straight person holding up a sign saying, "Use a condom, whatever it is that you guys actually do together."

I numbered each card by hand, so we could keep track of how many people we were reaching. I also had T-shirts made, white ones, with the words "I DO. DO YOU?" printed on them. They were a conversation piece at the bars, Our House and Discovery. I'd give them away, but they had to sign their card to get the shirt. People love free stuff, especially when the hot guys are wearing the shirts. Guys would ask me what the shirt meant. "Well, it could be, 'I believe in Jesus. Do you?' But between us, it's really 'I practice safer sex. Do you?'"

Then I'd pause. "Do you?"

"Well, I think I do," was the usual answer.

"Let's talk about what you think that means then," I'd say.

The whole point was not to limit pleasure but to help people decide what risks were worth taking for them. If you made sex taboo and equated pleasure with punishment, then congratulations, people were just gonna throw up their hands and say, "Forget it." I had to meet people where they were.

I got money to make safer-sex kits, which were baggies I filled with the guidelines, two condoms, a mint dental dam, and an alcohol prep pad. The alcohol was for putting on your hands—if something stung, it meant you could get the virus in your body through that point. I didn't think many people would really use the alcohol before they had sex, but it was there to give them an option. Or maybe give them a second to think about risk in general. I think the kits worked, because they were put together to be of real use. The health department was always doing things like ordering types of condoms nobody would use. One time they gave me these dark green ones, extra-thick. I opened the box and showed it to one of the workers by the loading zone I used as an entrance.

"I don't mean to embarrass you, and you don't have to answer, but would you use these?"

He felt one and laughed. "I'd just rather dip it in Weatherbeater paint."

I grew up in the country, and I knew how thick that paint went on. I had them sent back, and now that I had good kits, I asked all my guys where the big cruising areas were. "What, are you going to go there?" Billy asked. "Just hand out condoms?"

"Why not?" I said. "Fish where they're biting."

Boyle Park in Little Rock is an idyllic little area, near where I'd spent Christmas with those men who were living together and dying together in that house in the Hillcrest neighborhood. I'd been a couple times now, handing out the kits, so I had it down. I think Billy pictured me standing in the woods where the men met, like some kind of washroom attendant. "Would you like some lube, sir? See you tomorrow night."

No, this was a sacred space, and not mine. I wanted people to feel safe, and there were enough trespassers. The previous year, an Arkansas state senator, Vic Snyder, had introduced a bill to repeal the anti-gay law that made consensual sex between men punishable with up to a year in prison. He couldn't even get it out of committee, and I knew there had been a number of stings with undercover cops at the cruising areas. An arrest could mean loss of employment, custody, and visitation rights—their whole lives.

I would only allow myself to be in the parking lot. The men would always back their cars in, so they could keep an eye out for who was there and interesting, and also so they could race out if they needed to. They would see each other, one would walk into the wooded area, and one would follow him.

Today there were a bunch of cars, and just as when you were fishing, you had to know when to get out so you could get the most people. I knew to go to the best-looking guy first, because that's who most of them were waiting for to get out of the car.

I click-clacked over on the blacktop in my heels and hose, right to the driver's side. The guy looked at me. I smiled. "Can you just put the window down a little bit?" I said. I made an inch-measure with my long nails, painted a rose color.

He did, and I dropped a kit in the window. I didn't say a word, because I just wanted to be this little invisible person making deliveries, not ruining the mood. He looked at it, probably expecting a Bible verse. He smiled, perplexed, and I was on to the next car and the next and the next. If you pretend to know what you're doing and that you're supposed to be there, nobody asks any questions. Then I got back in my car and rolled out. The Lone Ranger. Who was that blond woman anyway?

I had a sweet guy hanging around Norman's office at Discovery. He was shocked that I was going to Boyle Park and other cruising areas alone and insisted that I let him go with me. He was sick and knew he was on the slide going down.

"It doesn't bother me," I said.

"No, I wanna go too," he said, adjusting the glasses that were becoming too big for his thinning face.

So, I let him, because I think he was just lonely. We'd meet in the park, and while we waited for prime time, we traded stories about our favorite drag queens, like we were comparing baseball card collections. I mentioned this one I loved, a Little Rock legend. She was wild, and I heard that she once went after a guy who'd superglued her makeup case shut right before a pageant.

"I heard she shoed him!" I said. "Took her heel and hit him so hard with it that it left something like nail marks on his face."

"Yeah," he said.

"I wonder what happened to that guy anyway," I said.

He lowered his glasses to show little pockmark scars on his temple. "It was me." He could at least laugh about it now. He loved giving out the kits, so it was odd one twilight when he didn't show up to meet me at Boyle Park. I figured he got busy.

The next day Norman told me our friend was dead. He'd picked up two guys the night before at a bar. Big guys, and he took them back to his house. They beat him to death with a hammer, and then said they'd panicked because "this homosexual" picked them up, and they had to beat him off to protect themselves. These giant men, and this sweet, precious guy who said he wanted to protect me. The talk was, "Well, he was a faggot, and they didn't know. Good Christian men!" Good Christian men indeed.

A call from St. Joe's was never good, but at least Allison liked the food there. The head chef, James, was a friend from school, and he would look after her for me. Give her a nice table and make her feel special. I could take her and act like it was a treat.

They had called me about a new patient and neglected to tell me that he spoke no English. Angel was a handsome guy who'd done who knows what while making it to Hot Springs from Mexico. There was work here, usually at the racetrack between November and April, or tree planting, which is what Angel was doing.

They'd diagnosed him with AIDS but couldn't explain it to him. They had him in this big isolation room, and he looked like he was going to kill somebody, just out of fear. I turned and left, running over to the racetrack to ask my friend Bob Holthus if he had a horse groomer who spoke Spanish and would be willing to come translate. Bob was the all-time winningest trainer at Oaklawn Park, and I knew he'd have somebody. He just pointed to a guy, gestured to me, and said to him, "Go."

We went back over to St. Joe's, and we were able to explain everything to Angel. My interpreter was more upset than Angel was, but he also explained that Angel's main worry was being deported. Eventually, I was able to take Angel home to the rooming house he shared with a dozen other men. It was a place from back in the 1930s, with one bathroom down a hall. It was designed to have only men staying there, because back then women weren't supposed to travel, and if they did, they were not considered the kind of women people wanted to help. I would end up with two other men from that house, Carlos and Antonio.

Angel was so hard to pin down, constantly playing a disappearing act on me. His instinct, whenever he was in danger, was to move. And he didn't have a car, so he just walked everywhere. I would be driving around, and I'd see him completely drunk, and when I slowed down I would see he was sick. Whenever I picked him up, I would end up rushing him to the ER, and we'd be there waiting for the doctor as he drunkenly sang Spanish love songs to me—"Sabor a Mí," at the top of his lungs. He would get admitted and then leave as soon as I went home. Later, through a translator, he would say it was my fault for leaving him alone.

I'd had it, and one time I just took his clothes home with me so he wouldn't be able to leave the hospital. I planned to wash them for him but also to leave him stranded so he could finish a course of antibiotics. Sure enough, they called.

"Did you take Angel home?"

I glanced at his clothes, a neat pile in a bag on the kitchen chair. "No," I said.

"Well, he's not here, and his IV bag is gone too."

"Oh Lord," I said. "Okay, I'll look."

I went to the rooming house, and there he was in his hospital gown, with his IV bag hanging up on a nail above his bed, empty.

"You are Houdini," I said. "Nude-ini."

He gave me a look. "*Loco*," I said. And he smiled. I loved him.

Angel was in again soon enough, this time with systemic herpes, painful sores like fever blisters all over his body. I was at St. Joe's visiting him, when we needed to sign some papers. We needed a witness, and God sent First United's new preacher, walking the halls with his chest puffed out, trying to look important. He was a pompous man who hated me. It wasn't a suspicion. A friend told me I had been discussed at Rotary. "Boy, the new pastor sure doesn't like you," he said.

Now I saw my chance. "Oh, wonderful," I said, "can you help me with something?"

He frowned.

"Just come in, I need you to witness something."

"Can't a nurse do it?" he said, visibly repelled by Angel and all his sores.

"No, no, we need someone important, like you. This won't take a second. Just need you to sign something saying you were here when he signed. I promise you won't have to touch anybody, just stand by the bed here."

I paused: this was the moment. "Uh, we just need a pen." The preacher had this Montblanc pen he was so proud of. He kept it sticking out of a pocket so you could see it. In case you ever wanted to write a check, I guess. "Oh," I said, pointing to the pen, its black and gold luster shining under the harsh fluorescence of the hospital lights. He reflexively covered it with his hand.

"Don't they have pens out there?" he asked, gesturing to the nurses' station. I gave him a look of confusion. Why ever would we need a pen when he had one for us to borrow? He hesitated and finally handed it to me. I think it was bad enough to him that *I* was going to touch the Montblanc.

And I handed it to Angel.

"Here, Angel, just sign here," I said. The preacher stared at this modern-day leper touching his precious pen. He took it back, though he looked like he didn't want to. The pen was too valuable to him to sacrifice. He looked at me, hatred in his eyes.

He left, and thinking of lepers made me remember the one Jesus meets in Mark's Gospel. Jesus helps him but is chicken about it. He sends the guy off, saying, "See that you tell no one." Well, the leper tells everyone he sees. Soon Jesus is no longer welcome in any towns, "but stayed outside in lonely places. Yet the people still came to him from everywhere."

Angel and I smiled at each other, together in our lonely place.

Chapter Twenty-Seven

I sat with Tim and Jim in their high-rise. Allison was on the floor in front of Tim. He was absently running his fingers through her long red hair. It was late March, and Tim and Jim had each been sick again with lung stuff. The last time he was in the hospital, Jim said he didn't want to do it anymore. He got me to help him sign a DNR, a "do not resuscitate" order. "I don't want any heroic measures," he said, using a phrase he'd probably learned on TV.

"I understand," I'd said then, knowing this was an escalation for Tim and Jim. Neither wanted to be the one left to grieve the other. They had a dream that they would die together, as close in death as they were in life.

"We'll be cremated," said Jim, "and then you can put us up in the urn together."

Tim piped up. "But you can also sprinkle us here and there. Take us to the park."

"Where you pick up people," I said.

"Exactly," said Tim.

"That'd be amazing," agreed Jim.

There was something I had to bring up, and I had to do it in front of Allison so it was real. "You know, when Allison's daddy died, we were able to get social security. It's what's saved us." I looked right at Tim but with gentle eyes.

I pictured his daughter and knew he was doing the same as he finger-combed Allison's hair. She was about Allison's age, close to nine. I pictured her blond like her daddy.

Tim shook his head, no.

"Would you ever let me talk to her mother?" I asked. "Just to let her know when she needs to know."

"She's better off poor and not knowing what her daddy died of," Tim said.

"I don't think that's true," I said.

"No," he said, flinty and final. "End of story."

I nodded. But I admit I tried again in the next couple of weeks. They were getting frailer, shedding weight and hair as the horse race toward death intensified. He refused to tell me how to reach out to them.

Tim went in to the hospital at the end of the first week of April, and I knew he wasn't coming out. It was in his dark eyes. They always stood out against the lightness of his hair, but now they seemed darker. In his hospital bed, he continually bent his wrists and elbows inward, his limbs a collection of hinges as he curled himself into new positions to try to get comfortable. I began to see death coming to call.

Jim was home and talked about coming to see Tim, but he was too weak. Not sick enough to get admitted but too sick to visit.

I felt torn about who to be with, but come April 10, it was clear Tim had hours. He was three days shy of turning thirty-two, and I knew he wouldn't make it. His jaw was becoming slack, his breathing slowing. We were downstairs at the hospital in a quiet room. I left only to call Jim, who cried but understood he couldn't make it to AMI hospital to say goodbye.

"We'll be with him," I assured Jim. "I promise you." Allison and I sat with Tim as the sun went down, and we talked to him with a light hand on his forehead or on his arm.

Meanwhile, over at the eleventh floor of Mountain View Heights, Jim Kelly, the beloved of Tim Gentry, made a decision. He swallowed every painkiller he and Tim had stored up, washing them down with gulps of whiskey. I see him standing at the window, taking one last look at the view they had come to love. The moon, full but for a small slice of shadow, cast light across the mountain.

As his body succumbed to the overdose, Jim fell backwards into the glass table we had picked up one afternoon at a dumpster when they were making the apartment a home. The force of him falling shattered the glass of the table. The shards cut into him.

The sound scared his next-door neighbor, an elderly woman who adored Tim and Jim. She went out, and a male older neighbor on their other side came out, to see what the fuss was. From the shared balcony, they could see in. She screamed, and he called 911.

The ambulance came and took Jim, resuscitating him and keeping him alive. Any DNR he had on file at the hospital didn't matter.

A nurse came to Tim's door. "They sent me down here," she said. "Uh, the other guy is here. ICU. Bad."

"Jim?" I said. "How?" I didn't even think of an ambulance. I had been the ambulance for so many people that it didn't occur to me there was another way that Jim could get here. Allison and I got in the elevator to the second floor. We could see Jim through the glass, in the small ICU, skeletal and bloody. He was just feet from us, passed out, with the tube still down his throat from his stomach being pumped.

And then he woke up.

Jim was a demon, furious that he was still here on this earth. He tried to sit up, then pulled at the tube down his throat, ripping it out and tearing one of his vocal cords in the process. Choking on blood, he tried to yell but could make only guttural, slurry screams of desolation.

I grabbed Allison and pulled her face to my chest to hide her. She pulled away. "I'm going back to Tim," she said, already taking off for the elevator.

I looked back at Jim, who met my eye briefly in hysteria. I never saw anything like that pain. I think they sedated him, or the fury left his body spent. He collapsed. I stayed for some time, then worried Tim would die while Allison was alone with him. It was too much. I went back downstairs, and we each held Tim's hands.

Tim died that night, April 10.

I visited Jim upstairs. His body was breaking down now that his spirit was gone. He remained angry, and I knew his soul would not rest until he left us. They wanted to go together but not like this. I couldn't be mad at the old neighbors who had saved him. They loved them so much, and they didn't understand he was ready.

It was too late for Jim anyway. He died two days after Tim, on April 12. Allison was heartbroken but tried not to show it. Even at her age, she just kept moving. Their pain was over, and if it meant hers had begun, then at least she knew they were at peace.

The work of caring for the living switched over to the obligations I felt to them in death. I found homes for Furball and her hamster babies, but Nelly, their cocker spaniel, was harder. She wasn't a puppy. I was at the bank, and something told me to tell a lady who worked there as a teller. I just knew I could drop little hints. "Oh, I've got to give away the dog," I said. "It's heartbreaking."

"Well," she said slowly, "what kind is it?"

"A cocker spaniel," I said. "A girl. Most beautiful dog I've ever seen."

She asked a bunch of questions about the dog's health and her temperament, but I knew she was stalling. Then she got to it.

"Is there any possible way to get AIDS from a dog?"

"No," I said. "That one I know. No."

"Did the dog lick them?" she asked. "What if the dog licks me?"

I assured her, but what really sold it was me bringing Nelly by the bank at closing time. She came out, and Nelly nuzzled her. I looked up at what I was sure was Tim and Jim directing her. "You look like a Nelly," she said.

"I think it's meant to be," I said. I had the dog bed in the trunk, along with all the food and treats she had—just in case this worked out. When she saw me get Tim and Jim's stuff out, she hesitated. She remembered they had AIDS, and I think she worried about what she was doing. There was a line in her mind, and she wondered if she could cross it. But she did, and I was so relieved.

I had all of Tim and Jim's forms ready, so arranging for the cremation procedure was fine. I went to Kimbo at Dryden Pottery, and asked if he could make me a special urn. By then he, of all people, knew what I was doing, this man who had given me chipped cookie jars for years.

"I would need a tall one," I said, and explained that Tim and Jim wanted to be commingled and know that they were going to be completely together for eternity. I offered to pay at least something, but Kimbo said it would be an honor. I started to tear up.

His father came out, "Don't you do that," he yelled at Kimbo. "You give her a broken one."

"No," said Kimbo. He lowered his head, his white eyelashes blinking at me. "I'm sorry for your loss."

"Thank you," I said, managing to just cry one tear before stopping myself with a nod. "They were really special."

They were special. Family to me, and so I decided to put their obituary in the paper. I listed their names, wrote how they were devoted to each other. I said they were going to be buried at Files, but I didn't dare write what they died of. I just thought it would open a can of worms.

I put their ashes in the urn Kimbo made for them, commingling them. It felt sacred to me, and I had to fulfill the promise I made to set aside some ashes to scatter around their favorite places. I knew they'd want to be close to Nelly, so we went to the house of the bank teller and stood on a rock to pour some over the side of her back fence. Allison whispered, "Your daddies are here, Nelly."

When the obituary ran, I got a call from a woman I knew who had family buried at Files too. "I want to know who you're burying in the cemetery," she said. "It's only for our families."

"One's my brother," I said.

"You don't have a brother."

"Well, he's my cousin. I'm sorry."

"I wanna know what you're doing."

"They're family, what am I supposed to do?"

"They're not some of them people that you're dealing with, are they?"

"Yes, they had AIDS."

"Well, my God, why you gonna bury them in that cemetery?"

"Well, I knew that with your husband being a doctor, and you being so kind and everything," I said, "I just knew it wouldn't matter."

She paused a long time. "Well, just this one time."

She wasn't the only one who heard, I guess. The night before we were set to bury them, I awoke to another cross burning on my lawn. It was lumber again, probably the same people who set the first one. Back then, I'd been determined to show they couldn't get to me, but this time I was really mad.

I could see all the lights on in my neighbors' houses as I doused the flames with the hose. When it was out, I saw a light go out like the show was over. It wasn't.

"Fine!" I screamed to the people, all of them watching me, as I felt five years' worth of rage, yelling at whatever version of the KKK I had burning crosses in my yard. "Fine!" I said again to them, marching to my front door. "You tell me what I am supposed to do!" I grabbed the tall urn containing what was left of sweet Tim and Jim. "Are you going to help me? Y'all come and get them." I placed the urn on the chair on the porch and turned the porch light on. "You can be in charge of them, if you think what I am doing is wrong. But you're not gonna scare me. And you're not gonna do anything to me or my daughter. So you may as well quit wasting your time."

I left the porch light on all night, Tim and Jim there in their urn for all to see. In the morning, I knew I would find them right where I left them. All the doctors had to see them as they passed by on their way to early rounds at the hospital. I took them inside, cradling them one last time.

We had a small service at Hot Springs Funeral Home. Tim and Jim didn't have much to do with the guys at Our House, so I didn't expect many people. I'd left a note on the announcements board in the lobby of their high-rise, just in case anyone wanted to come.

Allison and I were upstairs at the funeral home when the funeral director came in. "The rest of the family is downstairs," he said.

"Is there another burial here?" I asked. "Another family?"

"No, his family," he said. "James's."

"Jim? There isn't any family at all."

"Well, they're here."

We walked downstairs to find about eleven people with three teeth between them. Jim's brothers and sisters. How long had I been caring for Jim, and he had family living thirty minutes away, still in Perryville? It could have been a million miles away.

They'd brought a U-Haul down. "We came to get their stuff," said one. He hadn't bothered to bathe, but he did have a clean shirt on. He did do that.

What stuff? I thought. But I was suddenly panicked. I thought I was the only one, figuring he was an orphan. I needed their okay that he was cremated.

"Of course, I can give you the key to his apartment," I said. "There's just one thing I need from you."

I got a signature, but I warned them. "Jim was a simple guy," I said. "He didn't have a lot of stuff."

"You mean to tell me we wasted all that gas to come down here to not get a damn thing he's got?"

"My condolences on the loss of your brother," I said, handing them the key.

Allison and I drove up the hill to Files to the grave site. I didn't try to get a preacher to come, because I didn't want Tim and Jim to face one last indignity of being told no. It was just me and Allison, like it had been in so many twilight hours. Only today we were putting these souls to rest in broad daylight.

And then I saw them. Three cars, then four, coming up slowly. They parked. And out came a caravan of little old ladies. The women who lived in Tim and Jim's building, who had come to care for them in their time together, who had fallen in love with them just like I had.

There was a long line of them, walking slowly on the road to the entrance of Files. At the front was a developmentally disabled boy, about thirteen years old, who I recognized. He lived at the high-rise with his grandmother, and she had grown especially close to Tim and Jim. He walked kind of stooped over, in a white T-shirt and blue jeans. He held a large coffee can reverently, a gallon-size container they had covered in countless scraps of used aluminum foil to make a pretty covering. The shiny vase was filled with tiny little flowers that danced with every unsteady step he took. They were hot pink and yellow and blue—absolutely stunning.

This was the Hot Springs I loved. The one where you never went someplace unless you brought something to offer. They were going to the funeral, and they didn't have any money. But they knew of a field of wildflowers, and I have always wondered where they found that field, because we don't have a lot of those in Arkansas. They had gone that morning, and I can see them out in this field, picking flowers and putting them in that coffee can they'd covered in lightly used foil. It was the foil they'd balled up and then put in a cabinet, and when they needed it, they unwrapped it, so it was crinkled. Because you don't waste new aluminum foil. These women had lived through the Depression, and the Depression had never really ended in Arkansas. They must have had to search for all those scraps, probably gathered from other women at the high-rise. "Do you know those guys? Those two on the eleventh floor?" Gathering enough to make it nice.

I watched those wildflowers dancing around inside that can. They were alive, celebrating Tim and Jim. I took the bouquet I'd brought and quietly put it by my father and Jimmy. I wanted these gifted flowers to stand alone in tribute. Every flower that these people picked to show Tim and Jim how much they were loved and would be missed. They said that they sang gospel hymns while picking the flowers, lifting their souls to heaven. I asked if we could sing one together.

"Do you know 'It Is Well with My Soul'?" I asked. It was written by a man who lost his entire family except for his wife when he sent them ahead on a trip across the Atlantic. The ship sank, and she sent him a telegram: "Saved alone . . ." The song had brought me comfort these years, and when the music director selected it at First United, I thought it was God placing a hand of reassurance on my shoulder. The hope and duty of survival.

They started to sing, and I joined in. I pulled Allison close to me. It wasn't a religious moment. It was just a hymn of comfort. Tim and Jim were free now, dancing like those wildflowers in the light, caressing breeze of April.

Chapter Twenty-Eight

I walked in to Billy and Paul's house to find Allison standing in their living room, waving at an imaginary audience. She was wearing one of Billy's tiaras and holding an imaginary bouquet. I'd let myself in—a habit from taking care of people in a town of unlocked doors—so they didn't see me at first.

"One long, two short," said Billy. "One long, two short."

I watched for a few seconds, my brand-new ten-year-old looking so big.

"That's it," said Paul. "You're doing it." Allison beamed.

I put my purse down, and the thunk of its weight made them turn. "They're teaching me the Miss America wave," said Allison. She did it for me, slower than she had been. "It's one long wave, then two little ones, over and over."

"She's a natural," said Billy.

"Better than a lot of the new queens coming in," said Paul.

"Oh, show her the Queen's wave," said Billy. "The royal one."

Allison thought a moment, changed her carriage a bit, then began to wave with smaller movements.

"Elbow, elbow, wrist, wrist," Billy said.

"Elbow, elbow, wrist, wrist," she repeated.

I sat down next to Billy to join in admiring the royal procession. "Queen of the fourth grade," I said.

At the mention of school, I could see Allison deflate. It was June, so it would be over soon. When I asked her about friends or who she sat with at lunch, she changed the subject. There had been an opening on the school board, so I ran and got on. I hoped it would help me keep an eye on bullying, but it became an extension of my AIDS work as well. There was this awful woman on there whose daughter got diabetes, so we had to teach the kids what to do if her daughter passed out on the playground, though that had never actually happened.

I said, "Well, we also have to start teaching them about how you do and don't get HIV," I said. It was a Catholic school, so I guess she felt she had the right to jump all over me and say that what I proposed was filthy and nasty.

"You don't know," I said, "how many of these kids are gonna be gay when they grow up." That didn't go over well, no matter how true it was. The parents accused me of pushing an agenda, but the nuns at the school loved me. Maybe it was because I helped them make their fundraising goals at the annual bazaar, but also the principal, Sister Noeline Banks, was just a good person. She, along with a third grade teacher, Sister Cheryl, appreciated what I was doing for people with HIV and listened to my concerns about what Allison was going through at school. Yes, I was the only single mother at that school, and I had gay men and lesbians picking up my kid, like today, when Billy showed up. But Sister Noeline and Sister Cheryl waved at every one of them.

Paul got up to go to work, and I told Billy I had to drive up to Mount Ida to drop off my mortgage check. I liked to bring it right to the lady I bought the house from instead of mailing it, because I could visit with her and also take along someone who looked like they needed an airing. There is something about being in a car with the world hurtling by that helped people open up. I could always drive as fast as I wanted and not worry about cops, at least around Hot

Springs. They figured if I was speeding I had someone with AIDS, and they wanted no part of that.

"I'm just going up to Mount Ida," I would say to my guys. "Going out on the loop." Billy called the trips, "Going up the country." With him, I'd play the radio full volume, and we all sang along or talked about whatever late-night movie he'd watched that week.

That time it was *High Noon*, and he had a lot to say about hiding the light of Grace Kelly's blond hair under the bushel of a bonnet. But he serenaded us with the movie's theme. "Do not forsake me, oh my darlin', on this our wedding day," he sang. On a long stretch of two-way, I closed my eyes just for a second, so I would remember the moment.

Maybe I knew things were about to change. My ability to predict the time of death had somehow lengthened to another kind of mourning. Not long after that ride, Billy drove up to my house to visit me.

"When I look, I see spots everywhere," he said. "They're black."

I knew what it was. Cytomegalovirus retinitis. The CMV that would slowly take his vision like a curtain closing across his eyes. I got him an appointment in Little Rock right away. They prescribed a medication and told him he could never drive again. It was one more thing he was losing.

And then, slowly, it was his mind. Billy regressed once he started the eye medicine, but it was unclear to us whether it was a side effect or just the beginning of AIDS-related dementia. He became child-like quickly, talking as if he were a little boy. He had always been one to express wonder and excitement about things, so it was hard to tell at first.

I would take him out with Allison, and she bonded with Billy even more as she got used to him having the mindset of someone her age. I adapted, taking them to zoos and kid-focused performances. Places we could leave if he got restless.

At home he lived in a blue bathrobe, worn and soft, somebody's grandfather's robe. And striped pajamas with brown corduroy house slippers. He let the robe billow as he walked, ever the performer. He woke up one morning and announced to Paul that he had to have a cowboy outfit. "I'm a cowboy," he told him. "I need my cowboy boots." It was irrational, but Paul was already used to doing anything for Billy. So, if he wanted to wear a cowboy costume, let him.

Then it was very apparent something was wrong. One day Allison and I went over and we couldn't find him. We knew he was home, because he had just called us. We finally found him in a closet with the door closed, a bare light bulb on over his head. He was wearing a beautiful pair of sunglasses. "I'm getting a suntan," he said. Another time he decided their dog, Pepper, had fleas and tried to put her in the washing machine. He was stopped just as he emptied an entire bottle of shampoo over her and before he closed the lid to turn it on.

It was clear Billy could not be left alone, for fear that he would hurt himself or wander off, disappear like a wisp. Paul had taken additional work to care for Billy, so Paul and I arranged that Billy always have at least one person, preferably two, around. That wasn't hard, what with Billy being so popular and all the people Paul had helped out at one time or another anxious to return a favor. Billy's lesbian fans came over, and it was funny because they were the most anxious about his pill schedule. They were these cool girls in their twenties who'd never taken medicine and didn't have parents old enough to be giving them medicine. No matter how many times I explained it, they were scared they would give him the wrong dose, and they worried that, if Billy took his AZT five minutes earlier than he was supposed to, he would die.

These women and I got a better sense of each other as we cared for Billy. The lesbians who went to Discovery in Little Rock had always been a little standoffish with me. Norman had set aside a bar that was just for them, and it was the first space that they didn't have to share with men. And then a straight girl shows up talking about AIDS and dental dams.

"We thought you were a fag hag," said one. "Looking for a gay guy to do your hair and be your friend and dress you up like a doll. You know, all that garbage."

"They're giving out makeovers?" I said with a laugh. "Man, have I been missing out."

We learned from each other as we kept a watch on Billy. The lesbians taught me about the start of deer season in November, and how the society women who were "straight" in daylight rushed to the gay bar in Little Rock as soon as their husbands went off to deer camp. "The women come over, and they are just rabid," said one. "*Rabid!*"

In return, I taught them how to care for their brothers who were dying. These women stepped up to take care of Billy and all the others who were becoming sick. Billy was just the beginning at Our House.

The queens of course came around, and being with Billy seemed to give everybody a chance to work out their sorrows over people they had let slip away—the ones who'd left Hot Springs and hid as they died alone. Holding Billy's hand couldn't undo that loss, but it was a way for them to be present. To be a witness.

Despite his regression, Billy enjoyed his life. He never missed a drag performance, and when he was onstage he was his old self. He could play the "character" of Billy again, and people adored it. To his fans at Our House, he was a symbol that having HIV or AIDS did not mean that you had to go hide in exile. You could stay in the game, be social, snatch trophies and *live*. The literature about HIV that I read and shared, by gay men for gay men, emphasized a focus on living with HIV, rather than on dying. But that was all theoretical, just words, until they could see it in practice.

Paul talked to Billy's family, but they would not come down to see him. Paul's own mother, Georgeanna, would visit on random Sundays.

The first time she saw Billy in his new state, Paul told her, "His mother won't come down."

"That's okay," she said. "I'll hug him. I'll love on him."

She would sit with Billy on the couch, and he would be calm in her arms. His nervous energy quieted. She was not an overbearing person, and I saw so much of Paul in her. Never one to ask, "What do you need? Are you okay today?" Just simply there. Steadfast.

As he got weaker, Billy began to spout more of the lines he'd memorized from the old movies he loved, those with his favorite, Bette Davis. He would pick a role and just be that for the day. Bette saying, "*Cuuute*," just like she did in *The Cabin in the Cotton*. "I'd like to kiss you, but I just washed my hair." Paul told me how he'd taken Billy in to Our House when Twyman was sitting there, scowling. Billy took a few puffs on his cigarette and looked around. "What a dump," he said. Twyman had just stared at him, probably not knowing he was looking at Bette Davis in *Beyond the Forest*.

As the summer began to fade to autumn, Billy's episodes changed and became dangerous. He was afraid of hurting himself or someone else, and we learned that he could feel these episodes coming on. Doctors Hospital in Little Rock was a good hospital that had a lockdown unit. It was suggested as an option to him, and he took it. He said they were kind, and when he felt the violence coming, either against himself or others, he would ask to be taken there. It was an hour's drive, and he was scared to even be in the car with me alone, fearful that he would do something to drive us off the road or hurt me. He asked me to restrain him, tying his hands behind his back, and it broke my heart to do it. I began carrying silk medical tape in my purse to tie his hands. Then that too became routine. He would call me over, frantic, and meet me with his hands behind his back. "I need to go to Little Rock."

Billy began to get furious at even Paul, impatient that he worked all the time and wasn't home with him. He didn't think Paul was fooling around or anything like that. He knew he was doing any job that would pay him. "Paul won't come home from work," he said.

I winced at the idea of Billy calling around to all the places Paul found work, looking for him.

"Billy, he's busy."

"He works too much," he said. "I need you to come over."

I knew he had at least two people with him. I had people to see.

"Billy, I can't," I said.

"No, I really need you," he said.

I thought that was code for a trip to Little Rock. "Okay," I said. When I got to his door, he let me in, and sure enough, he had his hands behind his back. He was smoking, a cigarette in the corner of his lips.

He said in a singsong, mischievous voice: "I've got something for you."

"What do you have for me, Billy?" I asked, tired. I didn't feel like driving my best friend to Little Rock so he could spend the night in lockdown.

"It's something special."

"Well, what is it, Billy?"

He whipped out a can of lighter fluid from his behind his back and doused me with it. I screamed as he threw the lit cigarette at me.

I jumped back, and the cigarette hit me at an angle. It fell to the ground, missing a streak of lighter fluid on the floor. The two men who were with him jumped on him and held him back.

I stared at him, frightened. "I can't believe you did this to me," I stammered. "You know, you know, we've got to go to Little Rock."

Billy had a glimmer of recognition of what he'd just done. He turned around and put his hands behind his back. I tied his hands and left him with the guys for a minute.

I changed my clothes there, borrowing one of his T-shirts. In the bathroom I rinsed my face, using soap to try to get rid of the lighter fluid. It was no use. The scent of it still filled the air in the car as we drove to Little Rock. Even with the windows down, I could smell it the whole way. We both could.

It was Halloween, a few days before the 1992 presidential election, and Hot Springs had Clinton fever. Allison and I were getting ready to go to Paul and Billy's for a small party and were already in our costumes. I was in a Little Bo Peep outfit, and she was a sheep. But first we had to show a Northerner around. He came down in a shiny suit, wanting to open up an art gallery, and it was clear he was looking to make money on the Clinton name. I'd started selling real estate here and there, so we drove him around and showed him spaces. I knew we looked crazy, but at least he would know what he was in for if he came to Hot Springs.

Three nights later, Allison and I watched Bill Clinton get elected on TV. We wrote a note of congratulations to President-Elect Clinton, keeping him updated on AIDS in his true hometown. They called him "the man from Hope," but he was all Hot Springs. While campaigning, he certainly talked about AIDS. "I want to increase federal funding for research, prevention, and treatment," he said. I knew that states were seeing an increase in need by thirty percent but were dealing with twenty percent *cuts* to federal funding. I was desperate for someone to do something on a real, national level to help people. We were all running out of time.

I couldn't tell if the rate of people getting symptoms was going up in Hot Springs, or if people just weren't hiding now that Billy had shown them it didn't mean having to leave town in secret. The morning after the election, I went to see Jerry, who was an Our House regular. He had so little money, it was like he even owed God. But it was the hospital that wanted the money. I'd gone spare-changing to get him AZT, but there had been a treatment he needed, and it cost something like two hundred dollars, which might as well have been a million to him.

Twyman, the owner of Our House, had set up an AIDS fund from fundraisers. I went to him to ask if he could give some money to Jerry.

"He's down here every night," said Twyman. "He can afford his own goddamn medicine."

"It doesn't cost anything to come here," I said. "He doesn't go to the shows." Maybe he just drank water. Twyman of all people should have known that this wasn't just a bar. It was a home, a community center, and a church. But I was afraid to contradict him and be banned. Twyman was a vengeful person, and he would make sure of it. When I told Paul that Twyman had said no, he wasn't surprised.

"I asked Twyman for money when Billy and I needed help."

"Why didn't you ask m——"

He cut me off. "You've done enough. And you know how I don't ask anybody for help. We had that fund set up, and I thought, *Well, you know, do what you gotta do.* And I asked him. It was three hundred dollars I needed for that month, to finish paying bills."

Twyman told Paul he needed to ask his lover at the time, David. "I said to myself, *After all these shows and all the stuff I've done for you, I've probably raised all the money that's in that fund.*" Then Twyman called Paul back. "He said, 'Well, we talked about it and, yes, we'll give you the money, but you'll need to repay it,'" Paul remembered. "I said 'No, thank you. I don't need it. I don't want it.'"

And now Jerry was in the hospital, dying. He could move a little but was beyond talking. I knew he could hear me, though, and when I talked I could see him relax. There was less fear in his eyes. I spent the day reading the *Reader's Digest* to him. We had a raft capsize at the Crystal Rapid of the Grand Canyon; worked to save elephants from ivory poachers in Zambia; and kept losing and finding a seafaring dog named Santos, whose owner sounded like he would prefer the dog stay lost. I read it until there were no more words to read. "I'll be back tomorrow, Jerry." He gave the slightest nod, and I kissed his forehead.

When I picked up Allison at school the next day, I told her we needed to go see Jerry. "He's real bad, so we're gonna sit with him," I said. When we walked in, his head was turned to the window.

"Jerry," I said.

He didn't move.

"Honey, I think he's dead," I said. "You might want to stay out here."

"No, it's okay."

I went in and confirmed Jerry was gone. I had to see to his body, give him dignity. I turned to Allison. "He might make a noise when I lay him back," I said.

"I'm outta here," she said. She went and took a seat in the waiting area.

A nurse came in. "When did he die?" she said. "I kept checking on him. Please tell me you were in here when he died."

I lied and said I was. I could just tell she couldn't handle it. She shook her head quickly and blinked several times. "Okay."

"Thank you for looking after Jerry," I said. I wet a washcloth and asked if she would like one.

"Yes," she said. She was new, and I wondered how many patients had died on her. She was the same age I was when I first started. We remained quiet, washing him one last time.

Jerry's family wanted to do a funeral at Caruth Funeral Home, which surprised me, but I welcomed it. Jerry was very popular at Our House, so I invited everyone. Suzann, the traffic cop who also ran the flower shop in town, was really fond of Jerry and offered to donate a casket spray. Allison and I went over, bringing some pastries. We watched her put it together, taking flowers from here and there, creating this gorgeous huge spectacle of color and life. Yellow button and blue chrysanthemums, snapdragons of every color, pansies, white and pink roses, gladioli—it was a piece of art.

"I don't know how to thank you," I said.

"Casket sprays are usually the responsibility of close family," said Suzann. "And we were all his family."

She delivered the casket spray to Caruth's, but something happened to the flowers before the service. The head of every single flower was drooping, the leaves browning, as if someone had poured poison on them. Suzann gasped when she saw it. I know if the service wasn't about to start, she would have run to the shop and brought something else.

We and the Our House crowd sat in the back, taking up a third of the pews. More and more of Jerry's family came in, and it made me feel better. It was getting so crowded, and I kept thinking how much I'd misjudged his family. I had thought he was so alone in life.

Jerry's brother got up to do the eulogy. He was angry. He pointed to the casket, then opened the palm of his outstretched hand. "This," he said.

There was a pause. "*This* is what happens. This is the homosexual lifestyle."

It hit us like a slap, but the family seated before us nodded in unison. This wasn't a eulogy. It was a hate rally. "Jesus Christ gave my brother the greatest gift. Life. And this is what he did with it. If you sin like Jerry, you end up like him."

I wish I had said something. Later, we all had things we wished we'd said. But we didn't. None of us wanted to get whipped. Jerry—their brother, son, cousin—was a stranger to them, and our love for him was a threat. They were just looking for an excuse to hurt us. Poison us, just like those flowers.

Chapter Twenty-Nine

Allison and I both had the worst flu. She'd gotten it at school, and hers was at least on the way out the door, but mine was still heavy in my chest and sinuses. I hadn't been able to see any of my guys for two days, because if this had me in bed, it could kill them. Around three in the afternoon, I'd finally gotten to sleep when the phone rang. I worried it was an emergency.

It was Billy.

"I did something really *ba-ad*." He stretched out "bad" in a singsong, playful way.

I tried to sit up. "What is it, Billy?"

"I killed Paul."

"You did?" Now I sat up. "No, you didn't."

"I did."

"Why? How?"

"I stabbed him," he said, no remorse or sense in his voice. "Over and over and over . . . Stabbed him to death."

"Billy, stay where you are."

There was no answer. "Billy." I could hear him singing to himself, the sound getting fainter as he walked away from the phone, leaving it off the hook.

I hung up and called 911, telling them to send an ambulance and police to Billy and Paul's house on Oak Cliff. Out of caution, I told them that someone there was HIV positive. As I got dressed, I called Mother Superior, their roommate upstairs, but there was no answer.

I told Allison that Billy said he'd done something to Paul, and we needed to go over there right away.

"Is he serious?" she asked.

"I'm fifty-fifty on that one," I said more to myself than her. Billy was so frail, I just couldn't imagine him being able to hurt a big guy like Paul. But if he surprised him . . .

It was only mid-November, but I put the car's heat on full blast because I had chills from the flu—or fear. When I pulled up, I saw the cops were on the front porch, just standing there. "Allison, you stay in this car." I'd pulled all the blankets off her bed to keep her warm and did a fast tuck around her.

"I'm a friend," I yelled to the cops. "The one who called."

They stepped aside like I should let myself in.

"Well, did you knock?" I asked. "What's going on?"

"Someone answered," said the one with a mustache.

"He tried to spray us," said the other guy.

"Spray you?"

"He said that everyone who comes in has to be sprayed," said mustache cop.

"Oh God, that's hand sanitizer," I said. "He has AIDS, so it's just a rule they have. Everyone has to spray their hands because he's immunocompr—. Listen, can you just go in?"

Both shook their heads, no. I put up both hands. "I have to go in there to find my friend dead in there? Probably blood everywhere."

They shrugged. "Y'all are the biggest wimps I have ever seen in my life." I banged on the door. "*Billy!* It's Ruthie."

He swung open the door. I looked at him in his blue bathrobe and pajamas. There was no blood on him. I looked at his socks to see if there was blood. None. None on his fingernails either.

"I told them they needed the spray," he said.

I held out my hands for him to spray them. "Billy, where's Paul?" I called out his name. "Paul?"

There was no answer.

I pushed past Billy to walk into the house, my eyes darting everywhere. I didn't see any blood. I kept looking back. I could see Billy walking toward me. He'd left the front door wide open. The cops just stared, fear in their eyes.

"Pa-ul," I kept calling. "Pa-ul." The bedroom door was closed. I opened it, afraid of what I would see.

Paul was in bed. Snoring. I turned on the light and said his name firmly.

He woke up with a start and sat up, fast, completely confused. I asked him, "Are you okay?"

"Yes," he said. "What . . . what are you doing here?"

"Well, Billy called me and told me he stabbed you to death."

"Oh gosh," he said.

"I felt like I should check."

"No, I'm just getting a nap between work."

I turned to see Billy smiling. He clapped his hands together. "Fooled you!"

"Billy, don't ever do that again," I said. "I'm very sick, and I don't want you to get it."

I waved to Allison as I walked past the cops. Her face was pressed to the car window, and I could see her big eyes relax into a face that conveyed she knew all along that I would be fine. I wondered if it was real. I was fifty-fifty on that one too.

"False alarm," I said to the cops. "Sorry to put you through the trouble of doing absolutely nothing."

I got in the car. "It's fine," I said. "Billy was making up stories." I turned the ignition. "Never a dull moment," I said.

"Nope," she answered.

*   *   *

I invited Mitch to spend Thanksgiving with us, saying it would be nice if he brought his mother too. He was still Mr. Saturday Night, but I liked him enough that I had made a rule with all my guys that I was out of pocket from four o'clock on Saturday afternoon until Sunday morning. Those were the only hours I would be unavailable.

Mitch made it easy to stick to that. He employed my guys and went with me to the drag shows every two weeks. But he was always a plus-one, never a partner. If someone who he employed got too sick to work or died, he didn't show any sadness. It was the loss of a good worker, but predictable. "Well, you knew that was going to happen," he said once, when I was gutted to lose someone.

He called me Thanksgiving morning to say they weren't coming. I had already cooked more than enough for four people. I'd even set the table.

"Really?" I asked.

"Yeah, we can't make it," he said.

"Okay," I said, in a way that said it was not okay. But Mitch was so literal he thought it was. I hung up the phone and told Allison that Mitch wasn't coming after all. Maybe it was just too domestic for him. Too much like a real relationship.

The table now looked silly with its fine linen tablecloth, inherited from my grandmother. I'd ironed it to make it perfect. I'd set out two candlesticks, orange and black, to look festive. I planned on bringing the leftovers around to my guys tonight and tomorrow, but there was something about four place settings that makes you want to fill them. I thought about who was well enough to come over and would be willing to on short notice. Bonnie would know she was a replacement and would resent it, so she was out. I didn't want to intrude on Billy and Paul, because Paul took holidays seriously, and I knew he would end up hosting us.

I decided to go to the rooming house to get Angel and Carlos, the tree planters. Antonio, who lived with them, was in the hospital with pneumonia, so it would just be them. I'd purchased a Spanish dictionary, so when I went over I was able to ask them if they wanted to come over to eat Thanksgiving dinner with us. I stumbled through "La cena de Thanksgiving," but they were in. We all drove back to the house to find our cat FooFoo lying in the middle of the table like a turkey. He was luxuriating in a slash of sunlight through the window.

I didn't let them know I'd been stood up for Thanksgiving, but this was somehow better anyway, sharing this most American of meals with two men who probably missed the meals they had with their families in Mexico. I got out my little translation book to say a prayer. I stumbled, and Carlos helped me.

"*Gracias por todo*," he said. Thank you for everything.

"That covers it," I said. We ate and ate, and Angel sang to me and Allison, there and on the entire way back to the rooming house.

Chapter Thirty

The Monday after Thanksgiving was Billy's twenty-fourth birthday. He was having a party at Our House that night, but he had Allison over that afternoon so they could have time together. They picked her up at school, and I quietly let myself in to find Billy sitting up on the couch, two blankets lightly draped around him like he was a sultan. Paul sat next to Billy, holding his hand. Allison was sitting on the floor, doing her math homework on the coffee table. I stood there just a minute before saying hello and took a picture in my mind. These were the three people I loved most in the whole wide world. My family.

"Happy birthday," I said.

They all kind of perked up for a second, and I could tell there was news. Billy and Allison spoke over each other.

"Ms. Ingersoll . . ."

"Allie's teacher . . ."

Allison grinned and let Billy take the spotlight.

"I have been asked to come speak to Allie's class."

"About HIV?"

"Well, I think I have other things to talk about, but yes. Life."

She wanted him to come in the following Monday. It gave Billy a recharge for the week. His actions had been erratic, but he cared about two things: Allison and being the center of attention. This was a *performance*, and any time he got to do one he could perform on cue.

I checked with Ms. Ingersoll to make sure this wasn't just something Allison had cooked up. I really liked her as a teacher. She was new to the school, high energy, and eager to talk about the whole world with Allison's class, not just the one outside their window. She was the only person of color at St. John the Baptist Catholic School. She confirmed that she had asked Allison if Billy could come in and talk to the kids about AIDS.

"Gosh, I can't believe you're so open to talking about this," I said.

"Fifth grade," she said, trailing off. "This message is crucial." Talking to her gave me hope. The deal was that they would talk about HIV on a fifth-grade level the kids could understand but without getting into any kind of sex talk.

The day of, Billy was already in performance mode as we entered the school, like it was a theater. There was an energy coming off of him that I had missed lately. He wore a collared shirt and sweater, one that Paul had just bought him for his birthday. He sat in a chair in the front of the room, while I stood in back with Ms. Ingersoll. There were a few empty desks. Some of the kids' parents didn't want him in the classroom, so they'd held their sons and daughters out that day.

"Does anyone here know someone with HIV?" Billy asked.

Allison's hand shot up. I smiled and had to shake my head in wonder.

"Well, now you all do," he said. "My name is Billy, and I have HIV. HIV is the virus that causes AIDS, which can make you really, really sick. So, show of hands, who here knows someone with HIV?"

The kids all raised their hands, some slower than others. Everyone looked around. Billy looked right at Allison and smiled. This was for her.

"Okay, so I'm going to leave it to the grown-ups to talk to you about how you get HIV, but I can tell how you *can't* get HIV. You can't get HIV by breathing the air around someone. And you can't get it by giving someone a hug. We all need hugs." He talked about how you can't tell if someone has HIV just by looking at them, so the main thing was to be nice to everyone.

A boy in the back raised his hand. "Are you going to die?"

I remembered again why I am so selective in liking kids. I liked mine. That was it. But Billy smiled as if he'd been waiting for the question. The dying don't mind talking about dying; it's the living that can't stand it.

"There is a song I love called 'I Will Survive,'" he said. "Y'all know that song? I sing it, and I change the words to 'We Will Survive,'" he said. "As long as we know how to love, we know we're still alive. Love is really important for living. Now, how old are y'all? Thirty-six? Fifteen? What?"

Laughter and screams of "No" and "Ten!" filled the air. He was working that crowd.

"Oh, *ten!*" said Billy. "Good age. I remember ten. It was fun, but sometimes I felt lonely. Does anyone here ever feel lonely?"

No one said anything, but I sure nodded.

"I want you to remember," said Billy, "that no matter how lonely you feel, there is always someone who wants to help. Sometimes it's a stranger."

He looked up and smiled at me. I wanted to look away, because I knew I was about to cry. But this time I allowed the tears to fall.

"Sometimes it's just you," he said. And he looked right at Allison. "If you're ever lonely, you can be a friend to yourself and take care of yourself, just like you take care of a friend. You need to be as good to yourself as you would be to a friend. A *best* friend."

I tried to picture a time when Billy wouldn't be here, and I couldn't.

Billy thanked the class for having him, and Ms. Ingersoll wiped her eyes before stepping to the front of the room to put an arm around him. "Let's thank Allison's friend Billy for coming in," she said. The kids clapped, and Billy closed his eyes, drinking in the applause like Tinkerbell.

At pickup the next day, Allison had a huge bundle of construction-paper cards her classmates had made for Billy. We brought them right over to his house and sat down on either side of him.

"The reviews are in," I joked, as Allison placed the pile on his lap. Kids had cut out Christmas trees and wreaths, pasted them onto the cards, and written personal messages inside. He opened each one, and we took turns reading them aloud.

"Dear Billy, I hope you don't get sicker." He paused, his voice catching just for a second. "And I hope you have a happy New Year. I like football, especially the 49ers and the quarterback Joe Montana. Love, Leonardo."

"My name is Chris," I read. "How are you feeling? I hope you feel better, I might come see you soon. Your friend, Chris."

Two dozen messages of love like that. A girl had made a small envelope packet and glued it in the card. "Open this pouch for lots of joy," she wrote. She'd cut out a dozen little red and white paper snowflakes. Billy gathered them in one hand, raised it high, and sprinkled joy down on the three of us.

Billy's family came to visit him at Christmas. They had never met Paul or been to their home in the whole time they had been together. I popped in just for a second to bring some food by, but I left quickly. Billy's mother was strong, someone who was used to being the most beautiful woman in the room. She looked like an aged Elizabeth Taylor: dark hair, with red lipstick, impeccable makeup, and no need to ever share a stage. She and her husband were educated, and she was very aware that she needed to present a certain prestige to the world by always looking expensive and keeping an immaculate home. I could see Billy learning the power of glamour at her knee. His sweetness came from his father, a meek, quiet man who was used to finding a corner to stand in, holding his white cowboy hat down in front of him. Billy had a younger brother he was devoted to and missed dearly, plus two sisters, one nice and one wicked.

Paul said Billy's mother couldn't hide her surprise at how nice their home was. Craning her head around to take everything in. "This is a regular house," she said, meaning a house like hers. Nice dishes in the cabinet; no chains hanging from the ceiling.

The visit devolved quickly. As Billy sat, a shadow of who he had been, the family was loose in the house. Paul, a collector of beautiful things, could see the look of people shopping an estate sale. They got to picking things up to see the label beneath. "Oh, whose was this?" they asked. "And this. Who bought this?"

"Where's his clothes?" the wicked sister asked. Billy had that full walk-in closet of expensive gowns and clothes that were luxurious even just for the aura he left on them. She walked in, seeming like a thief in the temple, as if clutching a golden key taken from the hand of her dying brother. That was too far for Paul, who politely cut the visit short.

"There was just no compassion at all," said Paul, genuinely surprised.

I admired Paul's ability to still be shocked.

Chapter Thirty-One

"Misty, I need a dress," I said. It was after a Saturday night show, and Miss Misty McCall was still in her beaded gown. She had done Cher's "Save Up All Your Tears," and I was glad she had gotten so many dollars. It's always good to have someone in a good mood when you need a favor.

"What's the occasion?"

"The Inaugural Ball," I said, and we laughed together, the brown bangs of her wig shaking. Bill Clinton had invited me to attend the January 20, 1993, Arkansas ball at the DC Convention Center. "I was wondering if I could buy a gown from your drag closet. I have to pass with all these fancy people. And people who think they're fancy."

"I can help you," she said. "Can you come by on Monday?"

"With bells on," I said.

Misty lived out in the woods in a double-wide mobile home, and she had taken the wall out between two bedrooms to make her drag closet. All those loser dresses bought cheap from the fed-up dads of Miss Texas and Miss Arkansas hopefuls filled it. The place was like a showroom, with a top row devoted to wigs and hairpieces, tiaras set out on velvet cloth like crown jewels. Then there were all these dresses, separated not by color but by feel and theme. There was a gorgeous scent, one you couldn't place, because it was a mix of all the perfumes worn with the gowns. I had walked into beauty.

"That's the Cher wing," I said, seeing a mix of Bob Mackie peeka-boo gowns segueing into the leather and dark straps of her recent body of work.

"Yes," she said, "and here are some showstoppers. What's the look you're going for?"

"Oh," I said. "Sophisticated. Smart." I thought this would be an opportunity to connect with other people involved in AIDS. "A high neck. Sleeves—I know it'll be cold."

"Hmm," she said. She had me try on different looks, and I felt like Cinderella with her fairy godmother. Bippity, boppity, boo. Then I saw all these beaded gowns in neat piles on the floor.

"Why are they all on the floor?" I asked.

"You *never* hang a beaded gown," Misty said, ever so proper. "Because it rips at the seams." The weight of its beauty will tear it apart.

I was drawn to those, and she helped me into a beaded dress of such a pale salmon it was almost cream. It had a jewel neckline, and golden beaded designs that I first mistook for stars, then realized they were stargazer lilies. It was elegant and that perfect Southern word: *appropriate*.

"That's it," said Misty.

"It is, isn't it?" I said, turning in the spotless three-way mirror. We hugged.

"How much would it be?" I asked.

She paused. I saw her doing the math of discounting it down for me. "Two hundred dollars?"

"That's very generous, Misty." This had to be a six-thousand-dollar gown.

"You're very generous, Ruth."

"I will make you proud, I swear."

"Is Mitch taking you?"

"No," I said, trying to hide my real disappointment with a joke. "I think he thinks if he puts on a tuxedo it'll turn into a wedding."

"I can't believe that," she said. "What a fool."

"I know," I said. "But I love him, so who's the fool?"

President Clinton mentioned AIDS in his inaugural address, calling it a world crisis. It was a shot in the arm for me. I was proud that I had invested so much time in my letters to him through the years. How many men did he know only through the pages of my desperate letters. Now, I hoped, we would see change.

When I entered the ball that night, I immediately got flagged by a reporter. All the networks were doing live setups, trying to get a feel for the change in the air.

"Oh, oh, your dress," said a newscaster about my age. "Here, turn around. Where did you get this dress?"

"I bought it from a drag queen for two hundred dollars. Miss Misty McCall—"

"Wait a minute, I don't think we can say 'drag queen' on the air."

She listened on her earpiece. "No, sorry, we can't say 'drag queen' on the air, but can we get you live? Just go ahead and turn around for us."

It was a magical night, and I came home with pictures to develop to show Misty. "I passed with all of them," I told her. "*W* magazine asked me to pose for them! I was the best dressed there, thanks to you."

Allison and I sent the president peony bulbs to remind him of Hot Springs. He wrote back a note, thanking us. "I've asked the gardener to plant them right outside the Oval Office. They bring back such good memories."

I knew he had a photo of Ricky Ray in his office. Ricky was fifteen and was supposed to go to the inauguration but had died in December. He and his two younger brothers had hemophilia and contracted HIV from blood products before they were eight years old. *Life* magazine did an article on them, and it rang true for me, because it showed that these kids' biggest problem wasn't a disease, it was dealing with awful people. In 1986, their school in Arcadia,

Florida, kicked them out. A group formed, Citizens Against AIDS—which sounds promising, but its sole goal was preventing the Ray boys from attending school.

The Ray family got a court order after a year of homeschooling, forcing the school to let the kids back in. Ricky was ten that first day back, and he got beat up by two kids at recess. He couldn't fight back because it would violate the court order. By the end of the week, it got better, so the Ray kids were going to tough it out. So someone burned their house down. They fled to another town, and Citizens Against AIDS showed up to do an "informational session" on their first day at that school—about what a danger these children were.

Now, Ricky Ray was dead. He faced the same hate my guys did. If President Clinton saw him in a photo every day, I also wanted him to look out on those peonies and remember my guys too.

Later, when Misty was dying, Norman called me for help. "You've gotta come up here and see her," he said. "We've gotta get some things figured out for her." One of the sad truths was that Norman was a kingpin in the gay community, able to make miracles happen, but as a gay man, he had little power at a hospital. It astonished me that someone so powerful could be dismissed by a doctor or nurse.

I went up to Little Rock, and I knocked on the door of Misty's room. Two men answered the door, but they wouldn't let me in. I guess I looked like a church lady, and they didn't know me. I knocked again. "Norman sent me," I said.

Saying "Norman" worked like "open sesame." They let me in but said I was wasting my time. "He hasn't talked to anybody in five days."

I went to Misty's bed and saw that edema had made her arms and legs horribly swollen. "Rick, Rick, I'm here," I said, using Misty's given name. "It's me." The guys hovered, a look of "I told you so" all over their faces.

Then I said, "Misty, darling, it's me. It's Ruthie."

Misty opened her eyes and started sobbing, but she didn't have any tears because they were all collected in her arms and legs—that's where the fluid was. She was gurgling because her lungs had filled up with fluid. I lifted one of her arms to put it around my neck, so she could hug me and I could hug her.

"I'm here now," I said. "We're going to get you more comfortable."

I went out to the nurses' station. "Your patient is smothering to death. Can you come in and suction?"

"We're not gonna suction him," said the nurse. "He's dying. We're not gonna touch him."

"You're not gonna let your patient drown to death, are you?"

"Well, we're not gonna suction him. He has AIDS. It's a waste of time."

"I tell you what," I said. "Why don't you call the Suction Fairy and have her leave a suction kit laying around, and I'll do the suction." A nurse in the background heard me, and she left a kit out, right by Misty's door.

I told Misty that I was going to suction her. "It's going to be uncomfortable, but it will make it easier to breathe," I said, draping a towel below her neck. I sent the two guys out, because I knew this would be too much for them to witness.

As I inserted the suction tube, I had a flashback to doing this for Daddy when I was a little girl. I couldn't believe how much I had to do at such a young age. The smell now was horrible, and I began to gag. The kind of gagging where you have tears in your eyes and you can't talk because you're going to throw up.

We took a break, and I hurried out of the room and into the hall to breathe. Misty's friends saw me, and they burst into tears.

"Oh my God," one said, "he's *dead.*" I couldn't talk for fear of vomiting, and I tried to wave him off, like, "No, he's not dead." I finally got where I was able to talk. "No, he's not dead. I'm gagging from doing this."

"Oh," the other one said, so nonchalant. "Okay."

I went back in to finish suctioning Misty, and when it was over, I did the same thing again, excusing myself to gag outside. And *they* did the same thing, shrieking he was dead. And I gave them this look with attitude, shaking my head.

"Oh," said the nonchalant one. "Good."

Now Misty could talk, though she still sounded like she was gurgling. But she wanted to talk to her mother. We called her and got the answering machine, and I left a message. And we called again later, and I left a message. And we called again later. And I thought, *Well here's the deal. She needs to know.*

This time I put the phone up to Misty so she could leave the message. She begged her mother to come see her. She told her she was going to die.

I knew she was right. Misty died the next day. I called her mother again, knowing the number by heart from dialing it so much. I needed to get permission to cremate her. "You've got to call me back," I said. "You don't have to do anything, but you've got to sign the papers."

When she finally called me back, she said she'd had to wait until her husband, Misty's stepfather, had left. They had been home when her son called, and he wouldn't let her pick up the phone. They both had to sit there listening to Misty beg on the answering machine.

"I am so sorry," I said. I told her that we were having a graveside ceremony at Files.

"Can I come?" she asked.

"Well, certainly," I said. People knew she hadn't gone to see Misty, and I worried about how they might treat her. Misty's mother parked across the street from Files Cemetery and came out of the car along with Misty's sister. I went over to greet them and saw the crosses hanging from their necks. When people saw Misty's sister, even if they thought the family had something coming to them, it evaporated in an instant—because the sister looked exactly like Misty in drag. *Exactly*. Everyone was so kind and gracious to them, because it was like Misty was there with them again.

We buried Misty with a beautiful headstone Norman paid for. Misty may have been a Little Rock queen, but Hot Springs welcomed her with an open heart.

Chapter Thirty-Two

I drove Angel to Files Cemetery on a beautiful February afternoon. It was strangely warm for being around Valentine's Day, the temperature up in the sixties. He was calm in the car, not singing to me like usual. He had been sick again, this time with spinal meningitis that would have gone undiagnosed if I hadn't insisted that he was worth giving a spinal tap to.

It had taken a lot out of him, and I knew his end was coming. I had found a nursing home that would take him, and I think we both knew that he would not leave there. I wanted him to be able to choose where he would go in Files when it came time to bury him.

I carried my Spanish dictionary with me as we entered the gate, but we didn't need words. He walked everywhere, sometimes standing still for a moment and looking around. Then he'd move again. I sometimes told him the names of people as he approached them. Midway through the cemetery he stopped. He swiveled his whole body in place, taking in the view from that exact point.

"*Aquí*," he said.

"*Aquí*," I said. "Okay. *Gracias*."

He took my hand, and we walked to the car. He sighed, and I drove him back to the nursing home. Of all my guys, it was hardest to imagine him staying in one place, even in death. Angel remained my slippery guy, always keeping me guessing. Even in the nursing home, he managed to confound me. One day I didn't visit him at the usual time—there was always some emergency—and he got angry.

"He's up on the roof," said one of the administrators once he got a hold of me. "Climbed a ladder, and now he's threatening to jump."

"It's one story," I said.

"Well, he's sayin' he's gonna jump," he said. "Can you get over here?"

I did, and Angel was up there, yelling at me in Spanish. I found someone who worked at the home who spoke Spanish. I asked him to apologize to Angel for me and to say I got the point, so please come down.

When Angel refused, I got mad. "Hold on, one second," I said. I went back in to borrow the phone to call my friend Dub at Hot Springs Funeral Home.

"Can you do me a big favor and come by the nursing home?"

"Well, yeah," he said, and then got formal. "You have someone who needs—"

"No, nobody's dead." I said. "But I need you to drive the hearse, okay?"

I went back out to Angel and the interpreter. "Okay, Angel, go ahead and jump," I said. The interpreter looked at me like I was crazy. "No, you say it exactly how I say it, please. Angel, it's not nice what you're doing, but sure, jump. One story isn't gonna kill you."

Angel was shocked and looked at the interpreter, who nodded and shrugged, as if to say, "Yeah, that's what this crazy woman is saying." This went on for a while, Angel and me bluffing each other, and then Dub pulled in to the parking lot in the empty hearse.

"Okay, jump now, the hearse is here. I don't know how long we have it for." Now Angel and the translator were both shocked. "Or maybe you'll break your neck and end up in there paralyzed in a bed and not be able to move. I don't know."

Dub got out to look at the scene, and I yelled to him, "Just a second, he's deciding." Angel gave me an angry look, then his face dissolved into a grin and then a smile. He laughed, his scattershot cackle, and gave me a look that told me I won.

He started to come down the ladder, and I gave Dub a wave of thanks before I hugged Angel. Over his shoulder I said to the interpreter, "Please tell him not to try to out-bluff me ever again."

Angel hung on, but I knew how close he was to dying because his love song became just a whisper. Angel, my escape artist, became weaker, until he finally slipped away from me in the night. They called me to say he was gone. "It's just like you to leave when I'm not looking," I said, when I went to care for his body.

We buried him where he asked me to. And soon after, Antonio joined him there and then Carlos. They'd asked to be buried with Angel, trusting he would never have settled in one spot if it wasn't the best choice.

Billy's doctor prescribed pulmonary treatments to prevent him from getting pneumocystis pneumonia, but the medical center wouldn't let him do it on-site. They acted like they were doing him a favor, doing the treatments at his home with a nurse, but it seemed clear they didn't want someone with AIDS hanging around the office for three hours.

A breathing therapist came to the house, gloved up in a space suit, like the old days. She made it clear to Paul that she was the supervisor of this whole group that did this, and that none of the other nurses would come. So, as the boss, she *had* to do this. She sat for three hours on the edge of her seat, afraid to touch anything at all. The treatment was brutal; it involved filling his lungs with medicine and then him coughing his guts up for another two hours afterward.

She made no conversation while it was going on, offered no words of compassion. It was hard enough for Billy, but to have someone there who treated him like he was toxic made it that much worse.

Paul, ever the host, greeted her twice a week. "Would you like some coffee?"

"No."

Second week: "Would you like some coffee?"

"No."

Third week: "Would you like some coffee?"

She paused. "Yeah, yeah, I would. I *would* like some coffee."

Paul reenacted the moment for me at the bar. The way she surprised herself. "You could see it going through her mind like, 'I probably shouldn't. I'll probably get AIDS. But I want some coffee.'"

Paul said it progressed from there, her care of Billy going from, "Here, stick this in your mouth," to touching his back and saying, "It'll be okay." For me, that should have been the bare minimum, but they were starving for kindness.

In the springtime, I began to prepare Paul for what was to come. I gave him information as he needed it about what to expect. Billy now needed round-the-clock help, I told him, and it would come from friends, and Paul should accept their help.

"Now you'll have these groups of people," I said, "that will come and help you, and it will be surprising who it is. And you'll also have sightseers."

"Well, what's sightseers?" he asked.

"Those are people who just wanna come over and see what's going on. Then you'll have the people that you really thought would be by your side and really help you. Well, some of them will be gone. That's okay, because I know you will be supported."

There were some close friends who couldn't handle it, so I was glad I'd warned Paul. But there were plenty of people who came and stayed nights with Billy while Paul worked at the bar. So many men and women came and helped, but Billy had his favorites. One was Pancho, a Mexican man from El Paso. Paul and Billy hadn't known him that well, but Pancho and Billy discovered that they both knew a lot of old gospel songs, like "In the Garden." They would sit for hours, singing softly and reverently.

Of all the caregivers, Dusty seemed the most dependable. People had been mean to Dusty years before, when he first came to town, but Paul had taken him under his wing and got him started in drag. He had done quite well for himself, but the general consensus was that Dusty was in love with Paul. Paul was the only one who didn't see it. Paul was tired and just happy someone was coming over to cook that night. When the washer was broken and Dusty took their laundry to have it cleaned, Paul thought it was an act of kindness. Billy thought it was an audition for the coveted role of Mrs. Paul Wineland.

I often came over to find Dusty there. Billy whispered, "This one is Eve Harrington, mark my words." He lapsed into the cadence of Bette Davis's Margo Channing in *All about Eve.* "Waiting in the wings."

I didn't tell Billy that Dusty had indeed confessed his love for Paul one teary night at the bar. He said that he even wished he had AIDS, so that he could be as loved by Paul as Billy was. I told him that would be a lousy way to get a boyfriend, but I also knew he didn't have a chance with Paul. That didn't matter right now, anyway. I had enough drama, being on two tracks: one where my best friend was dying, and the other where I was helping the community prepare for it.

Even Mother Superior, who tried so hard to make everyone think he was an ogre, was wonderful. There were things you could never say to him, but Billy could say anything. When Billy regressed, it was like he'd taken truth serum. Mother, so big as Billy got frailer and frailer, would hold him in his arms like a baby. One time, Billy looked in Mother's eyes and said, "Girl, you're really good, you know. If you had lost a hundred . . ."—he paused—". . . a hundred fifty pounds in your day, you could have been Miss America." It was something the healthy Billy never would have said, and if anybody else had said that, Mother would have thrown them in the lake.

"Girl, you are so hateful," Mother said, in a soft voice suffused with love and kindness. "I can't believe you talk to your mother like that."

I was right that there would be sightseers. Mother brought over a friend, Scott, a big guy who had a whiny voice. He hadn't seen Billy since he got sick, and when he saw how thin he'd become, Scott went, "Eww."

Billy made a matching face, "*Eww.*"

And Scott said it again. That was it for Mother, who literally dragged him out and threw him off the porch. "I knew I should never have let you in here, making an ass of yourself. Get off this porch and get in the car."

Allison was right there, holding Billy's hand. She was family now to him and all the queens who loved Billy. They mentored her, offering her advice on how to hold her head up high when she was being bullied. She repeated one piece of wisdom over and over: "Be smart, be brave, tell the truth, and don't take any shit." Billy recalled a line he'd heard that he wanted her to commit to memory. We later traced it back to Elsie de Wolfe, the first American interior designer, but then it was pure Billy: "Be pretty if you can, witty if you must, and gracious if it kills you."

Billy was preparing to go. He began to ask Paul to take him home. "Call my mother," he'd say. "I want to go home. I want to go home."

Paul didn't think Billy's family was equipped to care for him, even if they wanted to, but he always did as Billy wished. Paul thought maybe Billy could spend a weekend there. Billy would have that time, and that's all he felt they could handle. But there was always a reason he couldn't come, Paul told me. "His mother says, 'Well, I've got this thing,' and 'I've got that.' And 'It's not a good weekend.'"

He finally went one time. They came down to pick Billy up on Friday, and Paul loaded him into their car.

His mother called Paul first thing Saturday morning. Paul had to drive back and pick him up. "She had him waiting at the front door with his bag. There waiting for me." When Paul asked if they wanted to try again, she just said, "You know, I've got other kids, and I just can't handle him up here."

Billy's mother would sometimes call me to check up on things. "Just how much longer is this going to go on?" she asked me. "We have a life we have to live. How much longer do we have to put up with this?"

Not much longer, I thought but did not tell her.

Billy would gather up the strength to perform at the drag nights, and he would wear a red ribbon pinned to whatever he was wearing. One night he wanted to wear the red strapless Victor Costa dress he'd promised me. We added invisible straps, and it was still falling off of him. So he made do, wearing smaller and smaller dress sizes but becoming transcendent as soon as he hit the stage.

Someone confronted Paul after a show. "Why do you let him do shows?"

"Because he wants to do a show," said Paul.

"But why would you let him come down here when he looks like that?"

Paul never showed anger, but he did then, slamming his fist down on the bar. "He has *x* amount of days left. If he wants to do a show, let him do a show. His fans don't care, his friends don't care. Who is it hurting?"

When it came time for Billy's last show, I don't know if he knew it was the final one. Paul and I knew it had to be. His health was declining so fast, there was just no way he could keep performing. There would be no way he could even leave the *house*.

When Billy came out that night, the applause wouldn't stop. The music hadn't even started, and people leapt to their feet, trying to outdo each other to show their love. He didn't smile, just stood there taking it in. He wore a black dress that looked so expensive, the long hair of his wig falling on his thin shoulders. Finally, someone placed the needle on the record. As soon as people heard the first notes of Whitney Houston's voice, the room fell into a reverent hush. "If . . . I . . . should stay . . ." People sat down, like we were at church. I stopped breathing and didn't start again until I had to take a huge gasp.

Billy moved around the stage, sometimes a step or two behind the music. Two or three times he tripped a bit, but somebody would steady him and give him twenty dollars. It just made us more determined to show our adoration, like we were willing him to make it. Even if we weren't near him, we would all lean forward if he started to stumble, each of us ready to jump across the room so we could be the one to catch him. The one to save him as he fell into our arms.

At the point where Whitney really belts it, the audience got up and started bringing their tributes of dollars directly to him. When his hands were too full, people simply threw wads of money onto the stage. The other queens had come from backstage to watch him, and some helped gather the money from the ground for him. Everyone was crying, except for Billy.

The song ended, but people wouldn't let him go. It was a blur after that; he had to do four more songs before they let him leave the stage. Two lines of people formed on either side of the stage, so he wouldn't have to move around. We all knew this was goodbye, and we were giving him his flowers now, while he could see how much he meant to all of us.

Finally, we let him leave. As the queens escorted him backstage, he turned and smiled. Every person in there thought that smile was just for them.

Chapter Thirty-Three

I brought Allison with me to see Billy after school on the first Monday of May. He was down to sixty-five pounds, and you could see every bone of his body. He was conscious but slept much of the time. A nurse was there with him. I had gotten him home care, the first nurses I found who would willingly take care of an AIDS patient in his home, so they were a godsend. And even though they were frightened, they listened to me. They had asked me a few questions, and I told them the truth. "You're gonna be scared the first few times, and then you'll realize there's nothing to be afraid of." They took turns with him during the day, administering medicine and keeping him comfortable. They were wonderful, and they of course fell in love with Billy.

Paul went into the kitchen to make coffee, and I joined him, leaving Allison with Billy. She held his hand and told him about her day. Allison never talked to me about her school day, but at ten she had learned from her mother how important it is for the dying to hear about the world beyond the room they are in.

"How are *you* doing?" I asked Paul.

He paused, as if the question had not occurred to him.

"Last night, I couldn't get Billy to take a bath," he said, quietly, so it was just us who could hear. "He didn't want to, so I said I would just, uh, rinse him in the shower. I carried him, and he felt so fragile I was afraid I was going to break his bones. I was afraid he was gonna fall apart in my hands. I just took him in my arms and took him into the shower . . ."

Paul's eyes began to well up. I had never seen him cry. He froze for probably five seconds, but it felt like an eternity. "I tried to wash him off, and about halfway through he went completely limp. I thought . . . I thought he died in my arms."

I walked over to lightly touch Paul's arm. "I just rinsed him off as good as I could and brought him to bed. And I saw he was breathing."

"Paul," I said, "you don't have to bathe him like that anymore. He can do sponge baths, okay? The nurses will do a wonderful job."

He nodded. I took a breath. "It's getting close," I said. "You know it's getting close."

We went back in, and the nurse said it was time for his CMV medicine. He was taking it by IV at that point. She quietly searched his arms for a vein but gave up. She moved to his legs and found one down by his ankle. She started to prep the area, when I spoke up.

"Stop," I said to her quietly. "Just one second." I raised my voice just a little. "Billy, honey, how long do you think you're gonna live?"

"Not long," he said.

"Then we're not going to go through this anymore," I said. "We're not going to do it. If you go blind, you go blind."

He nodded. The nurse started to cry. She had fallen for him like all of us.

Once he was off that medicine, Billy slowly emerged from being so childlike and started to come back to being the man we had known. It happened around the time Paul stopped shaving him, because it was too much to put him through even that, and Billy didn't care. His beard grew in dark, and it was amazing to have some of the old Billy back, if so much weaker. He was able to have conversations with people again, quiet and slow but meaningful.

We watched *Dark Victory* together, Billy murmuring some of Bette Davis's lines with her. It was real medicine, watching her as Judith, who was lied to that her brain surgery was a success, and everyone but her knew she was going to die. When she realizes, there is comfort there, and Billy said the words with passion: "What we have now can't be destroyed. That's our victory—our victory over the dark. It's a victory because we're not afraid."

Then that coherence began to slip away too. In mid-May, Paul told me Billy's mother called. "Is he still alive?" she asked him, her voice that of a Southern belle.

"Well, yeah, I would call you."

"You know that when he dies that you need to put pennies on his eyes. Because if you don't close his eyes and put pennies on them, they won't be able to close his eyes for the funeral."

Paul said nothing. She continued. "And make sure you straighten all his limbs out. Because they'll have to break his bones if you don't."

Paul, sweet, graceful Paul, thanked her for the advice.

On May 19, a Wednesday, I went over in the morning. Billy was in bed, moving to a fetal position. I knew what this meant but refused to fully understand it at the same time. He had been in and out of consciousness and was cold despite the blankets on him. I got into the bed to spoon him and keep him warm.

"Billy, I love you with all my heart," I said. "You have always known that you are special, I know. And you are. I am so thankful that you took me into your life. Sometimes I feel like Dorothy in Oz—my whole world went Technicolor the moment I saw you."

"I love you, Ruthie," he said softly.

He slept, and I continued holding him. We breathed in unison, a slow rhythm that I committed to memory, like a song I could remember for the rest of my life.

Billy took his last breath the next day at four o'clock in the afternoon. Paul was with him, holding his hand.

Paul called me. "Billy just died," he said. It seemed so bizarre that something so important, so monumental had happened and I didn't know. "It just happened," said Paul. "I didn't expect it. He was just gone."

I went over, leaning forward at the wheel and driving as fast as I could. It's strange now, realizing that I thought that maybe Paul was mistaken. That this was just something like a sleep. That I could revive Billy. How many times had I been in this exact scenario, knowing a soul had left a body? And now I couldn't fathom it happening to Billy.

But he was gone. I straightened him in the bed and closed his eyes.

"He knew who he was today," said Paul. "He knew who I was. He hasn't, but today he did. He knew he was loved." He started to cry, and this time he let the tears fall. "He even ate this morning. A little cereal, he hadn't eaten . . . uh, hadn't eaten regular food in a long time. I'm sorry."

"Don't be," I said. "I love you so much, Paul. And I know how much you loved each other. Don't ever be sorry for loving someone so much."

I worried about Allison losing Billy, and later I tried to talk to her. She was quiet, letting me go on. Then she said, simply and with sureness: "I'm relieved for him. He suffered so much." She was on the edge of eleven, and she already knew that it would be selfish to want people to live past the point that they were ready. I nodded, trying to take that in.

I called Mitch to tell him. He came over. "I'm sorry," he said. "I know how much Billy meant to you."

"I'm just so shocked," I said.

He made a face. "Well, this can't be a surprise. We'd known he was dying for months. Longer."

I shook my head because I didn't want him to see how much that hurt me. "I'm just gonna take a bath," I said.

I closed the door and turned on the water full blast. I got in right away, and the water began to envelop me. It was so hot it was almost scalding, but I didn't care. The room filled with mist, and the thunder of the water would hide the sound of my sobbing. I curled my knees up, and my whole body heaved with grief. It took me over, a physical pain so pent up and overwhelming I thought it would kill me.

I slowed my breathing to the rhythm Billy and I shared the night before, hoping that would help. It did not.

"We'll bury him up here," she said. This was Billy's mother. I had called to tell her he was gone. I winced when she said that. I had hoped to bury him in Files. She lived an hour away up north, the very place he had fled. I had only the slightest catch in my voice. "You know he loved it here . . ."

"Nope, our son died of cancer, and he'll be buried up here."

"I would like to come," I said.

She paused a long time. "You can come," she said.

"Well, I appreciate that."

"But I don't want any of those faggots at the funeral."

"Oh, okay," I said.

I clicked the receiver with a long nail to hang up on her. "Fuck you," I said.

When I got the details, I proceeded to call everybody I knew to tell them the plan. "If you can get a day off from work . . ." I said. Most of them worked nights or were too sick to work anyway. I had never really asked them for anything before, and even if I hadn't called in favors, this wasn't for me. They would have done anything for Billy.

The day of the funeral, I led a twenty-two-car caravan of the fiercest queens I knew up to Dover, just northwest of Russellville. I rode in the front of the line with Paul, Allison, and Bonnie, and it felt like I was leading a small army on Highway 7. It's a beautiful drive, going through the forests of the Ouachita mountains, mile after mile of pine tree plantations. They left the trees looking normal along the perimeter so people don't complain, but behind them they were chopping them all down. It was all about keeping up appearances.

I hit my turn signal to make a right into the parking lot of a Quick Stop. I knew they had a bathroom. All the drivers behind me followed suit, and I saw an attendant's face go through four stages of shock as all the queens that had crammed into the cars piled out at one time.

Marshall came up and put his hand on Paul's shoulder. "Girrl, this is *country* right here," he said. "I'm *scurrred.*" This got a laugh out of Paul, and Marshall doubled down once he saw Paul smile. "I bet they get their mail from a covered wagon. I feel like the only chocolate chip in the cookie. I don't know what they're gonna do to us up here. I know they have them meetings up here."

When we finally made it to the funeral home, I could see our entrance terrified everyone. We sat in the back and still took up half the seats. The funeral directors kept talking loudly, huffing that their reputation was ruined. It was bad enough they knew Billy had actually died of AIDS, not cancer. Now this.

Everyone was staring at Billy's mother, who refused to acknowledge us. She was dressed like this was a funeral on *Dynasty.* The amount of time she must have spent on her hair and makeup.

As each of us went up to see Billy in his casket, it began to pour outside. You could hear it on the roof. I knew that it wouldn't occur to Billy's family to let Paul have a moment alone with Billy before moving him to the cemetery. It was way out, probably an hour's drive, and most everyone we came with was going to go back to Hot Springs after the funeral home.

"Paul," I said quietly, "just sit in your chair until everyone's gone."

I went to the main funeral director, who was by the door, probably watching the queens to make sure they didn't walk out with anything. "I have a man here who was very close to Billy," I said. "He'd like some time alone with him after the viewing."

"We can't do that."

"What do you mean?"

"That's for family only."

I dropped politeness.

"He's more family to that young man than his family ever was."

"We would have to ask the family."

I almost grabbed the lapel of that funeral director's jacket. "Come on," I said. "*We* will do that then." I dragged him through the funeral home, to the back door, and I looked right at Billy's mother. "Tell him that it's okay for Paul to spend time with Billy."

She looked at me, and I wasn't sure if it was shock or just fear on her face. "Oh, well," she stammered. "I guess."

"See?" I said to him.

People started to leave, and Bonnie and Allison took a ride back with the queens, so Allison could go back to school. After the last visitor left, I went over to Paul. "I've talked to everyone," I said. "This is your time. Take as long as you want. I'll be outside when you're ready."

I stood outside the parlor with the funeral director as Paul had a private moment with Billy.

"How long is this gonna take?" the funeral director asked me.

I looked away. He wanted me to know he thought I was getting away with something wrong. I thought about the time Billy was sick and said he wanted strawberries. How Paul asked him, "Do you want them cold or room temperature? Cooked down or raw? Narrow it down, because whatever you want, I'll get it for you." Anything Billy wanted, Paul got, whatever it took. And this pathetic excuse of a man had no idea what that kind of devotion meant, and he didn't deserve an answer. The denial of real love—*that* was the perversion.

When it came time for us to go out to the cemetery, it was just the immediate family and Paul and me. It was pouring down rain from the thunderstorm, and we could barely see where we were driving. Still, the cemetery was in the mountains, and even in the rain I could tell it was the perfect place to leave Billy. If I'd had my pick, this would be it. He could be up here looking down on everyone.

There was a tent set up at Billy's grave, and his family was already in it.

Paul and I had one umbrella between us, and we rushed through the rain to get to the tent.

"This is for family only," Billy's mother said.

We stood there in the rain for a minute, away from them, huddling under Paul's umbrella. And I gritted my teeth.

"Paul," I said slowly. "Throw that umbrella away. We're gonna stand in the pouring rain, and we're gonna get as wet as God wants us to get."

I paused.

"And then we're gonna hug every member of that family, so they know what they did to us. So they can *feel* what they did to us. All of us. Because they are assholes."

Paul put the umbrella down.

"Ruthie, I love you."

"I love you, Paul."

We relaxed into the rain and let it fall on us. Anything for Billy.

Chapter Thirty-Four

Billy's breathing therapist sent Paul a letter. It arrived the day after the funeral, and he read it to me.

> I just wanted to send you a note to say I'm sorry about Billy's passing. I wanted to thank you because I've learned so much from taking care of Billy. I realize you're people just like everybody else. You get up, you have your coffee, your breakfast. You just want someone to love. You have a house just like mine. Everything is just the same. Billy was just a person like anyone else. Hopefully this will make me a better nurse and a better person and be able to take care of the next person.

Paul said he was going to save the letter. "Because I could have went off on her, and been mean, and said 'I don't want you here' and 'I'm gonna sue you.' Instead, all it took was a few weeks of, 'Would you like some coffee?' 'Would you like some coffee?'"

I smiled and thought how wrong she was about Billy being a person like anyone else. He was a comet that burned bright, appearing once in a lifetime to briefly astonish and live on only in memory. But I was glad she was there for Billy and that she had written to Paul.

Paul got another letter right after Billy died, one from the people that owned the house he rented. It said this was his thirty days' notice, that they'd sold the property, and he needed to move out. Mother Superior too.

"They had said I could live here forever," Paul told me. "I've had no reason to believe I wouldn't." He had a few weeks to move out a houseful of memories of Billy and find a place to start over in. His sister had a house on Hobson Avenue, and she had converted her garage into a sort of apartment. I helped him move in, and he gave me the red Victor Costa dress Billy loved so much.

"He wanted you to have this," Paul said. He seemed so sad, and I wasn't sure if it was because he was cramming his whole life into such a little space, or if it even mattered, because nothing mattered without Billy.

I was in a stupor for a long time, distracting myself with the needs of others. There was endless need to bury myself in. I gathered donations to pay for a trip to San Francisco to attend an AIDS conference on social work. It was easier than it used to be but not by much. One bank would ask me what the other had given me. "Well, they gave me three hundred and twenty-five dollars."

"Well, *I'll* give you three hundred and twenty-five dollars," said a rival banker. And then Turf Catering, Johnson's Cleaners . . . I marked each donation in my ledger and wrote my donors' thank-you notes, promising them all they were helping to save lives. Because I believed they were. Even if they just gave me the money to get me to go away.

I arrived at the Sir Francis Drake Hotel in San Francisco on June 23, so excited because there were going to be people there who I could talk to. The theme of the 1993 conference was "Building Bridges—Caring for the Caregiver." I had the packet with me as I walked in. "Dear Colleague," it read, "Welcome to San Francisco." I was a colleague.

I spent the day talking with people, just listening in the hotel's opulent, gilded rooms. Under the bejeweled chandeliers, there was a lot of talk about the international AIDS conference that had just happened in Berlin. People shared bad news about the preliminary results of a study on AZT, showing it didn't prolong the life of symptomless people. I still had hopes for a vaccine and cure, and that was scoffed at. They said it clearly: there was no reason to hope for a vaccine before the end of the twentieth century. We should understand that the best thing we could do was to learn how to cope with never-ending loss. Get used to it and focus on prevention.

I had planned to return to Hot Springs with news of hope.

A man came up to me. He was in a position of authority at the conference, so I was flattered. He said he was intrigued by my work in Arkansas. "I'm having some people up after this," he said. "A small group discussion in my suite. I have a conference room attached. I'd love to hear more about how we can all work together."

"Oh, thank you," I said. "That would be great. It's been really hard. I am just really desperate for help."

He told me the room number, and I went up there at the appointed time. The latch was turned out to keep the door open, so I thought it must have already started. I knocked and let myself in.

"Hello?" I said, Miss Professional.

He was lying on the couch in his robe. It was open, and he was touching himself.

I looked down. What little hope I had saved from that awful day of news left me.

I had dealt with weenie wavers since I was a kid. I'd learned to humiliate them so I wouldn't show how humiliated I was. I'd say, "I'd be too ashamed to have that out in public." Or, "Jesus Christ, is that all you got?" They'd get pissed and run off.

But that night I was just broken. "You're doing this to me at an *AIDS* conference?" I said as he covered himself. "I just lost my best friend. And before him, everyone that I cared for, and I know I will keep losing them. I am doing everything I can to survive this, so I can help people. And I keep losing them. I just keep losing them. And this is what you do."

I turned before he saw me cry, walking backwards down the hall in case he followed me. I hit the elevator button twice, then again, willing it to come faster.

I didn't tell anyone. I was too humiliated. I wanted to be a colleague.

Paul and I sat in lawn chairs in my yard, and usually we could cheer each other up by talking about Billy. It was September 1993, and he had been gone four months. We had started the thing you do, where you collect the stories you'll tell over and over again. You begin to polish the edges of a memory—something funny he said or a specific performance—until the edges are smoothed and the story is comforting.

But that day there was no breaking through Paul's depression. "I'm just miserable," he said. "I'm miserable where I live. I'm sad Billy's gone. I'm just sad about everything."

"Well, let's see what we can do about this," I said. "Let's take the first thing. You don't like where you live. Let me work on it, and I'll call you tomorrow."

I knew an elderly woman who was moving out of her place on Morrison Avenue, closer to where he had lived on Oak Cliff. I brought Paul there. It was the cutest brick house, built in the 1930s, with a gorgeous fireplace. You walked in the door, and it had a big living room, just waiting for you.

"Do you like the house?" she asked Paul.

"I love it, but I don't think I can afford it," he said.

"Well, God told me he wanted you to have this house." God was a better realtor than me. She asked him what he was paying now.

His rent was practically nothing, because it was his sister. He told her the number, and she said, "Well, that's what your rent will be here."

I looked at Paul and asked, "When are you moving in?"

When we got in the car, I laughed. "Now, what else are you sad about?"

Melba put the playing cards down on the tiny yellow checks of her plastic tablecloth. "You asked about Mitch," she said tentative.

"Yes," I said. I could tell something was up. Bonnie was with me; she'd come along with me when I brought Melba a casserole to last her through the week. When Bonnie heard the tone in Melba's voice, she shot me a look that said, "Careful what you wish for."

Melba didn't like to give bad news when she read people's cards. I'd brought some of the guys down to her place, and all she saw was death. She would talk about anything but, then mention they were going to go on a journey. Now, I could see she was choosing her words carefully.

"Uh, I see him with lots of wine and laughing."

"Wine?" Mitch only drank beer. "He barely drinks, period."

"Well, I see all this life," said Melba. "He is having a grand old time."

Bonnie laughed, her guttural chuckle. "Well, how do we get in on all this fun?" I gave her a look. "What?" she said. "I like a good time."

"Just ask him where he's been having this fun," Melba said.

I didn't. I kept telling myself that she had her psychic wires crossed, because Mitch wasn't a drinker. And he wasn't that jolly of a person. That was the dead giveaway.

A woman from town called me a few weeks later. She was one of the most beautiful women in Hot Springs, but she'd been dumped by a guy who turned out to be gay, so she turned on me because I was sort of the ambassador for the gay community. She was *breath-less*, so excited to tell me what she'd heard. She prefaced it by saying, "I hate to tell you this," which always means the person has been waiting for just this very moment.

"I heard that Mitch has a *girlfriend*," she said. "A doctor in Texas."

"Where did you hear that?"

"Well, we had a neighborhood meeting last night," she said.

"And I was on the agenda?"

"No, well, it came up."

"*At the meeting?*"

"After."

"Oh, did someone bring this up under New Business? Where did everybody land on it?"

She started to talk, but I stopped her. "Thank you," I said. "I know it gave you no pleasure to tell me about this gossip. I have to be going, though."

I wasn't going kill the messenger, because I didn't want to waste the ammo. I needed it for Mitch. I drove over to his house, and I let him have it right at the door.

"I hear that you've been on a mission to sow enough oats to qualify for a farm loan."

"Well, hello to you too," he said.

I pushed past him to let myself in. Four years, and I had only ever been here a few times. Our dates always ended at my house. "Some lady in Texas? Did you tell her you'd get engaged someday too?"

He didn't deny it, didn't say anything. I saw his eyes dart to something on a shelf behind me, so I looked. It was a picture of the two of them. They looked so happy. I had never seen him look happy like that, the whole time I knew him.

"Are you kidding me?" I said. "That's her?" She wasn't even pretty. Looked as old as his mother. It all spilled out of him. He'd been driving five and half hours to see her when he told me he was going to Texas for work.

"I hear she's a doctor," I said.

"A chiropractor."

"So not even a *doctor* doctor?" I yelled. "And on top of that she looks like your mother. I can't believe you left me for that."

"Well, can't I keep you both?"

That did it. "Screw you," I said.

I got so mad he ended up picking me up and carrying me out the front door. He slammed it, and I drove right over to Bonnie's.

"Well, Melba was right," I said when she opened the door.

"She usually is," she said. "Come on in."

I was already moving on. I didn't want to give him the satisfaction of a betrayal. I tried to change the subject, just like always. "I was wondering if you could help me with some letters," I said. "I have an idea to get the Downtown Merchants Association to do some stuff for World AIDS Day on December 1. It'll be Billy's birthday, so I want it to—"

"Ruth, I'm sorry about Mitch."

"Who?"

She laughed. I took her hand. "You know, that person, that man I used to date . . . He thinks I am going to come to my senses." She nodded.

"Well, I have," I said. "I would rather be alone than treated that way."

"And you're not alone."

"That's right. I have you. And I have my guys. And I have Allison. But I spent all this time believing everything I heard in church— that I need a husband to be whole, to have a family for Allison. And the whole time I've been creating one."

We were still for about ten seconds, and I sat up. "Now, these letters I want to write. I have to get the tone just right, so I need your brain . . ."

Epilogue

It's a few weeks shy of Thanksgiving 2019, and I am going through a box of old photos and newspaper clippings before I drive down to Hot Springs. Those letters I started writing with Bonnie that day got the Downtown Merchants Association to hold a World AIDS Day event on December 1, 1993. Billy's birthday. I find the full-page ad I tore from the paper, the one I got all three banks in town to pay for and sign their name to. "TIME TO ACT" it reads, with a giant red ribbon.

It was past time, but I was grateful. I also saved the letter to the editor that was sent to the paper after. Under the headline, "AIDS Awareness Overdone," George W. Wilkerson, owner of Paw Paw's Vintage Photos in Hot Springs, wrote that he had just withdrawn his membership in the Downtown Merchants Association, "because of their endorsement of AIDS Awareness Day." George, who I knew, wrote: "AIDS is a behaviorally-transmitted disease and does not need awareness or anything other than saying 'no' to homosexuality or drug use. How much does it cost to teach that?"

It's been nearly thirty years, and so much has changed and yet so little. After we lost Billy, there were many more deaths in the Our House family. I watched survivors become numb as funerals became commonplace. People asked if they could scatter the ashes of lovers at Files, and I said yes, feeling so guilty that I was running from hospital to hospital that I couldn't even be there. I was never able to get a job with an AIDS service organization and continued to do my work alone.

When researchers developed a new class of drugs in late 1995 called protease inhibitors, people started living with AIDS. It took some time for us to get the new medicines, but they came to Arkansas and with them the "Lazarus effect" I'd read about. People who were at death's door were suddenly going to live. This was the day my guys and I had dreamed of. But now people with letters behind their names, some who got into the "AIDS business" for the money, didn't need me to care for the dying anymore. I became functionally obsolete. "Thanks for your service. We'll take it from here." The experts knew best because they were paid to know best.

I made my own job, as a fishing guide, taking tourists out on the water for two to three hours. The flyers I put in the hotels read, "You ask, 'Can she fish?' You bet your bass she can." I did all right, but the tourists stopped coming to Hot Springs. I finally decided to move in 2000, loading everything into a gold Ford Explorer I packed to the gills. I felt bad leaving Files, but Hot Springs wasn't sad to see me go. A lot of the people either still hated me for helping the gay community, or they wished they didn't have a constant reminder of what they'd done to me—or hadn't done for others.

Before I left, Dr. Hays, our old preacher at First United, came up to me at a church dinner. "I want to apologize. I was wrong." He had reconciled with the lesbian and gay community in his head and decided they were true human beings worthy of God's love.

He was an old man trying to get into heaven. "No, Dr. Hays," I said, as kind as I could be. "I cannot accept your apology."

His face fell, and I continued: "It doesn't seem like my forgiveness to give. Every Sunday you were spot-on for whatever I needed to hear that week. My marching orders. And I thank you for that. But that forgiveness? That would be up to the men I cared for, and they're gone."

It wasn't just the people who died of AIDS. Even many who did not have the virus ended up committing suicide. They lived through the depths of the epidemic only to take their own lives. But I knew the memories they were living with, and why it might be too much to bear.

When I left Hot Springs, I didn't know where I was going. I just knew I would know it when I saw it. I thought I would probably end up in South Florida—probably Key Largo but maybe as far as Key West. That was where my Daddy's people came from, and I loved fishing, so I figured I could get a job working on a boat cleaning fish. And maybe I was re-creating the journey I'd taken so many of my guys on, reading them my guidebook of the Florida Keys. Key West was always the last stop—the place where nobody could judge or hurt you anymore. I was tired of hurting.

I didn't make it that far. I stopped in Orlando and noticed there was old moss on the big, big trees. And old roofs. I took those as clues that they didn't have hurricanes coming through there. I needed to go be someplace where something wouldn't just happen to take everything from me. They say, do what you know, so I got into the funeral business to make a living. It made sense to sell burial plots in God's waiting room. It was like time-shares, where you get to meet new people but never see them again.

Then, in 2004, Orlando got hit by hurricanes after all, so back-to-back that people didn't even bother to take the boards down from their windows between the storms. I took the hint and moved to where I live now, Northwest Arkansas—the land of Sam Walton—to be closer to Allison when she had her first child, a boy. Her three children, Jack, Ike, and Ella, call me Coco, because "Grandma" never really seemed to suit me.

In 2012, I had a stroke the very day my health insurance ran out. I had to learn to walk and talk again, and then I couldn't get insurance because I had a preexisting condition. As I recovered, I thought a lot about Bonnie having to cope after her surgeries. She was gone by then, her cancer finally getting her twenty-five years after she'd been given a three percent chance of living. I told her I could bury her in Files, but she wanted teaspoons of her ashes sprinkled in cemeteries around the world. I said that was a tall order, so she decided to donate her body to science. Leave it to Bonnie to have the answers even in death.

Mitch came back, though not in the way I thought he would. I'd erased him from my life and never even drove past his house again when I was in Hot Springs. He tracked me down through Allison, and I learned he'd had a stroke and was living with his mother, Donnie.

I agreed to have dinner with him and Donnie, if they were going to fry chicken and make biscuits for me. Mitch was in the kitchen when I got there, and I remember he was bent down to get the biscuits out of the oven. He looked up at me, and he was an old man, his beauty lost. He had this big tumor in his neck that was pushing into his carotid artery, and he couldn't take care of himself. He was dependent on Donnie.

I was going the next day to look at condos, and I asked if he wanted to ride with me. I had just signed the offer on one when he got the call that Donnie had fallen out of a chair and broken her hip. She died three days later, and we buried her at Files. Mitch couldn't take care of himself and didn't have an income, so I told him that he could stay at my house until he found a place to live. I didn't realize he'd already found it. I've kept him alive for years. He was diagnosed with calcium buildup in his basal ganglia, the part of the brain that controls movement. His symptoms are like Parkinson's disease and include dementia. So he became another patient for me. When I put him in the nursing facility, they assumed I was his wife, and I didn't say otherwise. We ended up sort of married after all.

AIDS followed me, of course. A year after my own stroke, I was minding my own business in my new home when a school district ten minutes north from where I lived told three foster siblings that they could not come back to school until they provided documentation that they were not HIV positive. An administrator had reportedly found out their birth mother was positive. These were disabled, elementary-school-age children—kids in foster care. I went on TV to go to bat for them, and soon word got out that I was not hirable. Nobody wanted to give a job to a troublemaker. I made do, focusing on my grandkids.

Recently, on a particularly warm day in October, Allison and I went tubing together. Out on the water, I asked if she ever wanted me to stop what I was doing when she was little. Someone had asked me, and I realized I didn't know the answer. She was insulted by the question.

"But why did you hide that you were so lonely at school?" I asked.

"I had nothing in common with those kids," she said. "My friends were the guys. That's who I played with after school."

I was quiet for a minute, the cool of the water contrasting with the heat of the air.

She continued, softer: "I didn't know a different life, and I was happy with it. And if sometimes it was hard, I wasn't going to tell you."

"Why not?"

"I was afraid you would stop what you were doing," she said. "And then what would happen to all these people?"

Neither of us was able to answer that question or even approach it. There was no one behind me. I had no choice but to help them. But I didn't say that aloud. Instead, we floated in the water, a mother and child after a war.

Now it's November, and I'm driving alone to Hot Springs. It's nearly a four-hour drive from where I live now in Northwest Arkansas. I still drive fast, so I can do it in three without really trying.

I pass Glenwood on my way to Hot Springs, so I stop in to see Chip's grave. My guy who made it all the way to DC, only to end up in the place he'd escaped from. I haven't been back to his grave since his burial in 1991, and for a moment I worry I won't easily find him. It's been twenty-eight years.

"Chip," I say to the air, "I need you to lead me to you."

I walk carefully around the graves where the ground has sunk. I trust him to bring me to him, calling his name from time to time. And there he is. I see the dip in his grave, the depression where the ground is sinking. His stone is leaning forward, toward the east, and the top is covered in lichen. But someone has left white flowers.

"I knew I would find you," I say.

I talk to Chip like I used to, and I want to ask him about the Doctor. Tell him that whatever their relationship was, I was glad he had it. Across the way, I can hear the thunder of an old-fashioned revival. A preacher is raving into a microphone, the sound so loud it carries all the way to here. It may as well be 1991.

When I get to Hot Springs, my first stop is at the house of Luke's family. I arrive unannounced, but his mother is gracious. Her husband has died, and I thank her again for being one of the only families to take in their child. She asks if I ever hear from Todd. I have tracked him down, still in Fort Worth, after years of never making more than a five-year plan. When I speak with him on the phone, he is sitting in the same house he and Luke were going to share.

When I leave Luke's mother, I notice they have laid down cement to dam up the creek in the spot where Luke was baptized.

On the way to town, I pass a strip club where Dolly worked, now called the Boogie Bar and Grill. On Central Avenue I can see the statue of Mary across from the Arlington Hotel, and I take a small detour to pass the place where Our House stood. I smile as I pass.

I make my way, finally, to Files Cemetery.

The carpet of pine needles crunches under my feet as I make the rounds. The mockingbirds still caw above me. I clear brush here and there on the graves, saying hi to Misty before walking over to see Angel, Carlos, and Antonio.

It's by Tim and Jim's grave that I see the little glints of rock shining in the sun. I kneel and move dirt to uncover them: quartz crystals pushed up from the earth. Perfectly clear, with tiny points. I gather some in my hand to take back to my grandchildren. Gifts from Tim and Jim.

I go to the grave shared by my father and Jimmy. The question I get most, the one I hate, is why I went into his room. And why I helped people. Again and again, "Why did you do it? How?" The answer is, How could I not? The real question is, How could *you* not?

"You started it all," I tell Jimmy. "Thank you."

I drive to the place I've rented on Lake Hamilton for the night. I can breathe better here, at the lake and woods that were my refuge as a little girl. The condo is on the water, with big bay windows facing west, so I can watch the sun set over the mountain and the bridge.

I am standing at those windows, admiring the expanse of blue, when the front doorbell rings.

"You're here," I say, almost dancing to the door.

I open the door to see him and can't raise my arms fast enough to take him into a hug.

"Hi, Ruthie."

"Paul, I am so glad to see you."

I usher him in, as if from a rainstorm, though it's a clear day. We talk over each other, saying how happy we are to see each other. He has brought two tote bags full of photo albums, and he lays them on the table by the bay windows.

For hours we sit, looking at each photo and letting the memories come. For years we suppressed them. I remark that it's nice to be with someone who understands how hard it is to think about those times, about these memories we don't want to have.

"They're too painful," he said. "It started back then. You had to put it all aside. I couldn't go to a job, and if they were like 'Well, why are you upset?' say, 'Well, I went to another friend's funeral who died of AIDS.' You could not do that. If you were in public, you just didn't do that. Now it's a little different, but people still don't want to hear it."

Paul found true love again, with Robert, who is lovely. Robert moved to Hot Springs from Oklahoma shortly after Billy died. He looked like Billy, only taller. People said it was too soon; they would come to me crying about it. But they were only mad because they all thought they were going to be the next Mrs. Wineland, and here was this queen who came from Oklahoma. Paul and Robert are still together, and knowing Paul was so well taken care of helped me leave Hot Springs when I did.

When Paul opens up the albums, Our House is alive again. The bar moved to a place on East Grand Avenue shortly after Billy's death. It wasn't the same. Everyone was dying. Paul stopped working there, and the Our House I knew was torn down. The albums Paul brought today end with Billy.

Looking at the photos of Billy, Paul tells me, "It's like looking at an old movie. He was so young. I keep thinking, *What was I doing with such a young man?* But I see I was young too. So that's okay."

He pauses, and I know we're both thinking about Billy's last days. We have become living memorials. No matter how happy a memory we allow ourselves to examine, the loss awaits us and the curtain falls.

"You were always so calm," said Paul. "Like somebody handed you a script. The funeral . . . I knew you had talked to whoever so I could be with him, I just didn't know the conversation."

"You didn't need to."

"You said, 'Do this. Do this. It will work out.' Looking back, I think, *Was she really this smart? Or was someone working through her?*"

"God was working through me," I say. "But it wasn't my time. It was your time. I was just there to keep the wheels going."

"You were the only one doing that for us."

Paul hands me a picture of me and Billy. "I want you to have this one." We are smiling in the photo, both so young. I think about the first time I saw him and then of us on that elephant, when we were both scared of what we knew was coming. Paul and I are quiet a moment, and I slow my breathing to the same rhythm Billy and I kept when I held him in my arms on his last night on earth.

I feel him with us, and I smile.

Acknowledgments

RUTH COKER BURKS

I first need to thank the people I cared for, and especially the men of Our House in Hot Springs and Discovery, in Little Rock. They took us both in, myself and my daughter, and they made a family for us. It is the honor of my life that you let me into your lives. I owe so much to every drag queen I have been privileged to know and watch. They taught me how to live while you're dying.

I am so grateful to Elisabeth Schmitz for reading the beginnings of my story and believing in us. She is a gifted editor, one who gave us the space and confidence to let us create the book my guys deserved. Everyone at Grove Atlantic has been lovely, and I especially want to thank Morgan Entrekin, Judy Hottensen, Deb Seager, Julia Berner-Tobin, and Yvonne Cha for their incredible work.

Thank you also to Kristin Lang, Anthony Roberts, and Esther Bochner at Audible for bringing this book to so many people.

It is difficult for me to find words to thank Kevin Carr O'Leary for putting his heart into this book. He knows how dearly I held the memories of my guys, and I believe they came to him to share their stories. He allowed me to visit with so many of the men I lost. They became so vivid I could smell their cologne, or reach out a hand to smooth their hair. He took on my soul.

There would be no book without Toni Long. Thank you for believing in me, and for sharing your guidance and friendship through these years.

Albert Lee at United Talent shepherded me through this process and brought Kevin to me. He encouraged me to have ownership of my story, and I am thankful for his care and attention.

I was on a plane when I met Jim Greene, a magical person who set so much of this project into motion. He did everything possible to connect me to people, including Toni Long. He's put such beautiful energy into helping this process along, and he's been a blessing. He makes me believe in angels, because he was an angel sent to me.

Paul Wineland and I visited the gates of heaven and the gates of hell together. Through all we went through, I never heard him complain. And I have never seen such devotion as he showed Billy. I am also so grateful Robert came into Paul's life when he did. He mended Paul's broken heart to the best of his ability.

Bonnie Slawson was my teacher before any of us knew what I would have to know how to do. In helping her navigate her cancer recovery—and with it the maze of health insurance and housing assistance—she prepared me for the work that defined my life.

Bonnie's doctor, Bruce Leipzig, MD, treated her like she had a million dollars. He was so invested in her health, and supported her decision that if it wasn't poison, she'd try it. He showed me what was possible in a doctor and did it with such grace.

Marcia Moore Hudson moved to Hot Springs from Denver when I was in the sixth grade. She was just a little older than me, and when she got on the school bus she saw me, this pitiful lost girl who nobody would sit next to. And she sat down with me. For many years, she was the only person who loved me. Before she passed from a brain tumor in June 2015, some of the last words she spoke to me were, "Now Ruthie, you write that book." She believed in me, and you would not be holding this book if she had not been so kind.

Matt Friedman was a rabbi who came into my life after the events of this book. He offered me emotional support while I was in the depths of grief. I am eternally grateful.

I am indebted to journalist David Koon for bringing attention to my story and to Files Cemetery in 2015. When we met, I only saw my life in black and white—he saw the technicolor. The care he put into his *Arkansas Times* article gave me the courage to face the pain of looking back on those years. He truly saved my life.

I want to thank John White at Storycorps for calling me at 9:30 one night in 2014 and asking me if I was that nurse who took care of AIDS patients in Arkansas. And I said "No, I'm not a nurse, but I did take care of people . . . " He asked if they could come down to Arkansas to record my story. He had urgency and he understood the value of this story. My dear sweet Liyna Anwar was the producer on the segment. Warm and funny and inviting, she sat with me, urging me to keep going. Liyna passed recently at the age of thirty, way too soon. But the good she brought to this world will go on for generations and generations.

During the events in this book, Doug Krile at KARK was the only reporter in Arkansas who would talk to me on camera. He helped me get the word out when no one else would. Laine Baker later covered my work while she was at KNWA, and I have since enjoyed watching her family through the years. Joel Kattner, a photographer from KNWA, has become a great friend. I am also grateful to Melinda Gassaway, the executive editor of the *Sentinel-Record* in Hot Springs, for all the times she listened when I said, "I just need five minutes of your time."

I am thankful that Norman Jones created spaces for the LGBT community to meet. He endured horrible insults, harassment, and violence, because he was the face of the community in Arkansas. I am in awe of his strength in living his dream. He is a hardass with a heart of gold.

I want to acknowledge some of the people of Hot Springs who would come to help me in meaningful ways. Wendell Workman was a lifesaver pharmacist who would give my guys hope in a bottle. As the president of the Downtown Merchants Association, Stueart Pennington was a great support, and also my funny friend. Suzann Franks and Debby Shackelford let me into their world. I am also grateful to Hot Springs National Park Superintendent Roger Giddings, and past mayors Melinda Baran and Helen Selig.

Owen DeVasier was my north star. He was a spiritual guiding light for me after I met him at the psychic fair in Hot Springs. He passed in 2005, and I will love him forever.

My cousin Raymond Lawler changed my life when he made me a blond all those years ago. We grew up apart, but every night as a child I would look at a photo of him and tell him good night. I loved him dearly from afar, and my worries about the safety of him and his friends fueled my need to help the LGBT community.

Scarlett Howell made me feel beautiful when I was so fragile. When I first sat in her stylist's chair, she gave me back my dignity. She has taken me under her wing and held me there.

Cheryl Stevenson is a wonderful friend and healer. People may mistake her kindness for timidity, but she observes everything and leads with her genuine heart.

Monika Miles has been my friend through hard times for both of us in the past ten years. I admire the graceful way she carries herself in life. She has a steel in her that is so strong that she doesn't need to let people see it to feel it. Her friendship and her sense of humor have kept me going this past decade.

I was privileged to have Suzanne Whiteman come into my life some years ago. She was the proud daughter of a Cheyenne medicine man, and she brought her beautiful family and Native American culture to me. I was honored that she chose to come live with me as she prepared for her death. She passed in January 2019, while I was working on this book. I was holding her hand when she passed, and her spirit remains with me.

Dr. Cara Riley, my doctor, did her residency at an AIDS hospice in Tulsa. She's an amazing doctor and I would not be here were it not for her care, compassion, and knowledge. I will love her until the end of time. Before Dr. Riley, I saw Jeff Jones, a PA who listened to my concerns and believed what I was telling him. He treated me as family.

I want to thank my daughter Allison for being with me on this journey. She was the girl who sat on the laps of people in the depths of despair and brought a light to their darkest moments. People shunned her, but she showed such resilience in holding love in her heart. I tried my very best to give her a life when she had lost so much.

I now have to speak directly to my magical grandchildren, so they will always have this. Jack, you are my first grandchild, and it is a joy to be your Coco. Ike, my Prince Ike, you are a remarkable young man. Don't ever let anyone take your twirl away. Ella, I see you carrying a journal and a box of pens everywhere you go. As you find the amazing life waiting for you, know that you will always be my twinkle.

When it comes to my parents, first I want to thank my daddy, because that will put me in the mood to say something nice about my mother. In 1957 he was the veteran of two world wars, and he was dying. He'd been diagnosed with emphysema and he and my mother made a business deal: They would marry and she would get a pension when he died. The clicker in the deal is that he wanted a baby girl. He wanted me, and he *loved* me. He died when I was five, but he's been with me the whole way. My mother was 39 when I was born, and she too became sick. She taught me how to fend for myself and not to take no for an answer. Did she teach me to be brave, or did she make me have to be?

KEVIN CARR O'LEARY

For decades, Ruth Coker Burks carried the weight of the memory of the men she cared for and laid to rest. It is the honor of my professional life that she trusted me to help tell her story and theirs.

I am deeply grateful to the many people at Grove Atlantic who took such care with this book, particularly our wonderful editor Elisabeth Schmitz. I have felt so fortunate to have her guidance. Thank you also to the team at Audible, who heard the magic in Ruth's voice. I am also indebted to Albert Lee for bringing me to Ruth, and to the United Talent family.

This book would not be what it is if Paul Wineland had not opened his life and photo albums to me. "I adore Paul," Ruth slips in every time she speaks of him, and now I do too. I am also thankful to Ruth's daughter Allison for being willing to open up to me. And to every single person in Hot Springs who spoke with me once Ruth vouched for me, thank you.

When I was twenty, I started reading *POZ*, a magazine about living with HIV. Its founder, Sean Strub, gave me an internship that became the best job ever. I am grateful to everyone I worked with as an editor there, and to Walter Armstrong, RonniLyn Pustil, Gonzalo Aburto, Dick Scanlan, Stephen Gendin, Jeffrey Hoover, Jennifer Hsu, LeRoy Whitfield, Bob Lederer, Laura Whitehorn, Greg Lugliani, Esther Kaplan, Kevin Irvine, Lady Catiria, and Shawn Decker.

Through *POZ* I met Barton Lidicé Beneš, my best friend. Losing him in 2012 remains the wound that helped me understand Ruth's loss of Billy.

I am blessed to have Kathleen Carr O'Leary as a first reader and mother. My father, Daniel Philip O'Leary would have loved Ruth. I also thank my brother, Dan O'Leary, for inspiring my love of books.

I would not have been able to devote these years to helping Ruth tell her story without the steadfast support of my husband, Brian Esser. I wrote the first chapter on my phone, lying on the floor of our son Keith's bedroom as I waited for him to fall asleep. And it was because of our younger child, Jason, that I could picture Allison so clearly as Ruth spoke. I love you all.